I0810053

IMAGES
of America

SHACKELFORD COUNTY

On the Cover: At the end of the long trails, American cowboys would often hold informal competitions among themselves and different outfits to see which group had the best riders, ropers, and all-around best drovers. It was from these competitions that the modern rodeo would eventually emerge. This unidentified man, a working cowboy from Lambshead Ranch, tests his skill riding a bucking bronco. (Courtesy of John A. Matthews.)

IMAGES
of America

SHACKELFORD COUNTY

Shackelford County Historical Commission

ARCADIA
PUBLISHING

ISBN 978-1-4671-3118-6

Published by Arcadia Publishing
Charleston, South Carolina

Printed in the United States of America

Library of Congress Control Number: 2013954932

For all general information, please contact Arcadia Publishing:
Telephone 843-853-2070
Fax 843-853-0044
E-mail sales@arcadiapublishing.com
For customer service and orders:
Toll-Free 1-888-313-2665

Visit us on the Internet at www.arcadiapublishing.com

This book is dedicated to all the citizens of Shackelford County for their interest, help, and support.

CONTENTS

Acknowledgments

Although the assembly of this book was done by committee, our small number cannot begin to take credit for all of the labor. This book was a true community effort and it would not have been possible without the help we received from so many different people. Our most gracious and sincere thanks go first to our many chapter authors: Sunday Tidwell, Jane Lenoir, John A. Matthews, A.V. Jones Jr., Jon Rex Jones, Wilma Jo Tucker Mitchell, Duston Brooks, Lawrence Clayton, and Melinda Lucas. Many of these same kind folks also pulled double duty as caption writers or editors. Carol Dromgoole and Betsy Parsons also provided additional, much valued editing help. Julia Putnam both wrote and edited numerous captions, and also did much to get the word of our photograph search out to the community.

Photographs came in from all quarters, and although we could not include them all we would like to thank everyone who shared their family treasures with us: Frank Andrews, Dee Balliew, Eddie Bartee, Sandy Conway, Betty Diller, the Fort Griffin State Historic Site, Jack Hopkins, Lea Clayton Hutt, James Garvin, Elizabeth Green, Nancy Green, the Jones Family, John A. Matthews, Byron Maxwell, Carolyn Maxwell Mitchell, R.P. Mitchell, Wilma Jo Tucker Mitchell, Byron and Laura Palmer, Hank Paup, Ted Paup, Julia Putnam, Joy and Wade Roberts, Cathy Rupp, H.R. Stasney & Sons Ltd., Clifford Teinert, and Anne Diller Wendt. Special thanks go to Duston Brooks and the Moran Historical Museum for providing most of the photographs for the Moran chapter, and to Watt Casey Jr., who provided the majority of the images for the modern times chapter.

Additional thanks for photographs go to the Robert E. Nail Jr. Archives at The Old Jail Art Center. Any photographs in the book that do not have a courtesy line can be credited to, and found at, the Archives.

All chapter titles are taken from the lyrics of popular *Fort Griffin Fandangle* songs.

Chapter six originally appeared in the *Handbook of Texas Online*: Lawrence Clayton, "Fort Griffin Fandangle," *Handbook of Texas Online* (www.tshaonline.org/handbook/online/articles/kkf02), accessed October 4, 2013. Published by the Texas State Historical Association.

The Book Committee of the Shackelford County Historical Commission was Gilda Brown, Molly Sauder, Saundra Nobles, Randy Bacon, and Julia Putnam.

Final thanks go to all the citizens of Shackelford County for their interest, help, and support.

Introduction

By Sunday Tidwell

It is early summer in Shackelford County, Texas. Tomorrow the mercury will hit 100 degrees Fahrenheit and return to that mark for many days to come, but today is mild. Mourning doves coo from a nearby live oak tree, a covey of quail amongst the prairie grasses and prickly pears gently whistle, "Bob White . . . Bob White," and the sizzling song of tiny cicadas reverberates through the clear, sweet air. White-tail deer are resting in the shade of mesquite trees, that ubiquitous, water-thieving source of green foliage and firewood that dominates our landscape. Behind barbed-wire fences, herds of fat beef cattle graze on native grasses fed by mineral-rich soil. Just before sundown this evening, western diamondback rattlesnakes with their bellies full of cotton-tail rabbits and field mice will slither from their earthen dens and stretch out on limestone boulders to soak up the radiant heat. Across the pasture, coyotes drink from a dwindling creek bed.

Such is life in Shackelford County. A mere 165 years ago, there was no Shackelford County as a geographical designation, no mesquite infestation, and no barbed-wire fence. The agricultural and industrial revolutions were hitting full stride in the Northeast, but west central Texas was still a wild, unsettled buffalo range dominated by an ancient race—the Amerindians (known colloquially as "Indians"), hunter-gatherers who had Asian origins and who had crossed on foot over a land bridge between Siberia and Alaska thousands of years ago. Scattering across the North American continent, the Amerindians splintered into hundreds of distinct cultures. The Plains tribes of this area (most notably the Apaches, Kiowas, Tonkawas, and Comanches) were hunter-gatherers; they followed the magnificent buffalo herds, and the buffalo followed the grass, which grew wherever the rains fell. It was a nomadic life that necessitated a fierce, hardy, and often cruel culture. The Comanches in particular had a reputation for rape, kidnapping, theft, torture, burning, and mutilation of their enemies. Other bands of Indians who lived in this area were the Anadarkos, Caddos, Wichitas, Wacos, Tawakonis, Kichais, and Kickapoos.

In 1845, Texas became the 28th state in the Union, and in 1849, Captain Randolph B. Marcy of the US Army became the first white man known to have explored what is now Shackelford County, although there were likely explorers, surveyors, and traders before him. At the time, he and his band of scouts rode their horses to within 20 miles north of the present-day boundaries of Shackelford County. The first white man to attempt permanent settlement in this area was probably Jesse Stem, an Ohio lawyer and friend of Rutherford B. Hayes, later to become US president. In 1851, Stem joined the United States Indian Service as an Indian agent, and in 1852, he established a farm on the Clear Fork of the Brazos, near the old Butterfield Stage Crossing, in what is now known as the Valley Pasture of Lambshead Ranch. He grew good crops of corn and oats. Stem dealt primarily with Comanches but with other tribes as well. In 1854, Stem was murdered by two Kickapoo Indians near Fort Belknap, Texas. On a subsequent trip to the area in 1854, impressed by the Clear Fork of the Brazos River, Captain Marcy and Maj. Robert S. Neighbors suggested to the US War Department that a Comanche Indian reservation be established and a military fort be built near the Clear Fork. The Comanche Reserve was begun in 1854, and by May 1855, the first Indians arrived there to live and be trained to grow and harvest crops.

Oblivious to or undeterred by Jesse Stem's murder, other white people looking for cheap, fertile, plentiful land began to settle. Ledbetters, Greers, Lynches, Jacksons, Matthewses, Striblings, and Jacobses became the first permanent families in the area. As Captain Marcy and Major Neighbors had hoped, the US Army provided protection for these settlers by establishing a military fort—actually in Throckmorton County—called Camp Cooper, on the Clear Fork of the Brazos in January 1856. In addition to aiding the settlers by putting down hostile Indians, Camp Cooper troops supplied and protected the hospitable Indians of the nearby reservation. Col. Robert E. Lee, who would go on to be a Confederate hero of the Civil War, commanded Camp Cooper for more than a year in 1856–1857.

In 1859, the Comanche Indians were removed from the reservation to Fort Sill (then Indian Territory, now Oklahoma), but Camp Cooper was to live on until 1861, when the Civil War began and Texas seceded from the Union. At this point the US Army ceded Camp Cooper to Texas Secessionist troops, who were soon called away to battle, not against the Indians, but against Union troops—their own brethren. With soldiers now away for war, the settlers were once again vulnerable to marauding Indians. Even though many Indians had been removed to Fort Sill, a few violent bands of Comanches and Kiowas remained, as did small bands of friendly Tonkawas. Some white families moved to Fort Davis, in present-day Stephens County, during the war years for safety. Others remained in the area and congregated in civilian forts.

The Civil War came to a close in 1865, and Texas reverted back to the United States. The national business of taming and populating the western frontier resumed, and Shackelford County, Texas, was about to be born. In 1867, a new US Army post, the legendary Fort Griffin, was established in the northern portion of the county. In reality, there were two Fort Griffins that blurred into one very colorful, raucous, and deadly place. There was the actual US Army fort, which lay on a tall bluff not quite a mile from the Clear Fork of the Brazos River, 15 miles north of present-day Albany. The other Fort Griffin was the Town of Fort Griffin, sometimes called Griffin Flat, Griffin, or The Flat. This town grew up in the flat river valley just below the army fort itself, so it was sandwiched between the military post and the river. It was a rough, primitive place, to be sure; transportation into Fort Griffin was only by horseback, wagon train, or the occasional stagecoach, as the nearest railroad was over 200 miles to the south in Calvert, Texas.

While the soldiers of Fort Griffin went about the task of subduing Indians, buffalo hunters in the area were killing the Indians' sustenance en masse. After thousands of years of existence, the southern herd of buffalo was hunted into near extinction by 1878. Gone with the buffalo were most of the Indians themselves and certainly the Indian way of life. What had been the buffalo range now became the path for Longhorn cattle being driven from South Texas to Dodge City, Kansas, along the Western Cattle Trail. Fort Griffin was the primary supply point for the cattle drovers, buffalo hunters, and soldiers. They were thoroughly taken care of in the local stores, brothels, gambling halls, and saloons, including the infamous Bee Hive Saloon. In 1936 in *The Early History of Shackelford County*, Ben O. Grant wrote: "Life in Fort Griffin could not have been dreary. The best mingled with the worst and life was cheap. No one cared for Fort Griffin nor regarded the future of it. It was a town where all lived in a wild flurry of the present."

As the population of Griffin exploded, life was becoming increasingly dirty and dangerous. Questionable characters abounded: Lottie Deno, Mollie McCabe, Big Nose Kate, Pat Garrett, Doc Holiday, Wyatt Earp, John Wesley Hardin, John Selman, John Larn, Hurricane Minnie, and Hurricane Bill. Fort Griffin did have its higher-minded citizens who did not live for whiskey, cards, and the fast draw of a gun. Frustrated with the outright lawlessness and spotty law enforcement in Fort Griffin, some of the cattlemen formed a secret, masked vigilance committee known as the Old Law Mob, and cattle thieves began to get their due by being hung from a tree by a lariat in the dark of the night. But this was not enough; it was time to do things legally, out in the open, and this would require political and geographical changes.

Before 1874, Shackelford County had existed as an attachment to three other counties—Bosque, Palo Pinto, and Jack—for judicial purposes. Traveling to Jacksboro to conduct legal business was long and hazardous, so, in 1874, residents of the area petitioned the county court of Jack County to organize their own county. Permission was granted, and it was named Shackelford County in honor of Texas Revolutionary War hero Dr. Jack Shackelford. Fort Griffin became the temporary county seat on October 12, 1874. But within a month, the founders of the new Shackelford County had called an election to determine a different county seat, 15 miles south of Fort Griffin, and the town was to be called Albany, in honor of Albany, Georgia. The sheriff of Shackelford County, Henry Carter Jacobs, just happened to already own land at the new town site. However, Jacobs did generously donate much of his land for public and civic use.

The political leaders of the county had a plan: Albany was to get a railroad and become the largest city between Fort Worth and El Paso. The Albany city fathers did indeed win a bid for the Texas Central Railroad by giving them $50,000. The Texas Central, coming by way of Cisco, reached Albany in 1881, the same year that the Army post of Fort Griffin was shuttered. The frontier era had ended, and the Wild West town of Fort Griffin would soon fade away as Albany grew and progressed in typical Victorian fashion. Homes were built, a school (later to become a college, then an orphanage) was started, churches sprang up, businesses opened, a two-story limestone jailhouse was erected, and a public water system was established. And to the south of Albany, the small farming towns of Sedwick and Hulltown (now Moran) also increased in population and services, due to the arrival of the railroad.

In 1883–1884, the leadership of Albany erected what remains the centerpiece of the county today, the stately courthouse in the French Second Empire style, with an exterior of limestone quarried from the nearby hills. The 130-year-old courthouse stands proudly in the town square, with its clock and 800-pound bell on top. By 2001, the courthouse was beautifully restored through funding from the State of Texas and is still in use for its original purpose. It well represents the spirit of preservation and perseverance that defines Albany today.

At the dawn of the 20th century, farming and cattle ranching continued to be the mainstays of the local economy. But the new stuff of Texas legend, petroleum, was discovered near Moran in 1910 with the Cottle No. 1 natural gas well, followed three years later by the nearby Edwards No. 1 oil well. Moran suddenly grew by thousands, as men and their families flocked to the area to get in on the boom. In 1926, a major shallow oilfield, the Cook Field, was discovered on the W.I. and Matilda Nail Cook Ranch near Albany. For many years, the Cook Field was the largest shallow oilfield in the world, and to date it has produced over 35 million barrels of oil. In 1929, Matilda Nail Cook, with a portion of her petroleum royalties, built a hospital in Fort Worth, now the Cook Children's Health Care System. Oil boom towns in the county flourished in the 1910s and 1920s, but then withered by the end of the 1930s. Only Albany (population 2,000) and Moran (population 250) remain as viable towns. Although the petroleum industry is notorious for its boom-bust nature, Shackelford County continues to benefit from oil and gas revenues. Wind energy has gained a foothold in the county as well; in December 2007, the Lone Star Wind Farm began operating newly-built turbines on the hills west and southwest of Albany.

Shackelford County has dodged or rejected that which some counties have embraced, such as interstates and big-box stores. With an emphasis on heritage tourism, there has been a deliberate effort to maintain a sense of frontier history while promoting education, culture, the arts, technological advancements, small businesses, and the tranquility of the natural world. There is an unwritten preservation code: Save what can be saved, and build modern structures to blend harmoniously with the old. The limestone quarries that were used to build many of the original structures in the county still yield a dense, high-quality rock that is used locally and trucked all over the state and beyond. Lueders stone is the benchmark in the limestone industry.

The late playwright, Princeton alumnus, and native son Robert Nail wrote *The Fort Griffin Fandangle* in 1938 for the Albany senior class play. Much of the script was drawn from *Interwoven: A Pioneer Chronicle*, a book by early area resident Sallie Reynolds Matthews about life on the rugged Texas prairie. The original show, performed by seniors and underclassmen at the high school football stadium, was called *Dr. Shackelford's Paradise*. It was enlarged into a community-wide production and performed again two months later as *The Fort Griffin Fandangle*, still the name of the show and still performed by local unpaid actors, from babies to old timers, and with real livestock, including fast horses and a graceful herd of longhorn cattle. Narrated from the viewpoint of early Anglo settlers, the *Fandangle* holds the distinction of being the oldest outdoor musical in Texas, having been performed 61 of the last 75 years. In 1965, the show was moved to its permanent two-acre grass stage, the Prairie Theater, where it is performed for six nights every June. Local resident and longtime *Fandangle* veteran Jon Rex Jones said of this historical pageant: "It has taught us to cooperate. People from all walks of life—cowboys, engineers like [G.P.] Crutchfield, and others—coming together to do something, and that has taught Albany to not take sides, to all come together and support common goals, and this has been something that has benefited us with the creation of the Old Jail Art Center, and the downtown Aztec venue, and things like that. The Fandangle taught us how to do that."

Robert Nail's nephew Reilly Nail, also a Princeton graduate and artistic visionary, inherited in 1968 the elder Nail's two-story limestone office building. Built in 1877–1878 as the first permanent jail in Albany, it housed law breakers for over 50 years, until 1929. The old jail was purchased in 1940 by Robert Nail for his personal use. Reilly Nail, a former CBS-TV executive producer in New York, was an avid art collector who retired to Albany in the 1970s and dared to convert the decrepit old jail into a small museum. Reilly and his cousin Bill Bomar of Ranchos de Taos, New Mexico, and both of their mothers, contributed portions of their art collections and historical archives to found the Old Jail Art Center in 1980. With the aid of volunteers and benefactors, the Old Jail is today a more-than 14,000-square-foot, modern, nationally accredited art museum that houses in its permanent collection works that span Asian, European, American, and pre-Columbian art. Notable holdings are by Amedeo Modigliani, Paul Klee, Pablo Picasso, Georges Braque, Joan Miro, Henri Matisse, Thomas Hart Benton, Grant Wood, Alexander Calder, Henry Moore, John Marin, Rembrandt van Rijn, Francisco Goya, Pierre-Auguste Renoir, Gustave Caillebotte, and Henri de Toulouse-Lautrec.

The Old Jail has an active acquisition policy, with a focus on collecting the work of contemporary Texas artists. The museum also hosts a variety of exhibitions, gallery talks, performing arts events, workshops, tours, distance-learning classes, and web-based lessons. The Old Jail is home to an abundance of local historical artifacts—books, photographs, letters, and news clippings. Maintained by a full-time professional archivist, these intimate objects can be accessed for scholarly and historical research.

Whether for the quaintness and wide-open spaces or for the culture and sophistication, Shackelford County has attracted and nurtured an inordinate number of intellectuals, creative types, prospectors, and businessmen. As we move through the second decade of the 21st century, it is our pleasure to share in print over 200 photographs from the past two centuries of these courageous and colorful people and our beloved county.

One

A Prairie Plain, A Bright Blue Sky

By Jane Lenoir

The area of north central Texas now known as Shackelford County has a long and fascinating history. Archaeologists chart it through traces of older cultures. Comanche, Kiowa, Apache, and other tribes have oral traditions, and Spanish and French explorers left accounts that detailed their crossings of the prairies. But the area's history, for most of its residents, arrived with settlers from Europe and the eastern United States. They came to Texas for many reasons—land, adventure, opportunity, escape—and many turned back, daunted by the harsh realities of life on the prairie. Others stayed to face the hardships. For many in Shackelford County today, those tough-minded pioneers are their ancestors.

In the 1840s, Capt. Randolph B. Marcy's trail for settlers headed to the gold rush in California crossed the northwest corner of the county. The 1850s brought Fort Phantom Hill to the south; Indian agents Jesse Stem and Robert Neighbors, the Clear Fork Comanche Reserve, and Camp Cooper to the north in Throckmorton County; and the Butterfield Stage, the Peters colony, and establishment of Shackelford County, originally part of Bosque County. Early settlers J.C. Lynch and George Greer started ranches in the southeastern part of the county. More ranches and settlements sprang up as families decided that, although they had to fight Comanche and Kiowa, this land was home.

By the 1860s, with the Civil War on the horizon, a number of once-optimistic settlers packed up and went back East. But the true pioneers stayed. Some volunteered for the Confederacy, while others mounted a home guard to protect against Indian attack. In 1864, the Elm Creek Raid in Young County prompted many of the area families to "fort up" for protection, some just over the Stephens County line at civilian Fort Davis, others at Fort Mugginsville, Fort Hubbard, and several ranches in southern Shackelford County.

Following the Civil War, in 1867, a fort was built in northern Shackelford County on a rise overlooking the Clear Fork of the Brazos River, first called Camp Wilson and then renamed Fort Griffin in honor of Maj. Gen. Charles Griffin, the late commander of the Army's Department of Texas. For 14 years, it housed, at various times, troops of the 4th and 11th Cavalry, and the Buffalo Soldiers of the 9th and 10th Cavalry and the 24th Infantry. The soldiers provided escorts and helped build roads and telegraph lines, but their main job was to patrol and fight Indians. Many battles in the 1870s culminated in the Red River War and the defeat of the Comanches in Palo Duro Canyon in 1875.

Civilians, relieved by the Army's protection, moved back to their ranches and farms, and some settled beneath the hill. By the early 1870s, this became the town of Fort Griffin, or The Flat. Businesses that sprang up along Griffin Avenue served new settlers, ranchers, and soldiers. Soon, the vast herds of buffalo on the prairie drew the buffalo hunters. Tradesmen, gamblers, and ladies of the evening followed. Ranchers who moved thousands of longhorn cattle on the Goodnight-Loving and Great Western Trails came to get supplies. Soon, there were drugstores, hotels, stable yards, dance halls, restaurants, and even an ice-cream parlor. Huge stores such as Conrad & Rath, F.E. York, Frankel's, and Hamburg's outfitted the hunters, bought hides, and sold goods to thousands of settlers passing through on their way west. Well-known figures, with good reputations and bad, visited, including Pat Garrett, Bat Masterson, Doc Holliday, Big Nose Kate, Wyatt Earp, John Wesley Hardin, and Lottie Deno. Some of these personalities stayed for a while. The wild settlement earned the nickname "Babylon on the Brazos." The great slaughter of the buffalo was underway, and Fort Griffin Flat, now a true boomtown, boasted a transient population of 3,000 to 4,000.

By 1874, the military declared martial law and ran many lawbreakers out of town. The county was organized, with Fort Griffin as the county seat, but leaders soon decided Albany was a better choice. Many merchants and residents of Fort Griffin moved to the new, more civilized town. By 1878, the millions of buffalo were gone, and the boom was over. The wild bunch in The Flat headed for greener pastures. In 1879, the *Fort Griffin Echo* reported a population of about 500. The Army closed the post of Fort Griffin in 1881, and The Flat faded to a small farming community as the railroad came to Albany. Some of the huge herds of Texas longhorns now went north by rail, avoiding squabbles with Northern ranchers over tick fever. The railroad brought supplies, more businesses, and more people, and Albany had a nice little boom of its own. But that is another part of the story.

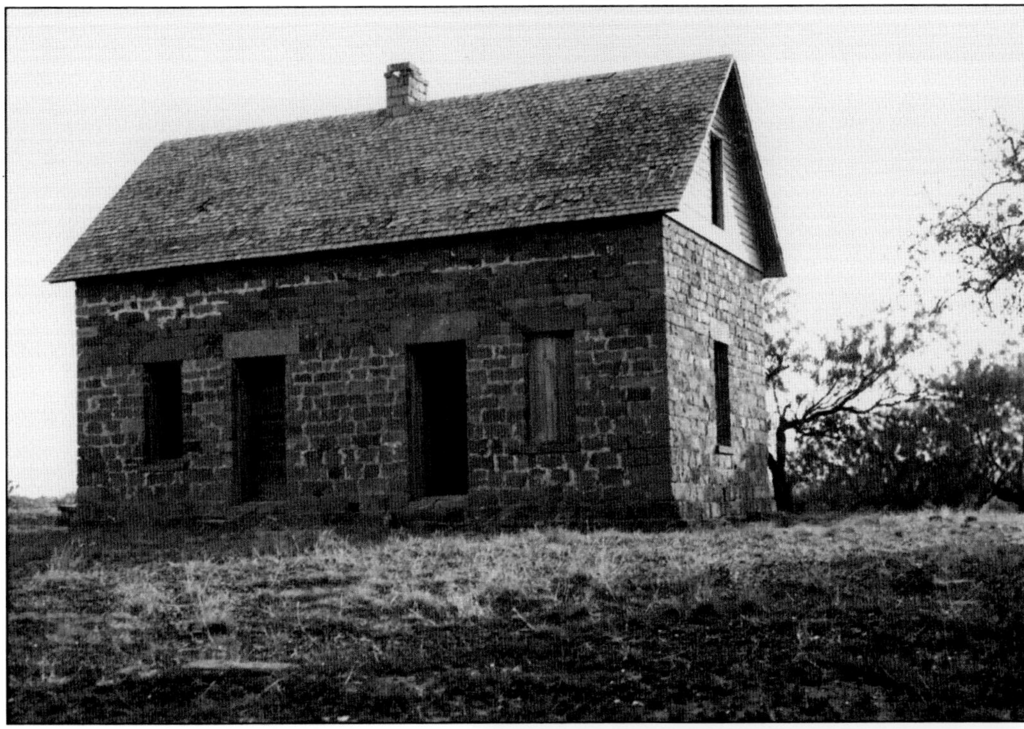

The first house built in Shackelford County was the home of George Washington and Sara Greer. Built in 1862, it was located on Hubbard Creek, approximately six miles north of Moran. It was a two-story rock structure with an outside staircase leading to the second floor. The home served as a way station on the old military highway to Waco. The nearby Greer Cemetery contains the oldest burial ground in the county.

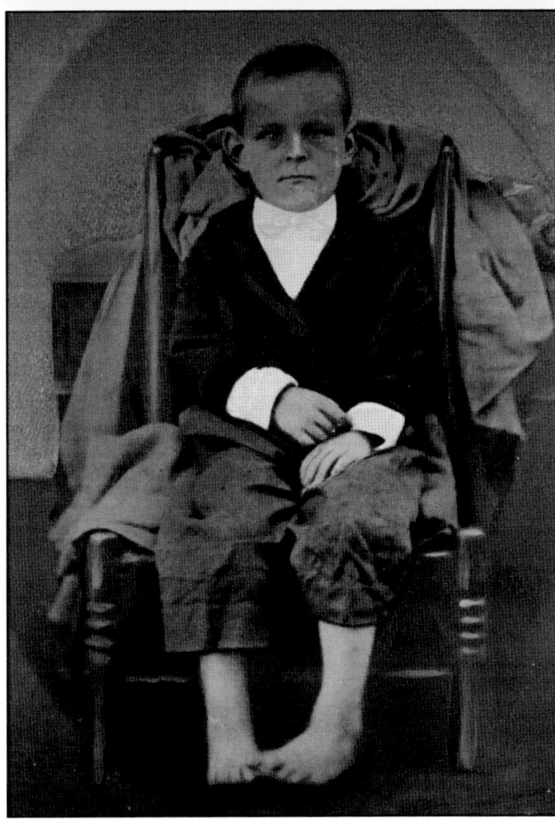

John Calvin Ledbetter, son of Mr. and Mrs. William H. Ledbetter, was age nine in late 1870 or early 1871 when he was abducted by Indians near Judge J.C. Lynch's home in southern Shackelford County. In 1881, he appeared at Fort Griffin. A mark on his shoulder convinced the family that he was their son. However, Johnny denounced his Ledbetter heritage, claiming instead to be S.W. Wesley from Missouri. (Courtesy of Lea Clayton Hutt.)

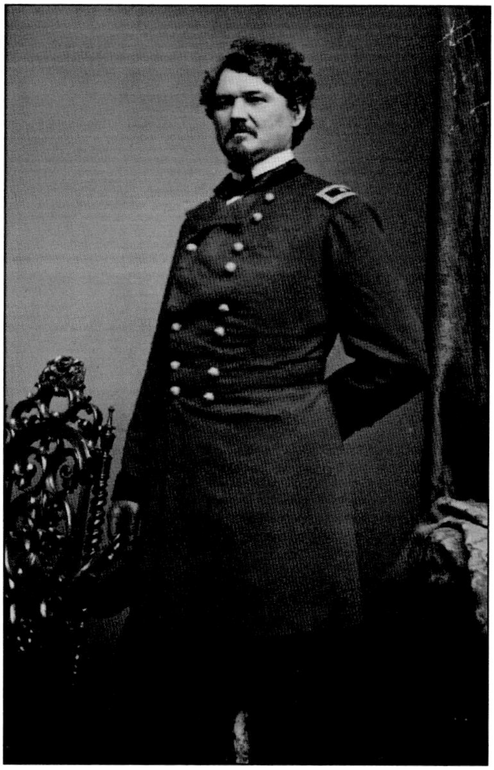

In 1867, Lt. Col. Samuel D. Sturgis, veteran of both the Mexican-American and Civil Wars, arrived in northern Shackelford County with the 6th Cavalry. Beside the Clear Fork of the Brazos River, the unit established Camp Wilson. It was moved in 1868 to a high plateau and renamed Fort Griffin, in honor of the late Gen. Charles Griffin, commander of the Department of Texas after the Civil War. (Courtesy of Fort Griffin State Historic Site.)

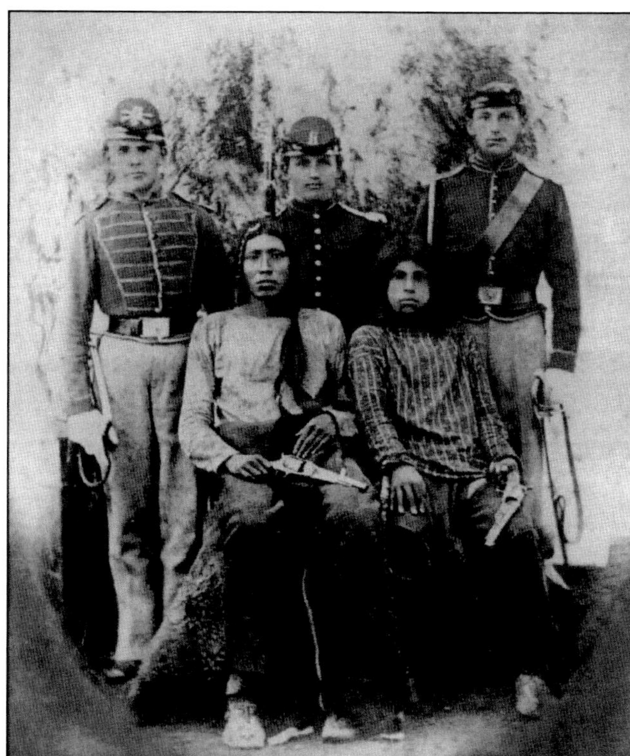

The three cavalry soldiers in this photograph still wear Civil War–style uniforms. New uniforms were not available until 1872. The man on the left wears the uniform of a bugler. The two Tonkawa scouts, if standing, would have been taller than these young men. Small riders, though, were less of a load on their mounts, and so could travel longer on patrol. (Courtesy of Fort Griffin State Historic Site.)

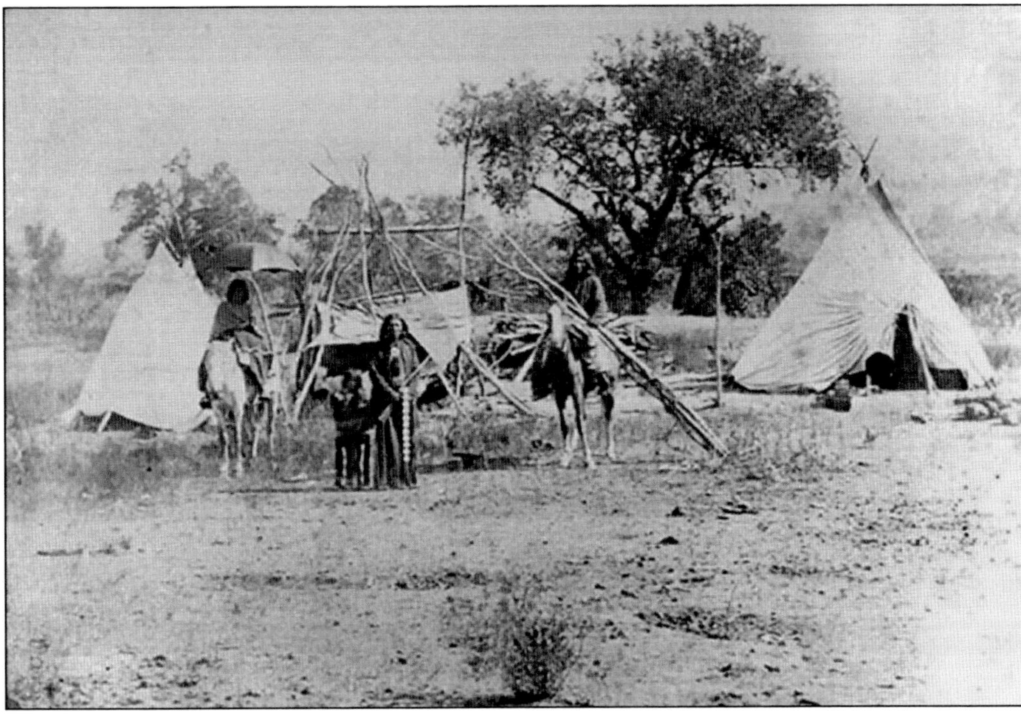

The Tonkawa and Lipan-Apache camps were on the Clear Fork, northeast of the main portion of Fort Griffin Flat. Moved from the Upper Brazos Reservation in 1859, the Tonkawa were almost wiped out in an attack by other tribes. Allowed to move back into Texas, they served as scouts for the Army at Fort Griffin, Fort Richardson, and Fort Concho in the 1870s. (Courtesy of Fort Griffin State Historic Site.)

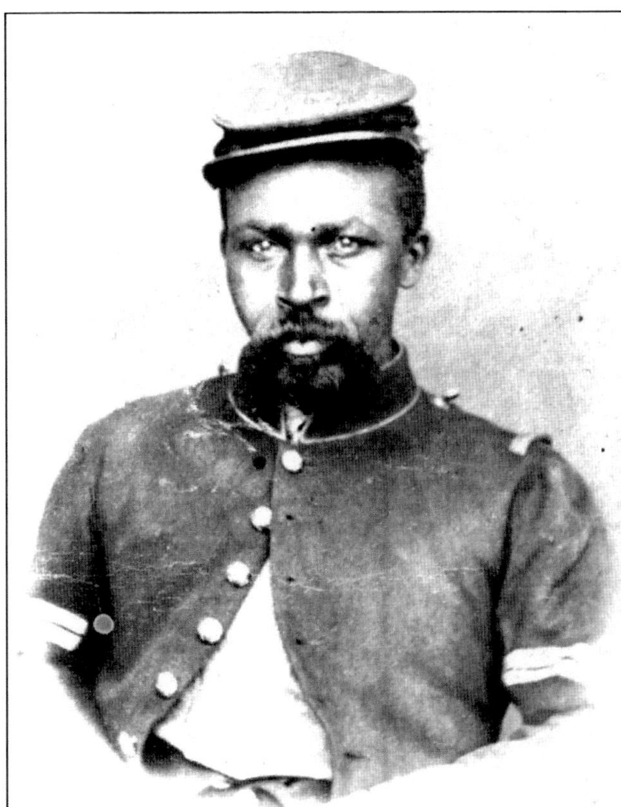

Former buffalo soldier Elijah Earl settled near the crossing of the Clear Fork and worked as a barber in the town. Highly regarded and described as "very intelligent and likable," he was a prominent member of the African American community. The *Fort Griffin Echo* mentioned his rousing speech at the 1879 Emancipation Day picnic and his well-attended 1880 Christmas party.

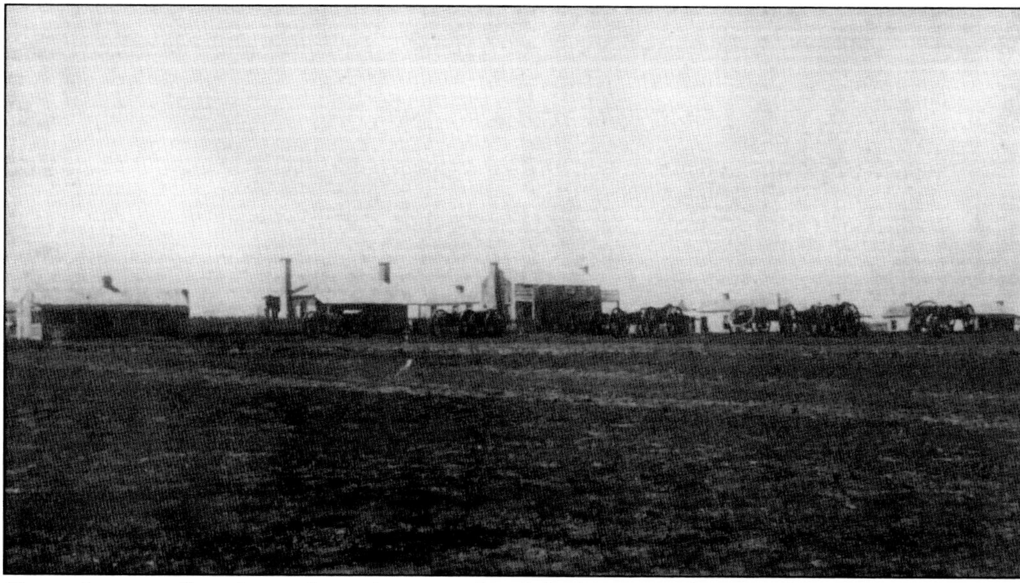

Shown here is officers' row along the east side of the large parade ground at Fort Griffin in the 1870s. Due to lack of construction materials in the area, abandoned farms and ranch buildings were sometimes disassembled and brought to the fort, which may account for the great disparity in style of these quarters. The two-story structure was the unmarried officers' barracks. (Courtesy of Fort Griffin State Historic Site.)

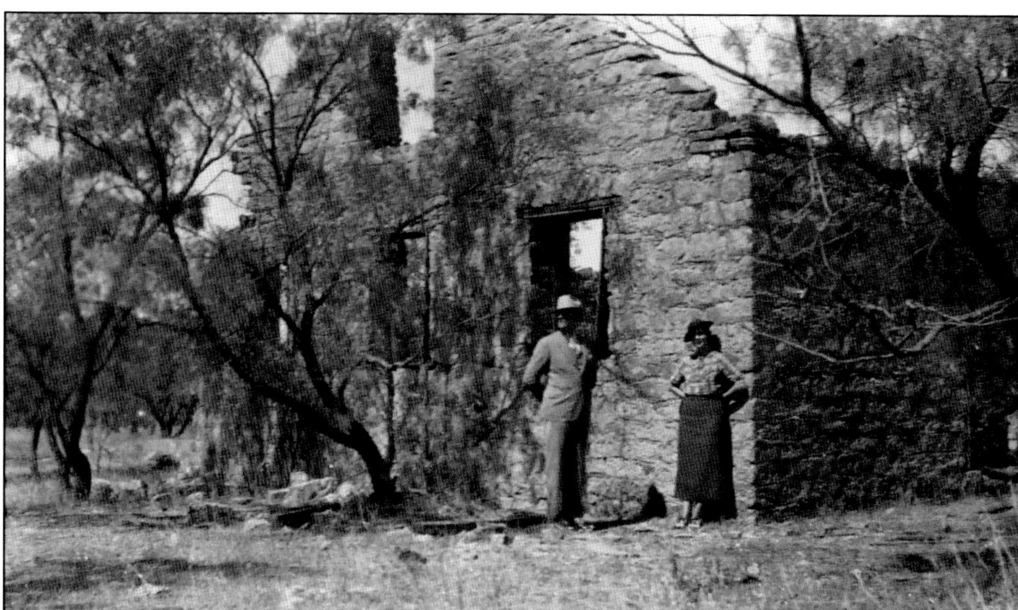

Shown here are the ruins of the Post Trader store at Fort Griffin, originally built and run by Frank Conrad and Charlie Rath. The store sold an enormous range of goods to soldiers, buffalo hunters, and cattlemen. In the late 1870s, it was the only good provisioning point on the Western Trail in Texas. This photograph is from the late 1930s, before the site was cleared and the ruins stabilized by Civilian Conservation Corps (CCC) crews.

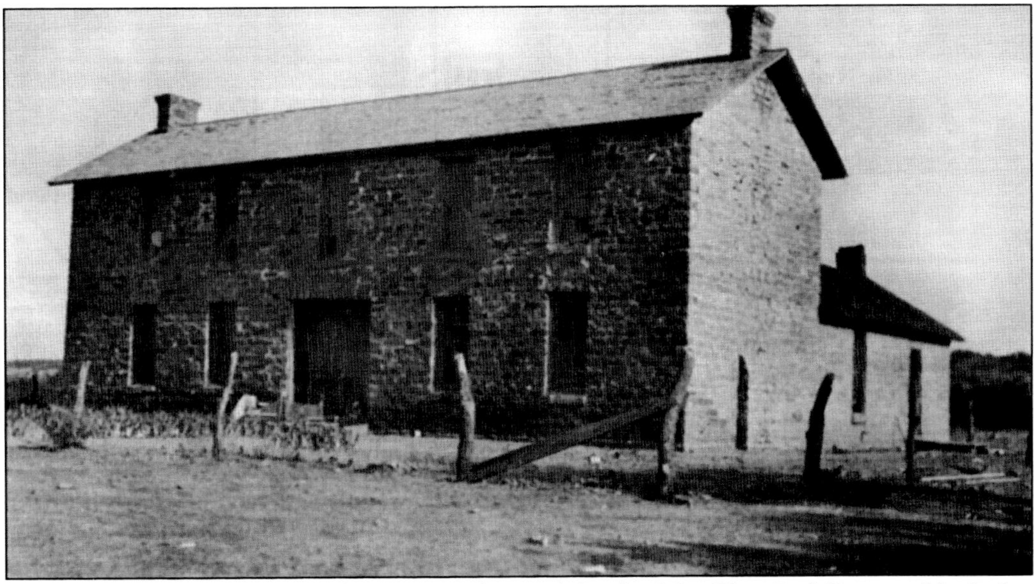

Tryal E. Jackson purchased land in 1870 on the south bank of the Clear Fork River and built this two-story rock home in 1874. When he relocated to Albany a few years later, he sold the property to Samuel Ward. Bud Martin, from Albany, purchased the home from the Ward heirs in 1943, and later sold it to the State of Texas. (Courtesy of Fort Griffin State Historic Site.)

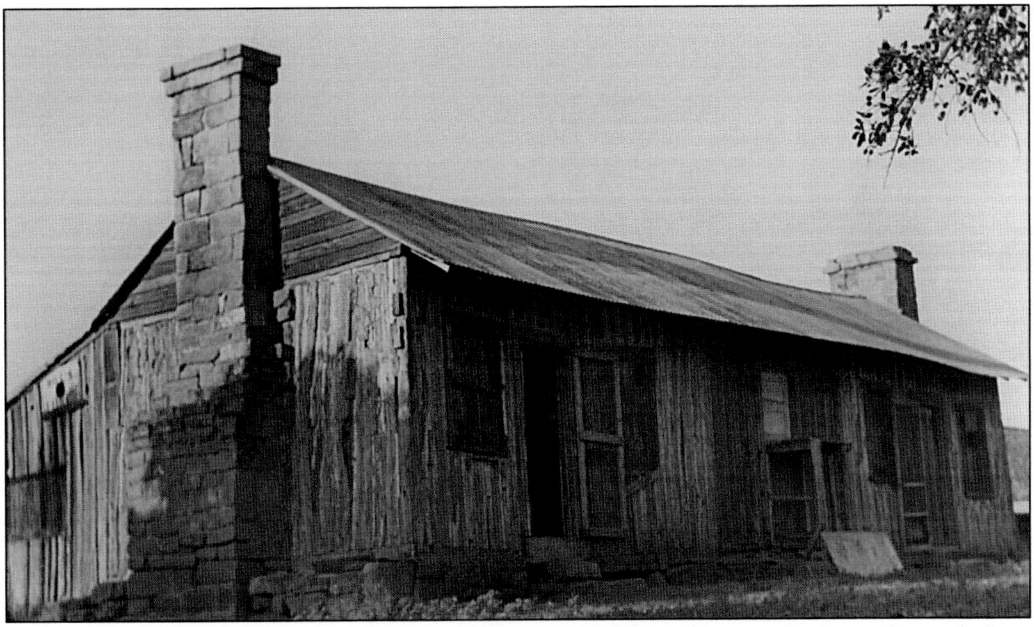

Typical of early homes in the area is the William H. Ledbetter house, which was located along the Clear Fork River, near Fort Griffin. Built between 1874 and 1877, this structure contains two rooms built of vertical logs, called pickets, separated by an open dog run. A bedroom occupied one side, and a kitchen/dining room was on the other side. Today, the restored dwelling stands in the Bank Park in downtown Albany. (Courtesy of *Albany News*.)

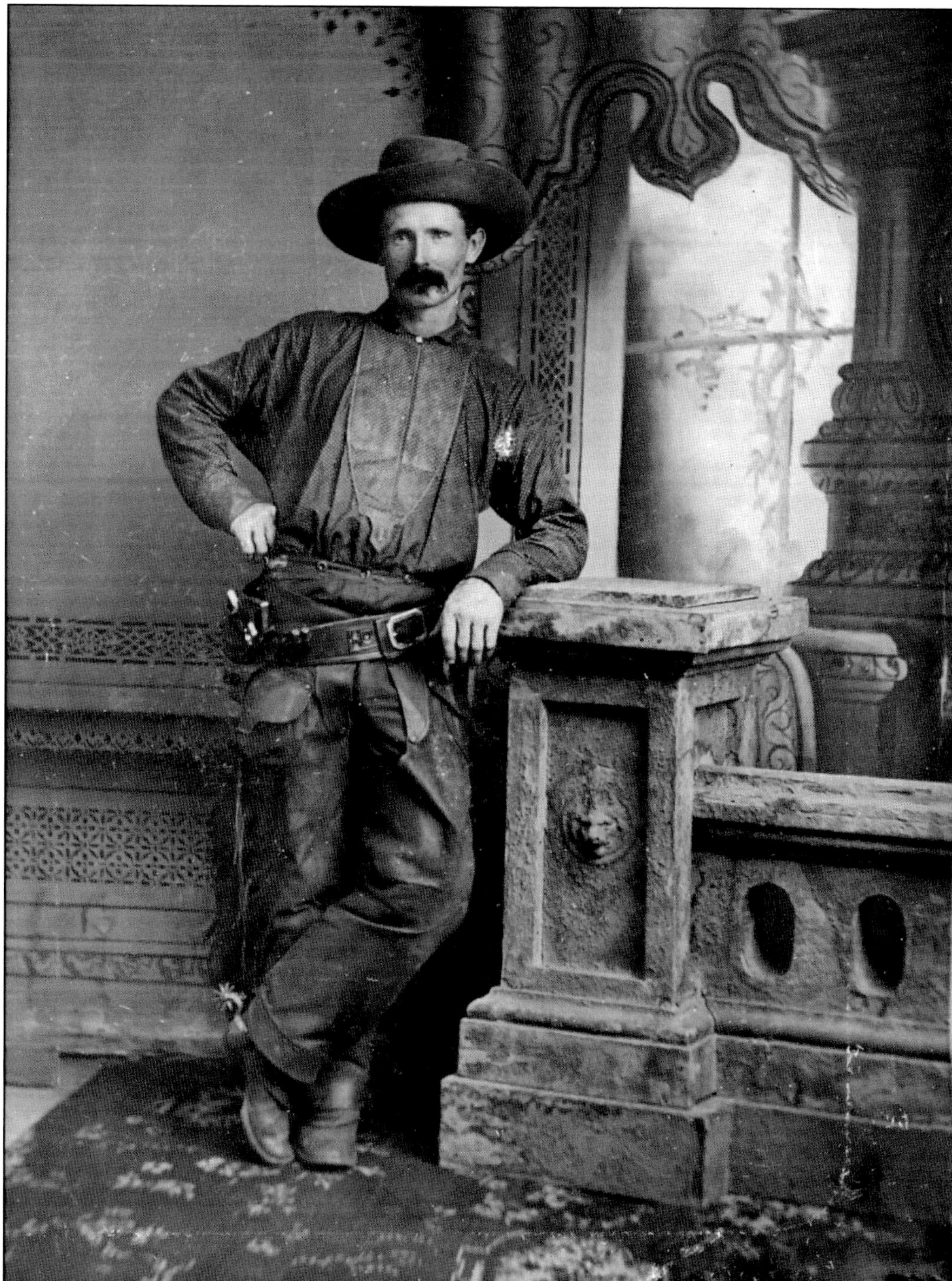

D.A. "Dutch" Nance (1845–1910) was a Fort Griffin merchant, cattleman, Confederate veteran, and Indian fighter. Raised in Young County near the Lower Brazos Reserve, he was the only white man to speak the Tonkawa Indian language. For a number of years, he was the only cattle buyer operating between the Clear Fork and the Rio Grande. His general store, in Fort Griffin, was a popular place with the Tonkawa Indians.

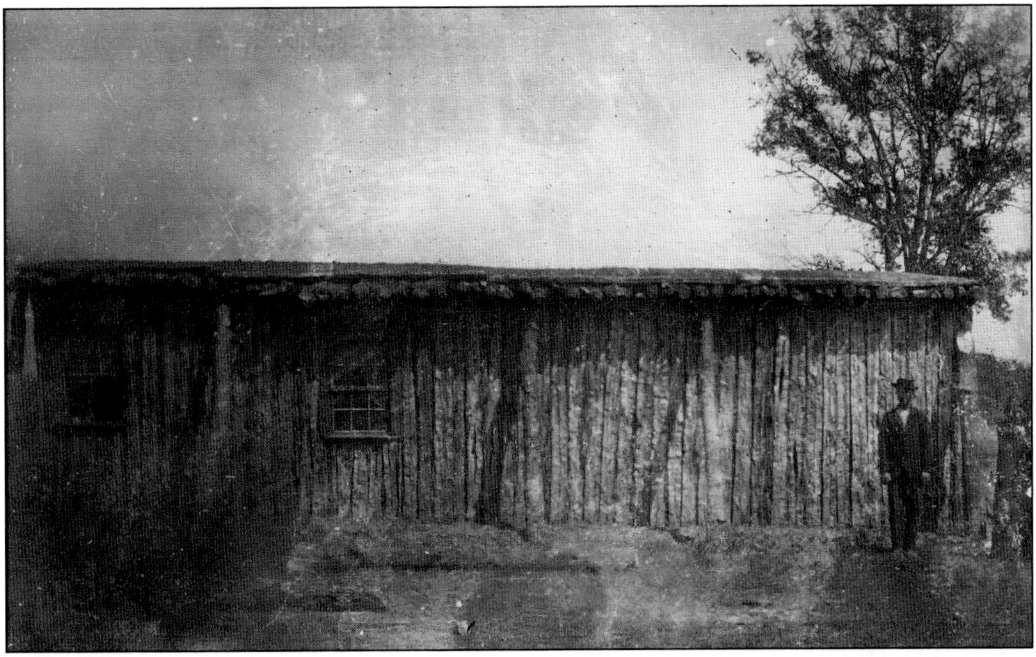

Dutch Nance stands in front of his mercantile store in Fort Griffin while a Tonkawa Indian peers around the corner. Nance opened his store in 1868. Built of picket construction, it had no locks on its doors. Living quarters were located in the back of the store. The Tonkawa Indians visited Nance's store daily, chiefly to buy raisins and lengths of bright calico.

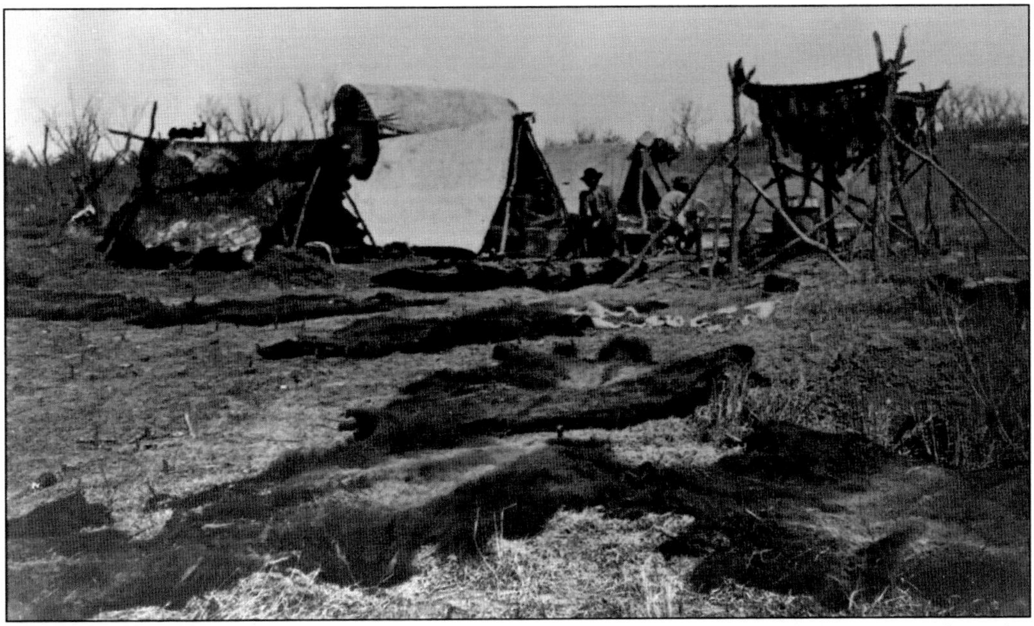

This is a buffalo hunters' camp near Evans Creek in Taylor County. Hides were spread on the ground to dry, and tongues were hung on racks. Begun in earnest in 1874, the "Great Slaughter" of the buffalo of the southern plains was accomplished in just a few years. Fort Griffin Flat was the supply point for over a thousand buffalo-hunting crews spread across the southern plains. By 1878, the great southern herds were gone.

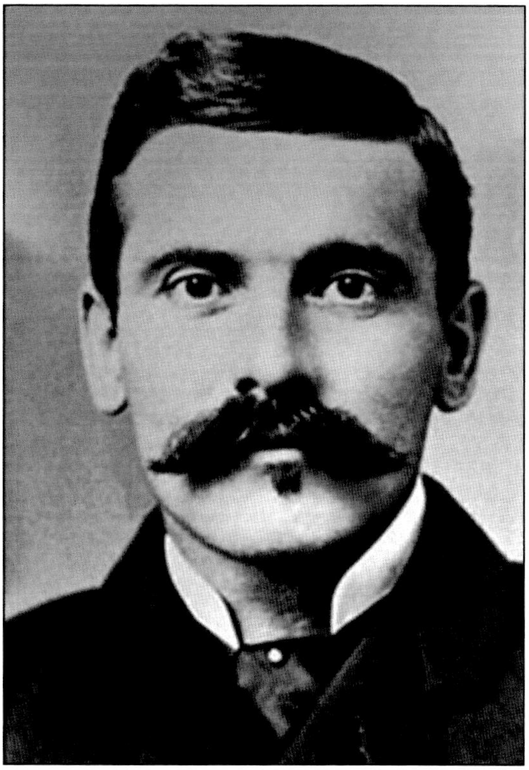

John Henry "Doc" Holliday, dentist, gunman, and gambler, was at Fort Griffin for a time. Arrested for a gambling and liquor charge, he was held in the Planter's Hotel until Big Nose Kate set fire to a shed, distracted his captors, and freed him. Most of his legend was fiction; although he injured several men, thus far, there is proof that he killed only two. (Courtesy of Fort Griffin State Historic Site.)

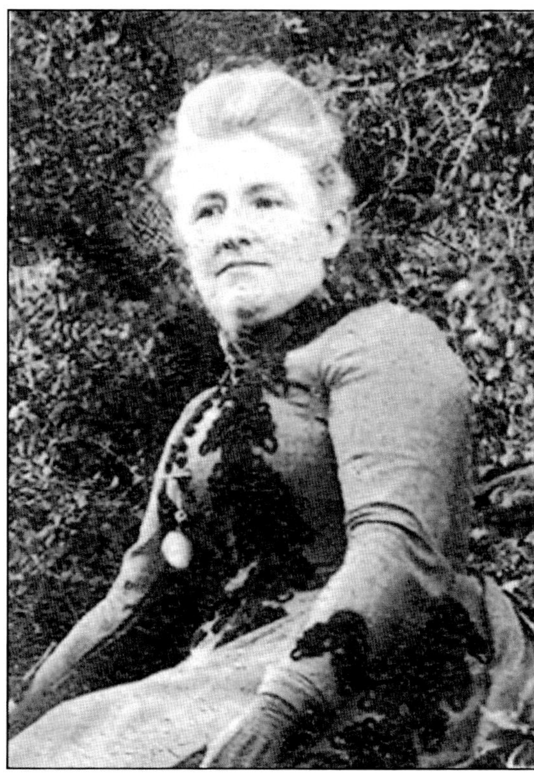

Lottie Deno was born Carlotta Thompkins in Warsaw, Kentucky, in 1844 to an affluent family. She was left to care for her mother and sister after her father died. Gambling her way from Chicago, down the Mississippi River to Fort Griffin by the 1870s, she became part owner of a boardinghouse and saloon. Legend says she left town because of a broken heart; actually, it was because of legal and financial problems. (Courtesy of Julia Putnam.)

John Larn (1849–1878), second sheriff of Shackelford County, served from February 1876 until March 1877. A member of the Old Law Mob, Larn was a cattle inspector for the longhorns passing through Fort Griffin, and he furnished beef to the military post. Accused of cattle stealing, Larn was killed in the Albany jail in the early hours of June 24, 1878, by 12 masked men, presumed to be the vigilance committee.

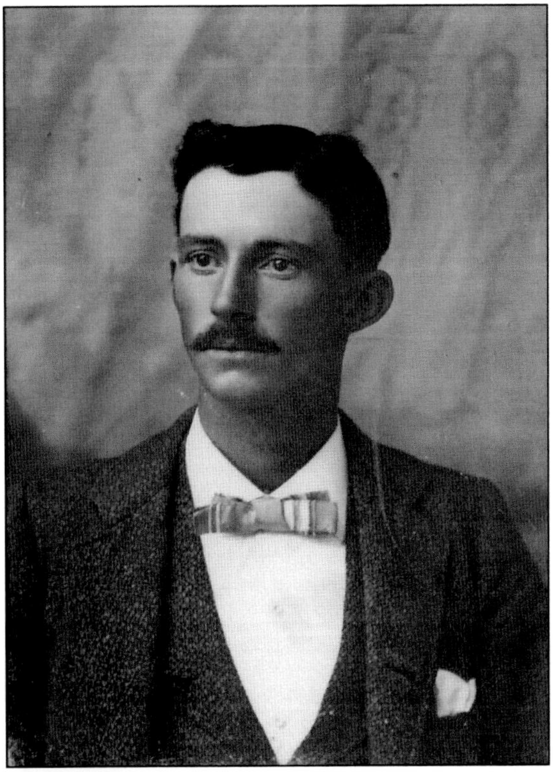

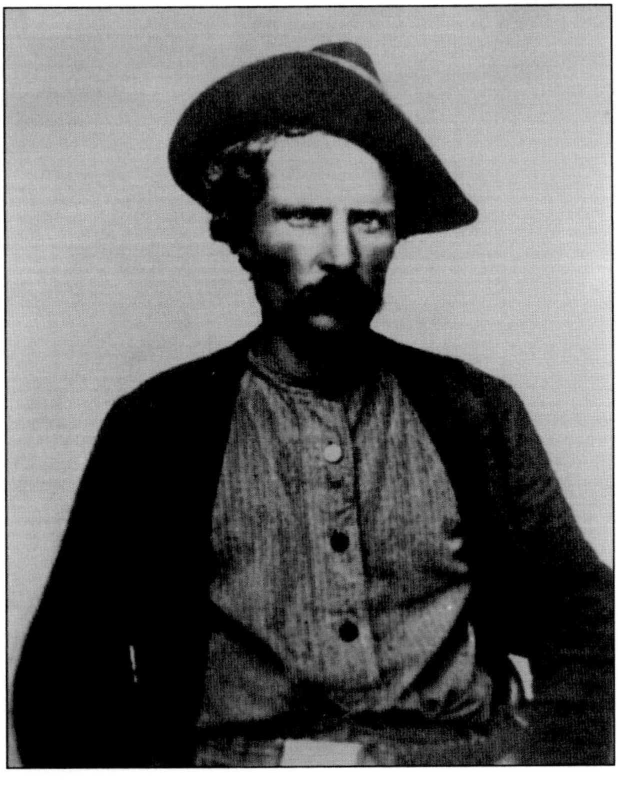

George Kisinger was a sergeant in Lt. George W. Campbell's Company B, Frontier Battalion of the Texas Rangers in the late 1870s. In 1876, at the request of Judge J.R. Fleming, Lieutenant Campbell, with a force of 30 to 35 Texas Rangers, set up camp north of Fort Griffin to help quell the vigilance committee violence. Lt. George Arrington took over from Campbell in the spring of 1878. (Courtesy of Fort Griffin State Historic Site.)

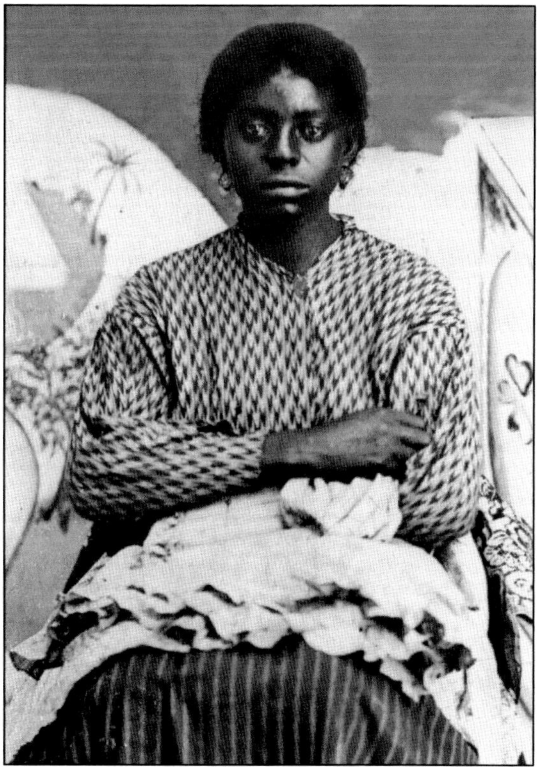

In 1863, at age 16, Mahala Cook Cass Dedmon and her 10-month-old daughter, Rose, were sold for $3,500. After the Civil War, she worked as a laundress at Fort Griffin and for Henry Palur in The Flat. She was probably in her mid-20s when this photograph was taken in the 1870s.

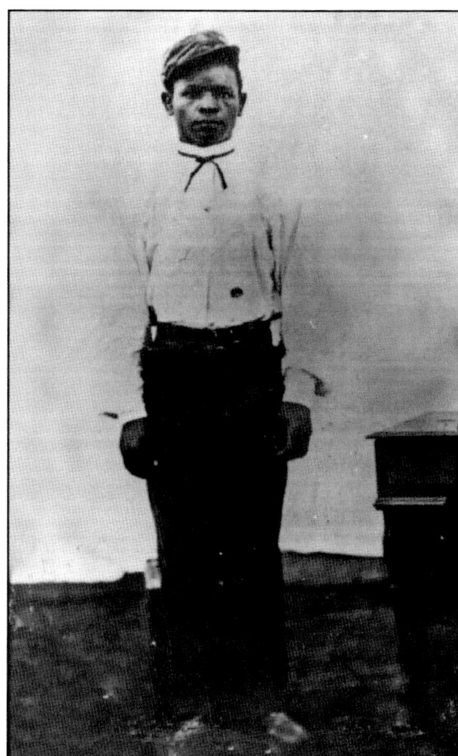

Born a slave in Kentucky, 1st Sgt. Lawson Gratts, 10th Cavalry, was enlisted by his master in the Union Army. Gratts became a first sergeant in Company C, 114th Colored Infantry. He was present at Appomattox when Lee surrendered. Freed, he served at Fort Sill in the 10th Cavalry. After being discharged, Gratts moved to Fort Griffin and worked as a freight hauler for Henry Palur, where he met his wife, Rose Ann.

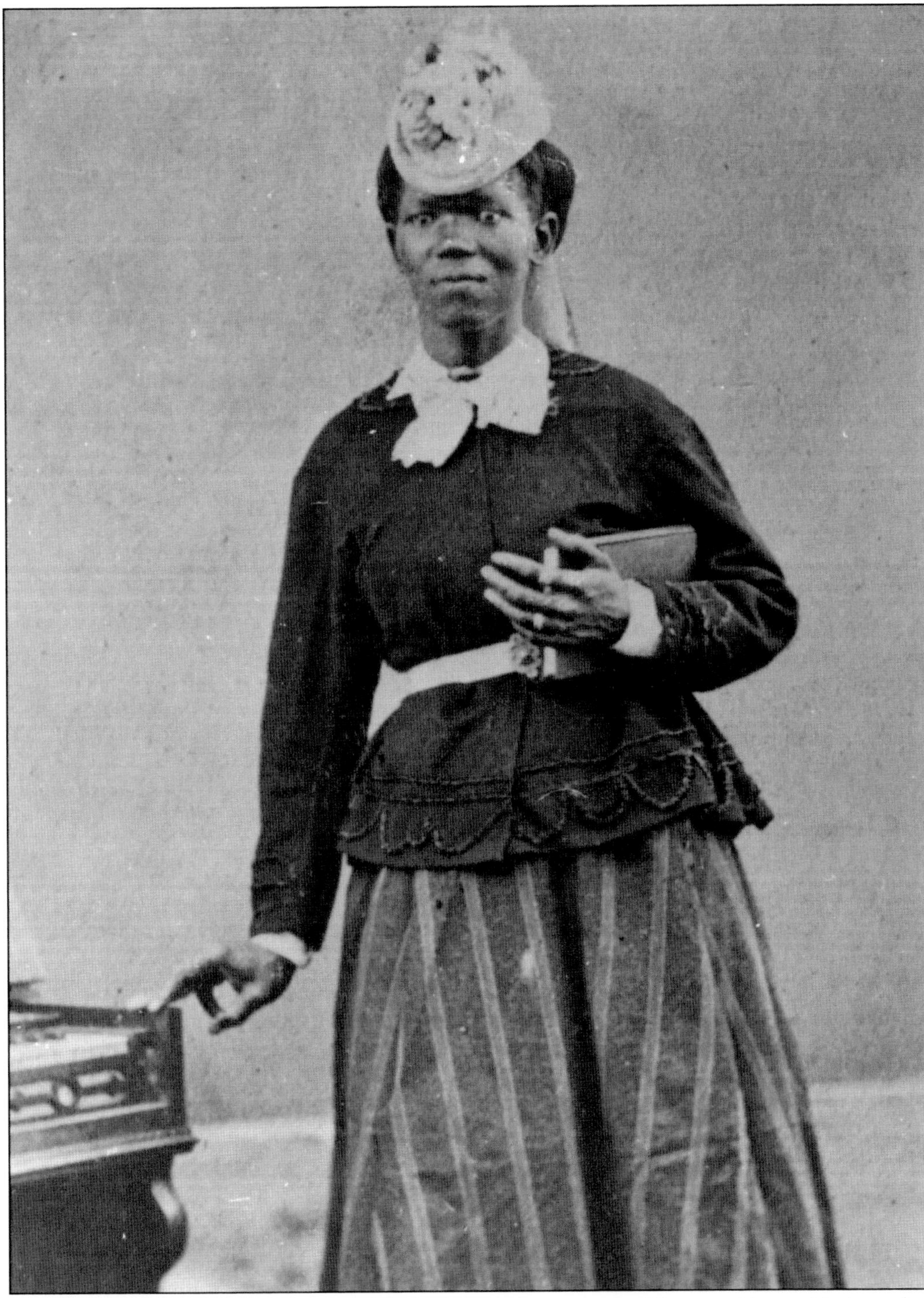

In 1877, Rose Ann Cass, daughter of Mahala Cass Dedmon, married Lawson Gratts, 42. According to records, she was 16 at the time. They were married for 32 years and had 14 children, about half of whom were born at Fort Griffin before the family moved in 1892 to Parker County. Rose Ann looks to be in her 20s in this photograph, so it must have been taken in the 1880s.

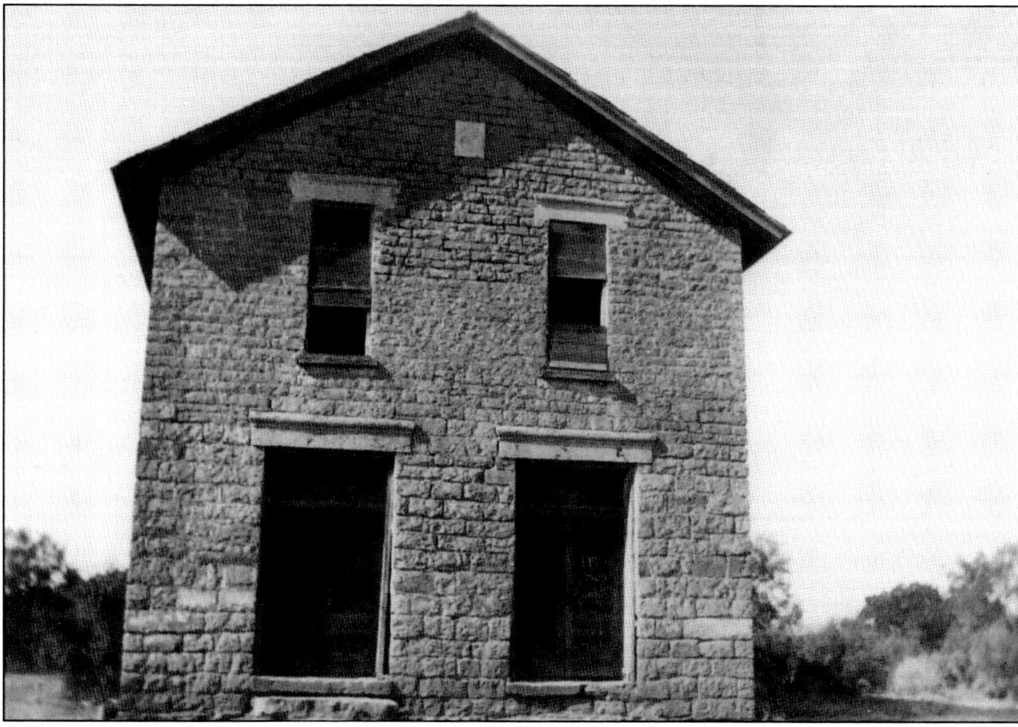

C.K. Stribling, first presiding judge and second county judge of Shackelford County, built this rock structure in 1877 for Fort Griffin Masonic Lodge No. 489. It was built with volunteer labor using rocks quarried from nearby Collins Creek. The lodge held meetings upstairs, while the first floor was used for church services, school, and civic affairs. Public school was held here until 1937. Today, it is privately owned and has been restored. (Courtesy of Lea Clayton Hutt.)

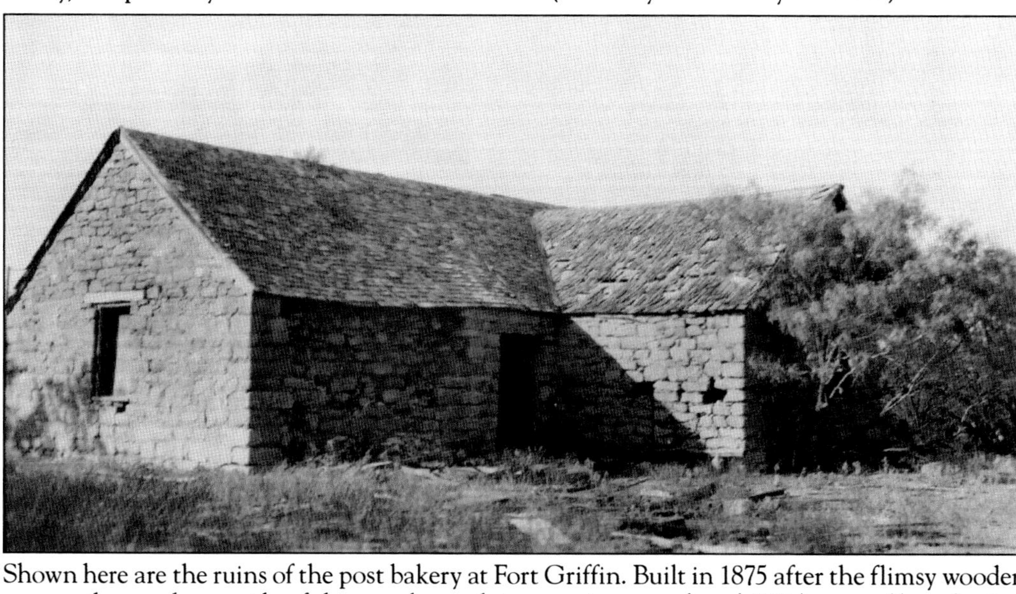

Shown here are the ruins of the post bakery at Fort Griffin. Built in 1875 after the flimsy wooden one on the northwest side of the post burned, it sometimes produced 800 loaves of bread a day. The roof collapsed in 1935, but, through the efforts of local groups, the bakery was rebuilt in the 1960s. The Texas Historical Commission did more restoration in 2013.

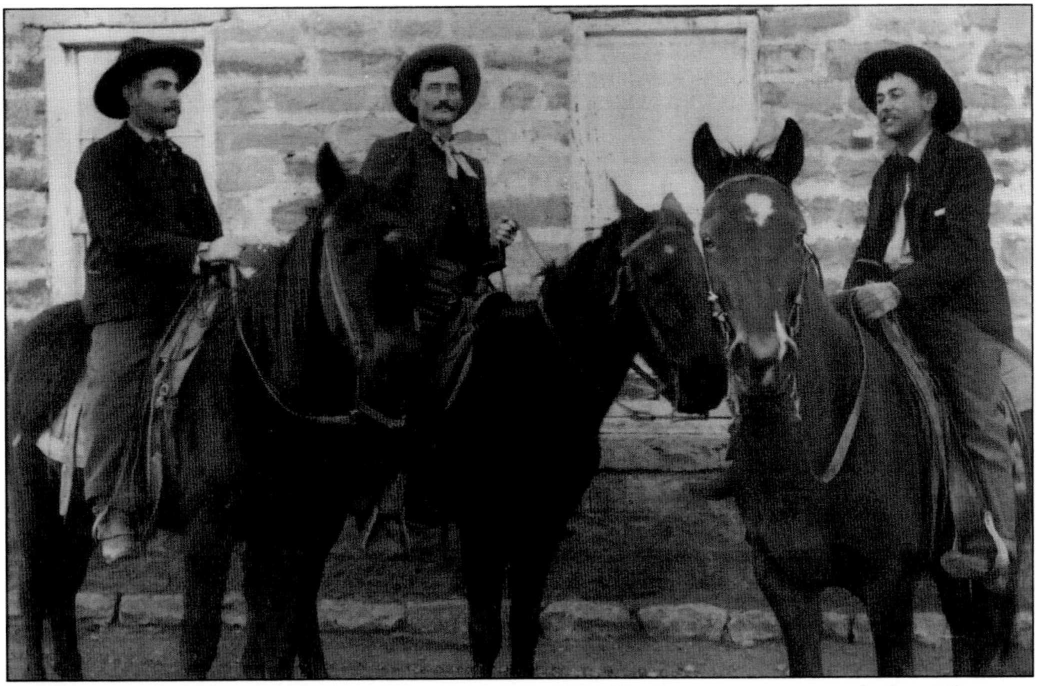

These cowboys, seated astride their horses, are dressed in Sunday-go-to-meeting clothes. They are, from left to right, Berry Campbell, Lee Tuton, and Tul Newcomb. According to Albany resident Emalyn "Sam" Gillispie, her uncles Tul and Berry were cowboys on the Matthews Ranch.

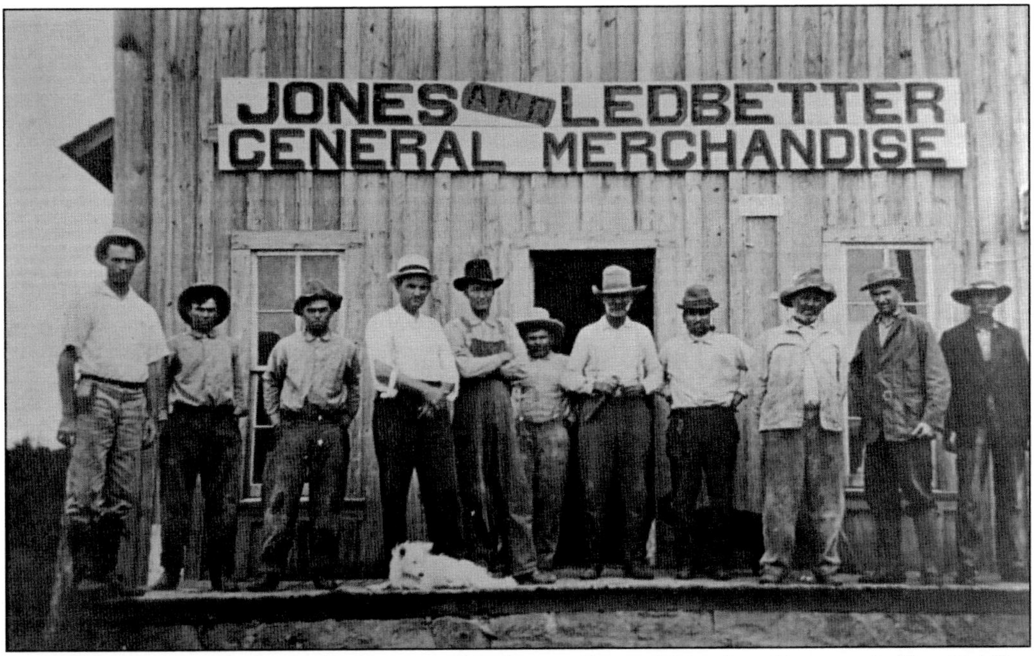

This 1915 photograph shows the Jones and Ledbetter General Merchandise store in Fort Griffin. From left to right are Claud Ward, Gene Pickard, Earl Pickard, Adam Jones, Seaborn Ledbetter, H.C. Pickard, Jim Alley, Elmo Murphy, Kirk Ledbetter, Elbert Sanders, and Lonnie Sanders. Adam Jones's dog lies in front of him.

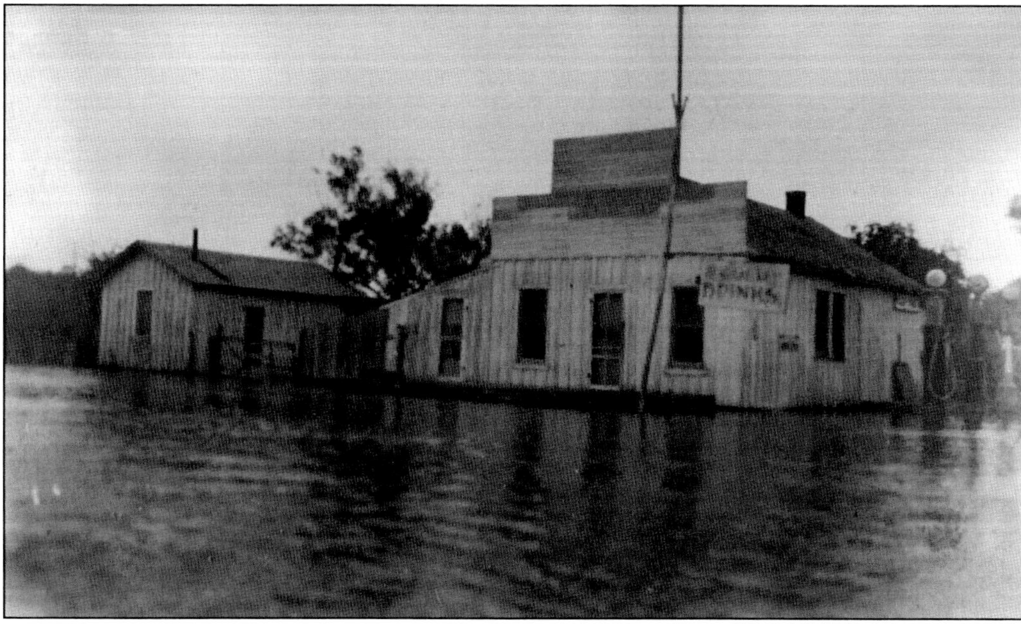

Floods in Fort Griffin were not uncommon, thanks to the town's proximity to the Clear Fork of the Brazos River. Here, the river waters lap up against the Fort Griffin General Merchandise Store in the early 1930s. (Courtesy of Lea Clayton Hutt.)

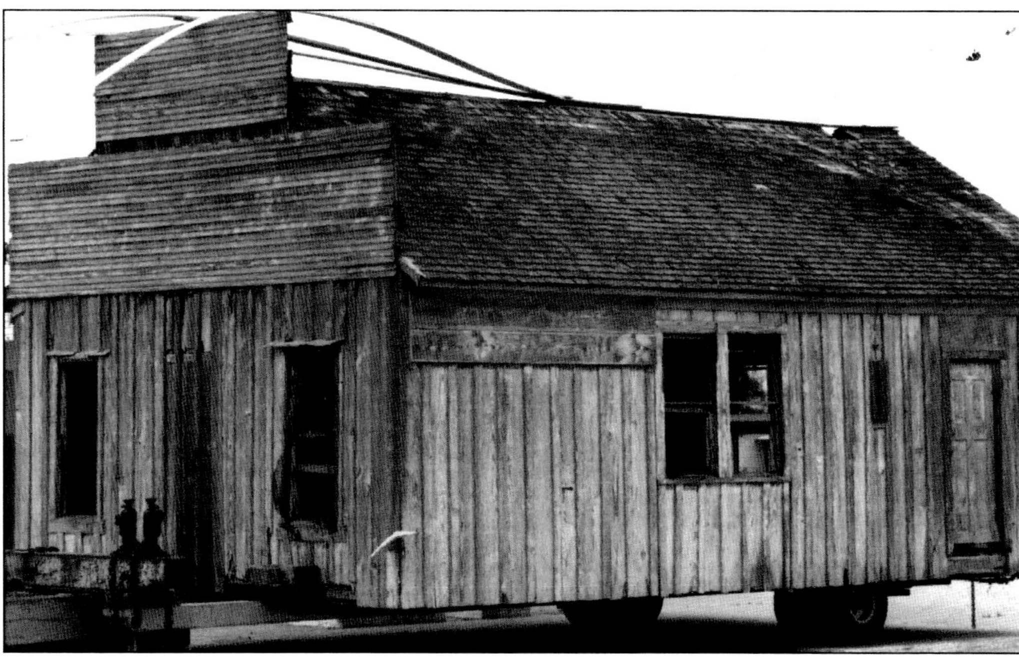

Jacked up and ready for transport to its new location in Albany in 1976 is the Fort Griffin General Merchandise Store. Located on the south end of Griffin Avenue, the establishment was built in 1901 and closed in 1951. Among those who owned and operated businesses in the structure were Theron Fincher, Sam Newcomb, and Harvey Herron. The building is now part of the Fort Griffin General Merchandise Steak House in Albany.

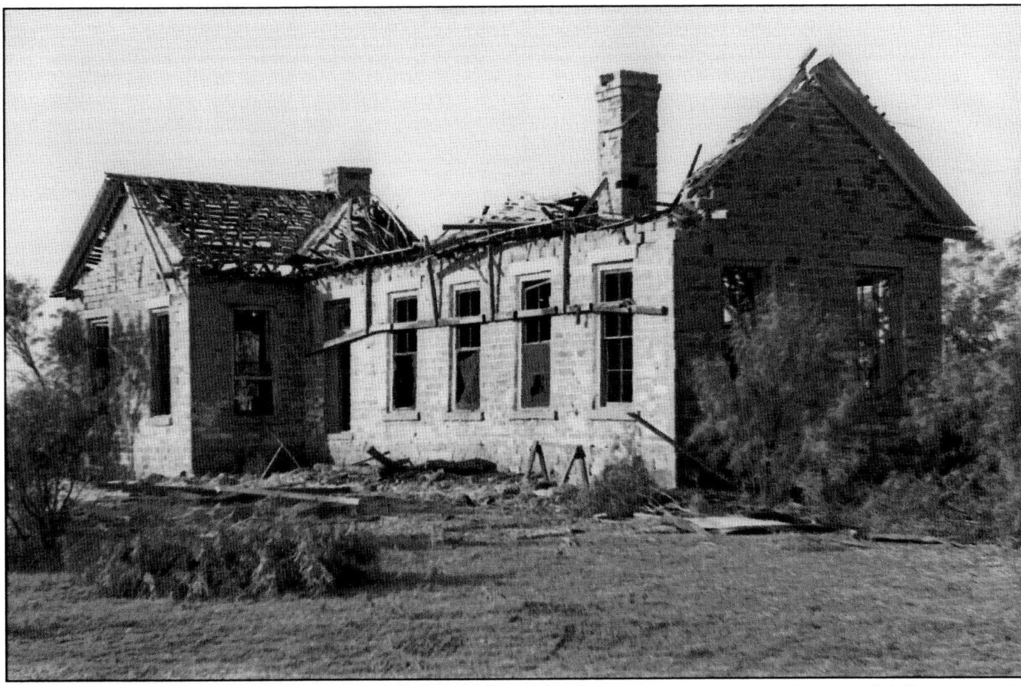

This early 1880s rock house was built by Gabriel Jordan nine miles southeast of Albany in the Vesta Community, later renamed Sedwick. In 1890, Jordan's widow sold the property to John F. Sedwick Sr. of Waco, whose son John F. Sedwick Jr. moved his family into the home in 1897. The Sedwicks moved to Albany in 1902, and John Jr. became well known in the banking business. (Courtesy of Moran Museum.)

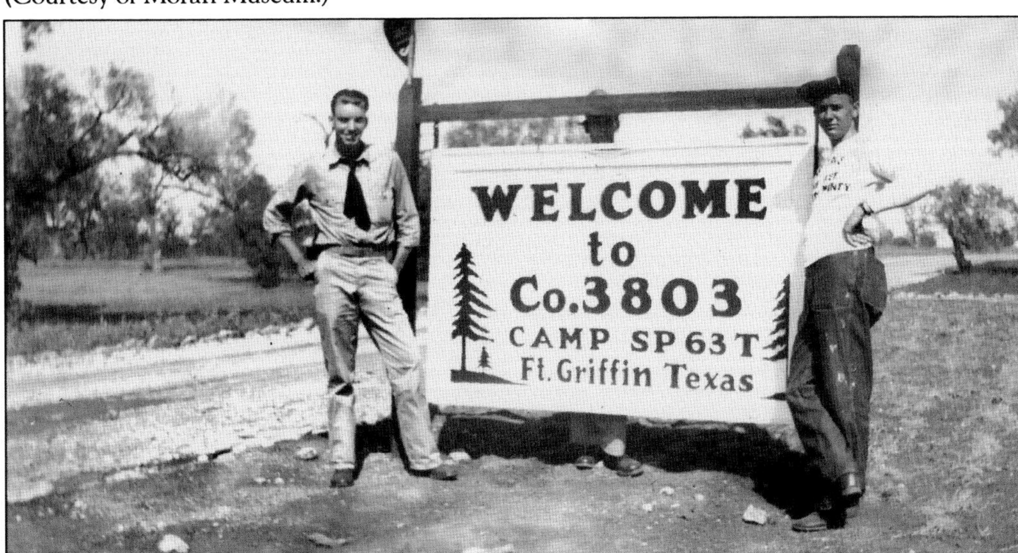

Most projects prompted by the Dust Bowl concerned soil conservation and erosion control, but 25 divisions built national, state, and local parks. Fort Griffin was one of the last sites worked on, and because World War II was imminent, many of the planned improvements were left undone. At the site of this camp, south of the fort area, paths and footings are still visible. (Courtesy of Fort Griffin State Historic Site.)

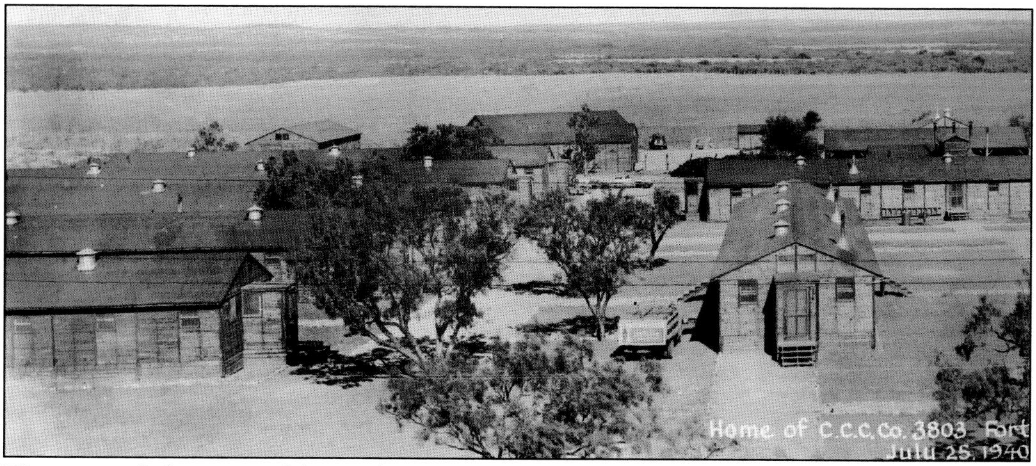

This is part of a long view of the Civilian Conservation Corps camp at Fort Griffin. The photograph was taken from the camp's water tower in 1940. Work projects such as the CCC employed about 2.5 million young men aged 17 to 25 from families on relief, helping to provide money to needy families during the Depression. The workers made about $30 a month, $25 of which was sent home to their families. (Courtesy of Fort Griffin State Historic Site.)

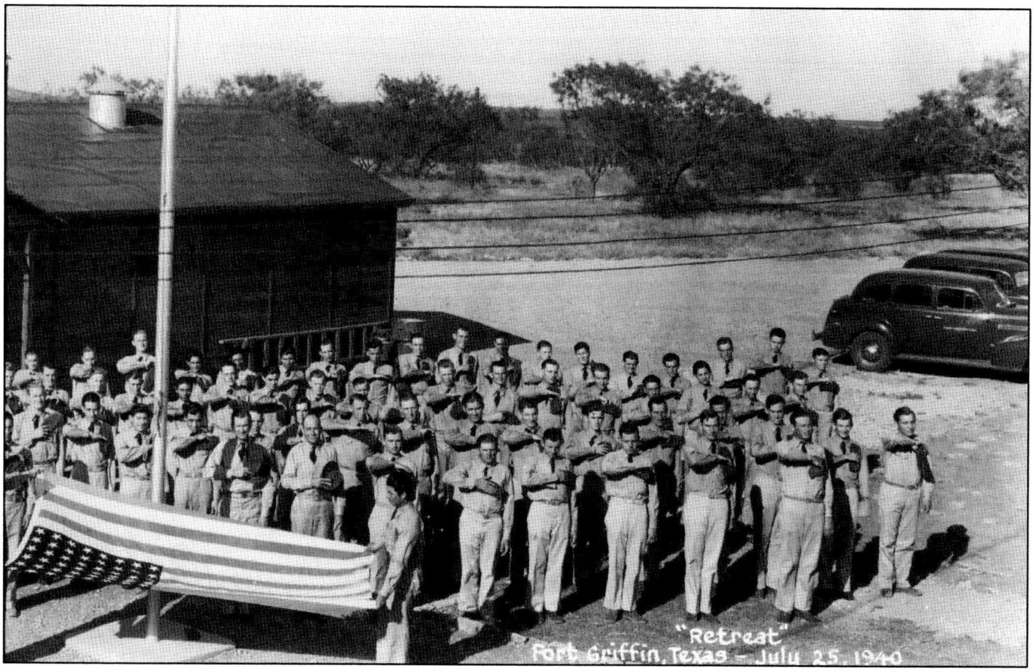

This partial group photograph of the CCC camp's men was taken on July 25, 1940, during a retreat. Standing on the far right is Albany native and longtime resident Ed Tackett, who has served the town as both chamber of commerce president and mayor. (Courtesy of Fort Griffin State Historic Site.)

Two

Let's Settle in This Country

By John A. Matthews

Shackelford County, carved out of Bosque County in 1856, was not organized until 1874. A visitor surveying the land at that time would have seen open grassland that looked like a rancher's dream. As seen on a map, the area stretches about 70 miles north to south and 40 miles east to west. The limestone-dominated land is fairly rough, too rough for much farming, but ideal for ranching. The Clear Fork River runs through the northwest part of the county, along with many smaller creeks that feed into it. Hubbard and Deep Creeks run in the southern part. Unlike today, there were numerous springs. The country was mostly open, with short grasses such as Indian grass along the draws and rougher slopes. Mesquite, at that time, was not dominant as it is now, possibly due to grass fires set by lightning, Indians, or campers. In addition, the large prairie-dog towns kept their areas clean.

Settlers were coming into this country and setting up homes as early as 1858. They brought horses, cattle, hogs (the ancestors of today's wild hogs), chickens, and whatever else they needed to thrive so far from the comforts they had enjoyed back East. Ranching consisted of cattle running on the wide-open range. There were no fences, so big roundups were held, at which calves were branded and some were sold. It was hoped that, at the next roundup, missing cattle would show up. Indians and rustlers could take a heavy toll. Barbed wire changed the situation. The ranchers were able to control their herds, the Indians were gone, rustling was under better control (although it still exists to some extent today), and ownership of the land was settled.

The ranching industry from 1900 to today has experienced ups and downs and has broken a lot of ranchers, while others have hung on. The early 1930s were very tough, with steers bringing 5¢ a pound and drought taking its toll. In the 1950s, drought and a market breakdown were disastrous. However, oil leasing and hunting have saved the bacon for many in Shackelford County in the last few years. Among old-timers still around and newer arrivals are Reynolds, Caldwell, Matthews, Nail, Davis, Snyder, Elliot, Sloan, Jones, Diller, Casey, Akers, Jackson, Compton, Green, Miller, Stasney, Musselman, and Poindexter. Apologies for any left out of this list.

Typical for life in a settled country, residents lived off the land. This was possible due to the variety of game to be had, with buffalo being the most plentiful. In addition, there were deer, antelope, hogs, fish, and small game, plus wild fruit and other staples. The ranching industry in the area had a slow start, as there was little demand, except from the Army and the small number of local residents. However, in 1865, George Reynolds drove a small herd southwest to Fort Concho, then to the Pecos River, then north to Santa Fe, and he made a nice profit. The success of this drive caused other ranchers to put together herds for California, Colorado, the Dakotas, New Mexico, and, later, when the railroad came west, Kansas. Thousands of cattle coming up from south Texas on their way north came through Albany and Fort Griffin. These drives continued until rail service was gradually established. The Texas Central came to Albany from Waco in 1881. Shipping pens were built on the west side of town, and, through the years, thousands of cattle were shipped out. The expansion of the railroads ended the long cattle drives and greatly simplified ranching. The railroads have, in turn, been replaced with trucks.

A tall sign reading "Home of the Hereford" has been at the bridge going to Abilene for a long time. When it was first erected, Albany could say that Herefords were indeed the predominant breed in the county, as nearly all the ranches ran them. The Dodson and Alexander registered operations were known over a wide area. However, due to several factors, including pinkeye, hybrid vigor, rate of gain, and grading "choice" in a shorter time in the feedlot, the Hereford has lost ground to other breeds. Looking at the sign from a different perspective, it brings back memories to many older citizens, and I hope younger ones realize they are driving under a bit of Albany history.

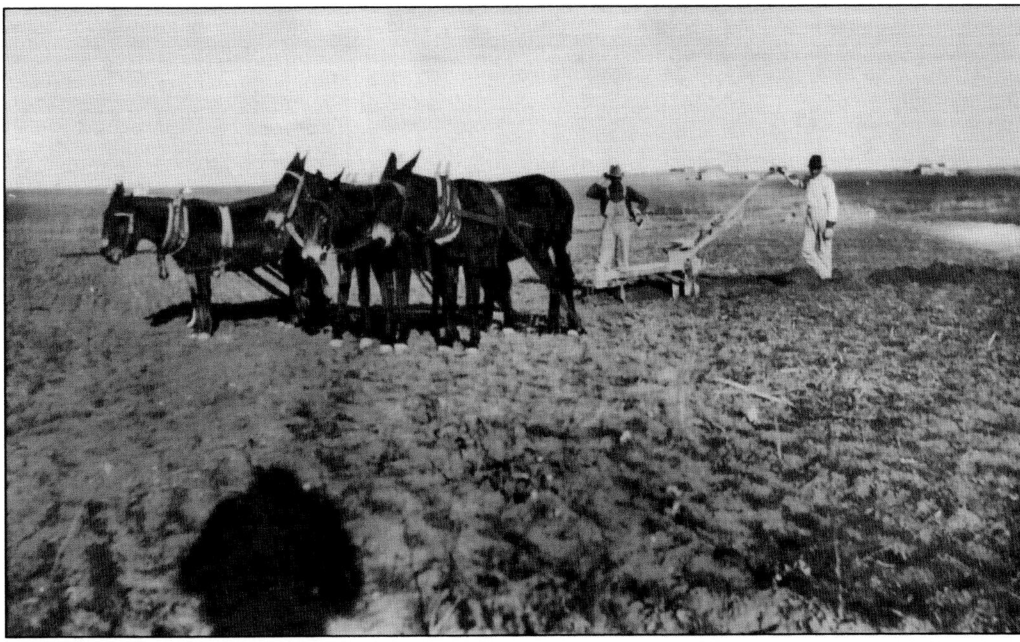

West Texas farmers and ranchers were struggling to survive the effects of a prolonged drought in 1886–1887, when Rev. John Brown appealed to Clara Barton and the American Red Cross. In January 1887, Barton arrived to survey the drought-stricken area. On her way home, she visited the *Dallas Morning News* and left a personal check for $20, encouraging the editor to solicit funds to help the farmers. (Courtesy of Kristen Landry Guerin.)

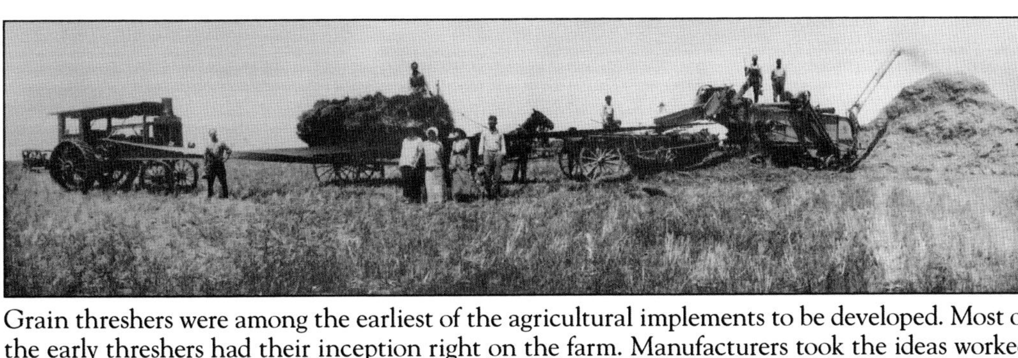

Grain threshers were among the earliest of the agricultural implements to be developed. Most of the early threshers had their inception right on the farm. Manufacturers took the ideas worked out by the farmers and developed them into working machines. The Sanders thresher is seen here. Wesley Miller Sanders is in the center, without a hat. (Courtesy of Lea Clayton Hutt.)

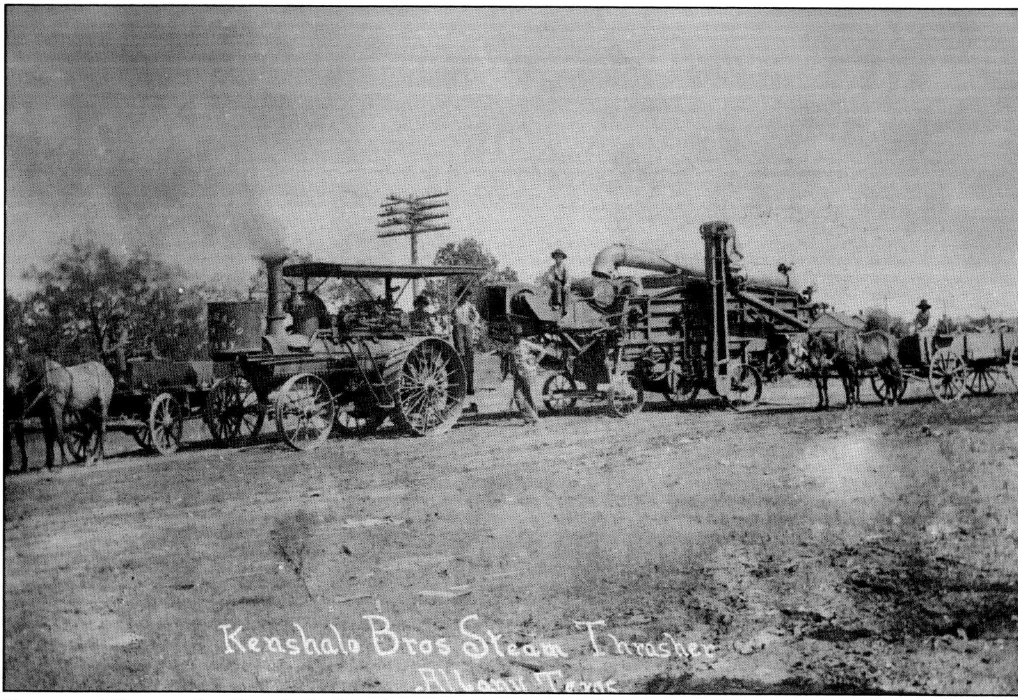

Born in Albany, the Kenshalo brothers, Pete, Charlie (1861–1941), and Ben (1880–1936), were pioneer grain threshers who owned one of the first gasoline tractors brought to Shackelford County. Ben was also superintendent of the Albany city water system for a time. This photograph was taken in 1901.

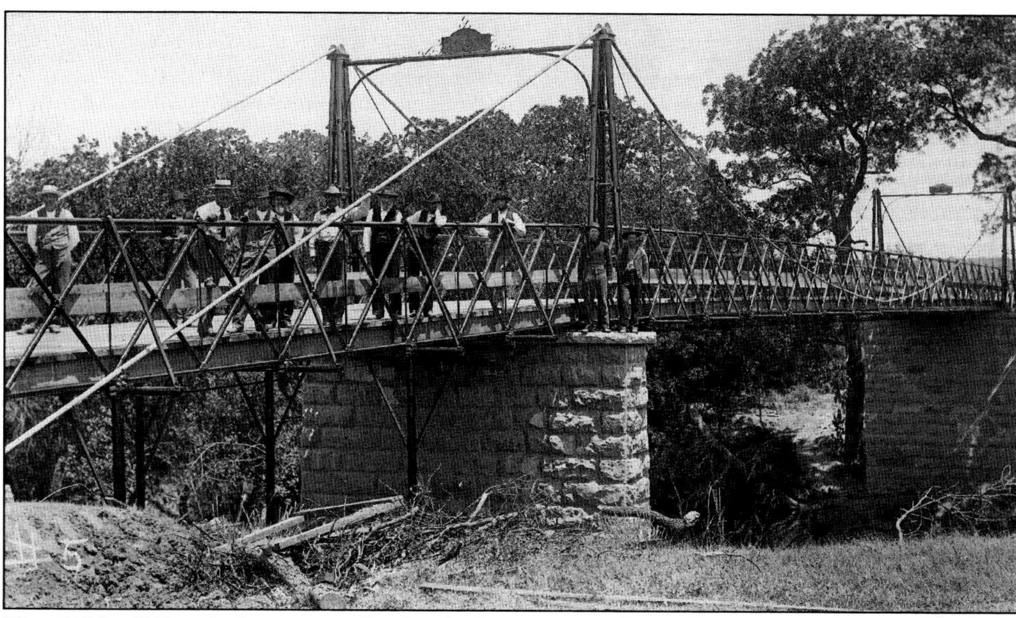

The Caldwell Ranch Suspension Bridge, built in 1896, is located 16 miles northeast of Albany, on the Clear Fork of the Brazos River. Men identified in this photograph are Judge J.C. Lynch (fifth from left), Judge J.A. Matthews (sixth from left), and Luther Hollowell (eighth from left). (Courtesy of John A. Matthews.)

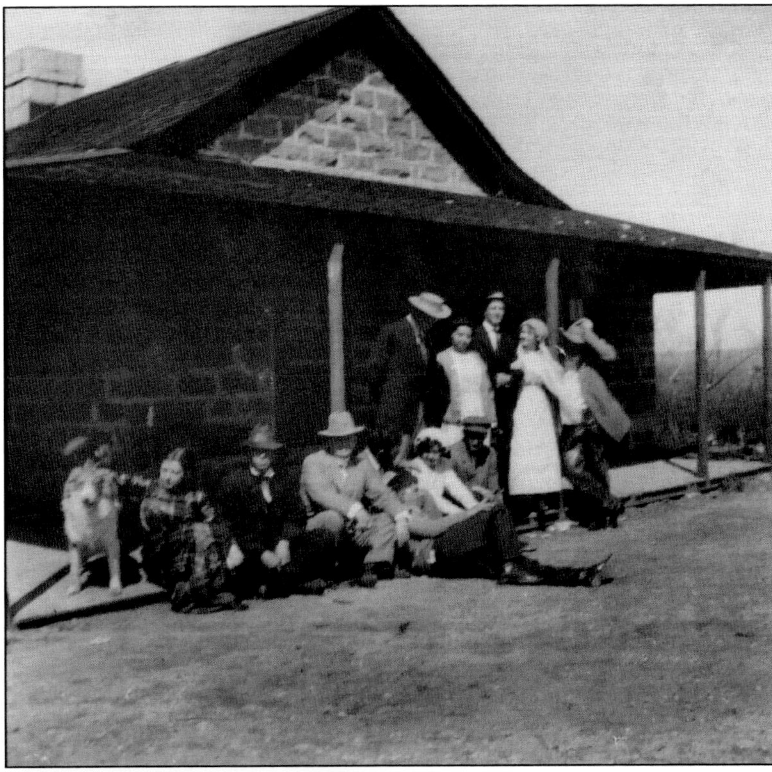

This 1913 photograph shows the Chimney Creek rock ranch house built by Joseph Kite in 1875. After Kite's death, Frank E. Conrad took control of the historic portion of the ranch. At the time this photograph was taken, two of the Conrad children, Louis (1888–1969) and John (1886–1945), were entertaining a large party, which included members of the Webb family. (Courtesy of John A. Matthews.)

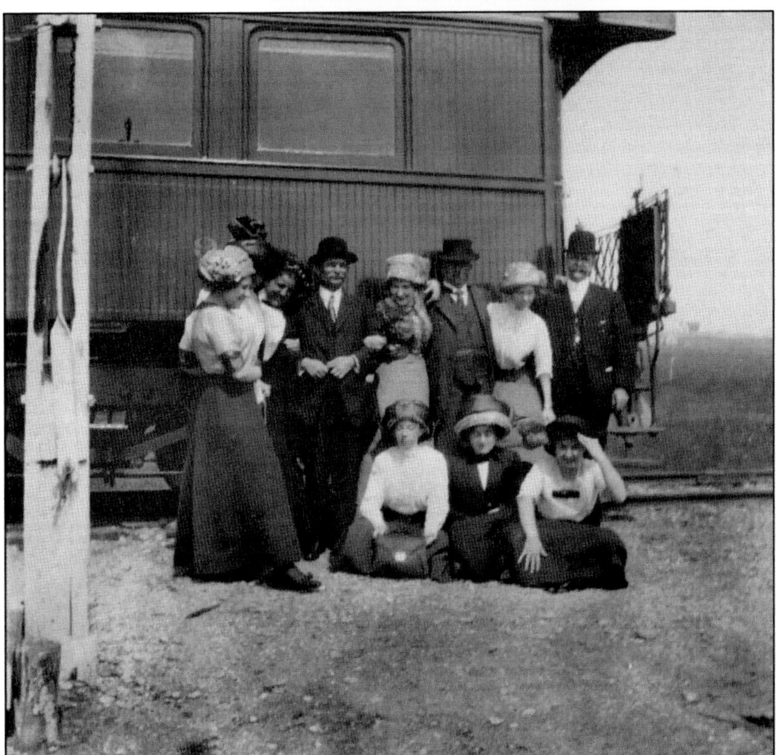

Arriving by train in 1913, the entire Webb house party was invited out to the Chimney Creek Ranch by John and Louis Conrad. In 1920, the ranch was purchased by G.R. Davis from the heirs of Ella (Matthews) Conrad (1865–1945), John, Louis, and George Reynolds Conrad. (Courtesy of John A. Matthews.)

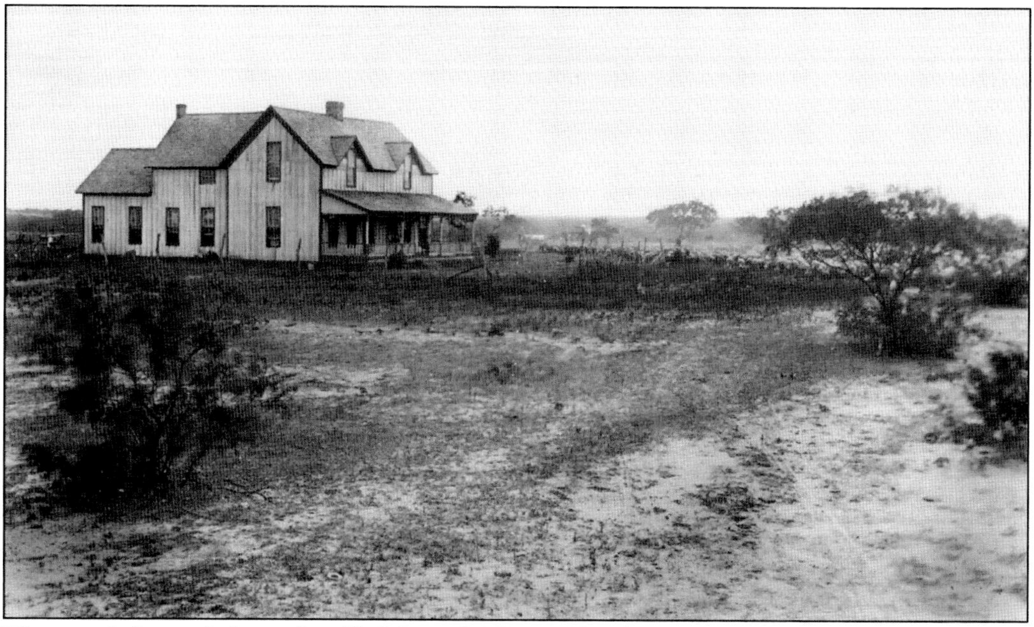

This ranch house belonged to Eli Meyer (1858–1927), who came to Fort Griffin in 1876. He later moved to Albany, where he established a sheep ranch three miles west of town. In 1891, he married Lulu P. Nance. After the construction of the new Presbyterian Church was completed in 1898, Meyer purchased the original wooden church and moved it to his property, where it was used in the construction of his ranch house.

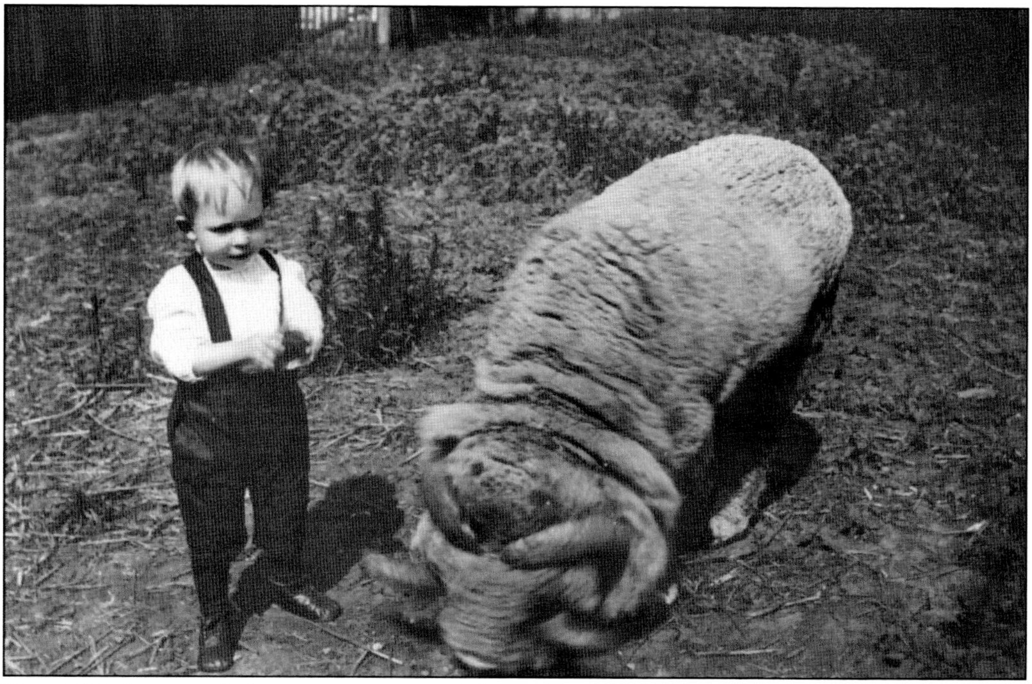

This 1896 photograph shows young Peyton Meyer, son of Eli Meyer, with one of his father's rams. Eli Meyer owned and operated one of the few successful sheep ranches in Texas. Today, Helen and Stanley Ivy own the property.

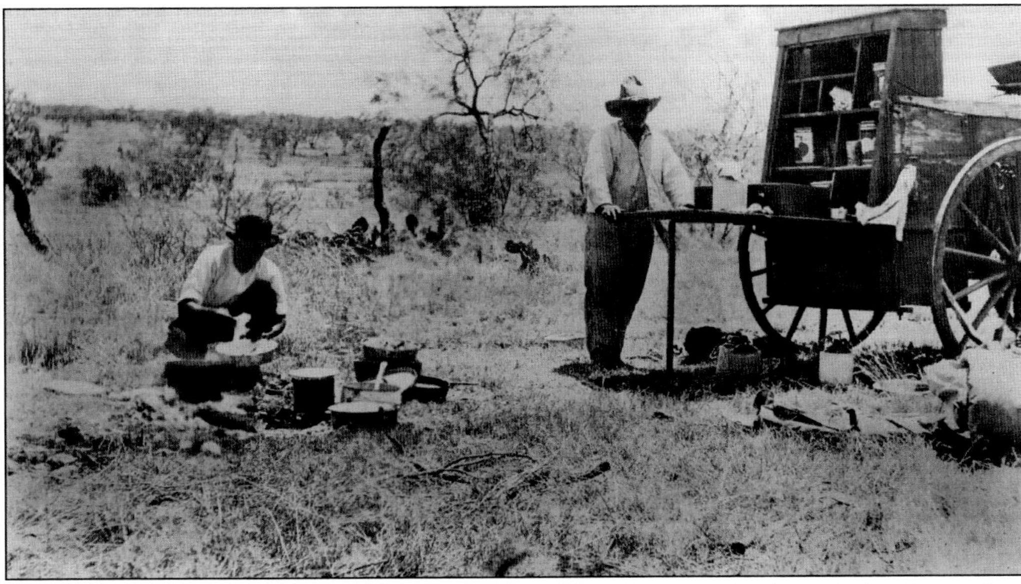

In this undated photograph, Joe Thomas (left) and Pete King get lunch ready for the cowboys on the J.A. Matthews Ranch, commonly referred to as Lambshead Ranch. The invention of the chuck wagon is attributed to Charles Goodnight, who introduced the concept in 1866. Originally called trail wagons, they accompanied riders on cattle drives. (Courtesy of John A. Matthews.)

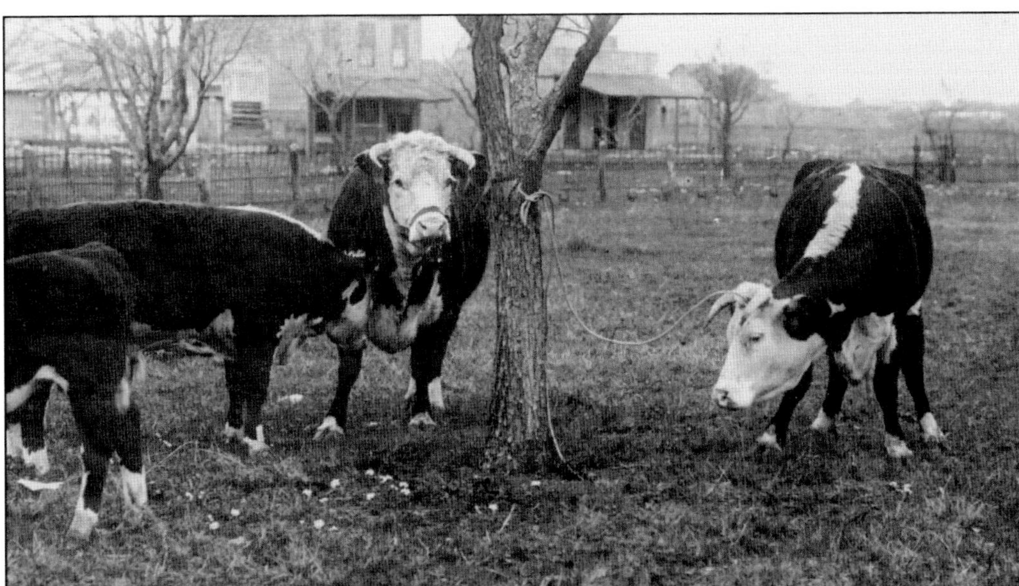

Henry Herron brought Herefords to Albany in 1910. He paid $250 a head for three, which was an unheard of price back then. These Herefords, shown on the courthouse lawn in an undated photograph, belonged to the Reynolds Brothers Cattle Company.

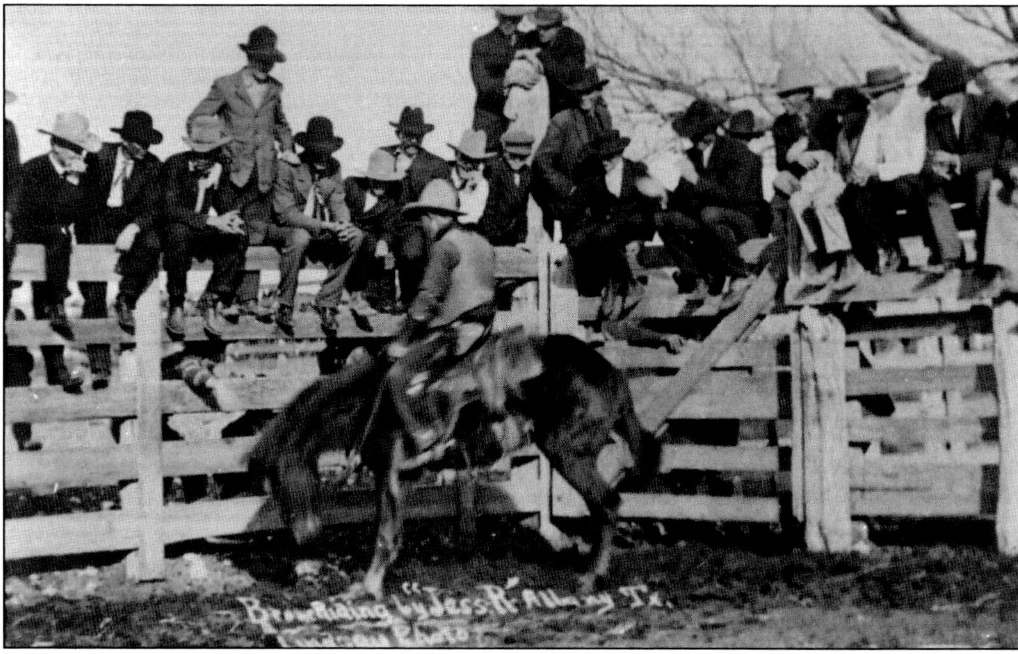

A cowboy identified only as Jess R. busts a bronco. Saddle bronco riding is steeped in a rich and varied history straight from the ranch. A wild, fiery bucking horse could be found on nearly every ranch in the world, and brave cowboys hopped on and hoped for the best. Saddle bronco riding was a pure test of strength and skill, and only the best cowboys stayed aboard for a full eight-second ride.

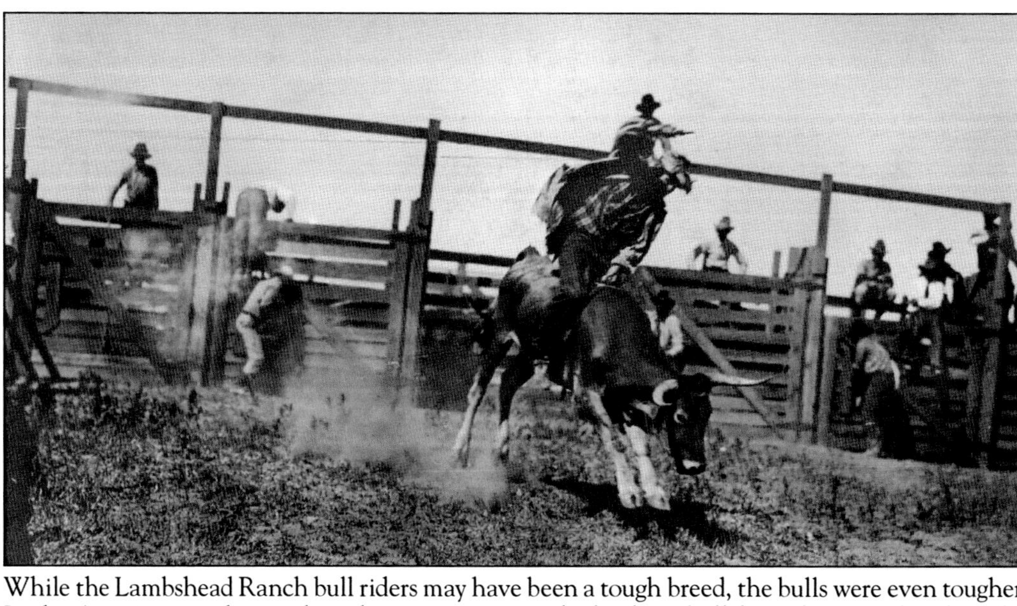

While the Lambshead Ranch bull riders may have been a tough breed, the bulls were even tougher. In the American tradition, the rider must stay atop the bucking bull for eight seconds. The rider tightly fastens one hand to the bull with a long braided rope. The risky endeavor has been called "the most dangerous eight seconds in sports." (Courtesy of John A. Matthews.)

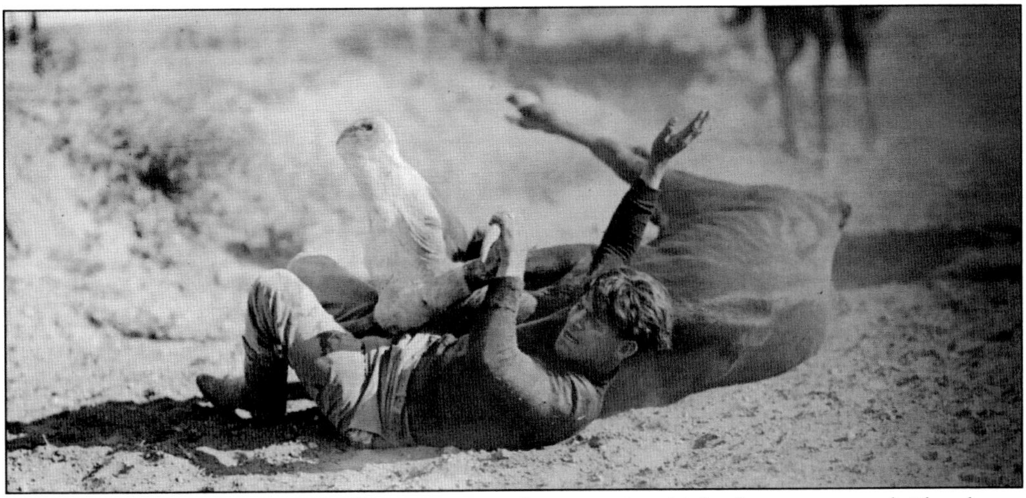

Steer wrestling, also known as bulldogging, is a rodeo event in which a horse-mounted rider chases a steer, drops from the horse to the steer, and then wrestles the steer to the ground by twisting its horns. Historically, steer wrestling was not a part of ranch life. This unidentified bulldogger was a working cowboy from the Lambshead Ranch. (Courtesy of John A. Matthews.)

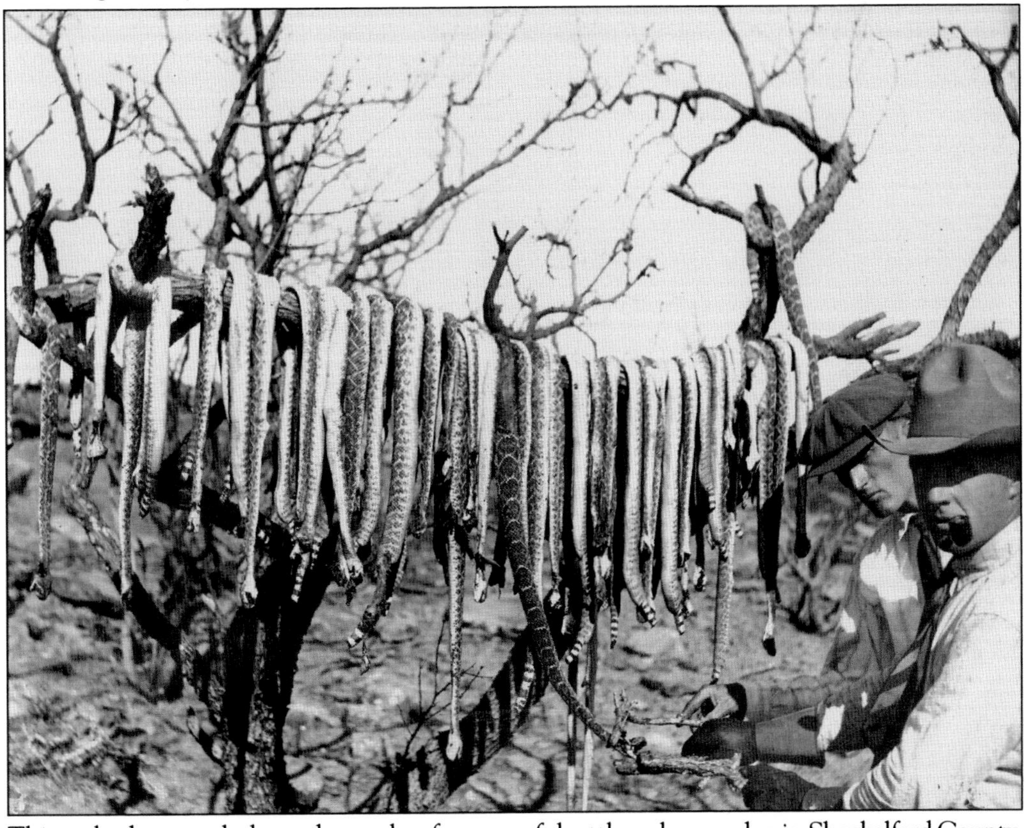

This early photograph shows the results of a successful rattlesnake roundup in Shackelford County. The snakes were smoked out of their dens and then captured. Rattlesnakes, and their stories, have long been an exciting and colorful part of Texas history. Many stories of snakebites ended in tragedy, since most of the cures were primitive and unreliable.

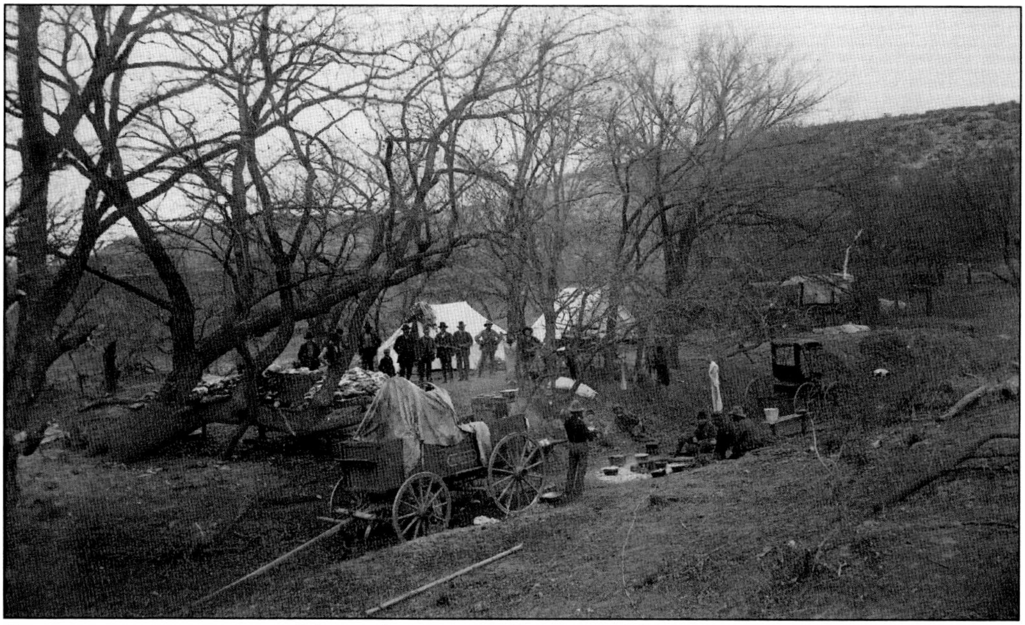

An important game meat of the early Texas settlers was wild hogs. In this photograph, L.H. Hill is identified as the man left of center, wearing a coat, with his hands behind his back. Butchering hogs was often a neighborly affair, with several ranchers working together. The meat was hung up to cure in a barn or smokehouse. Fried ham, biscuits, and red-eye gravy was a common breakfast meal for pioneers.

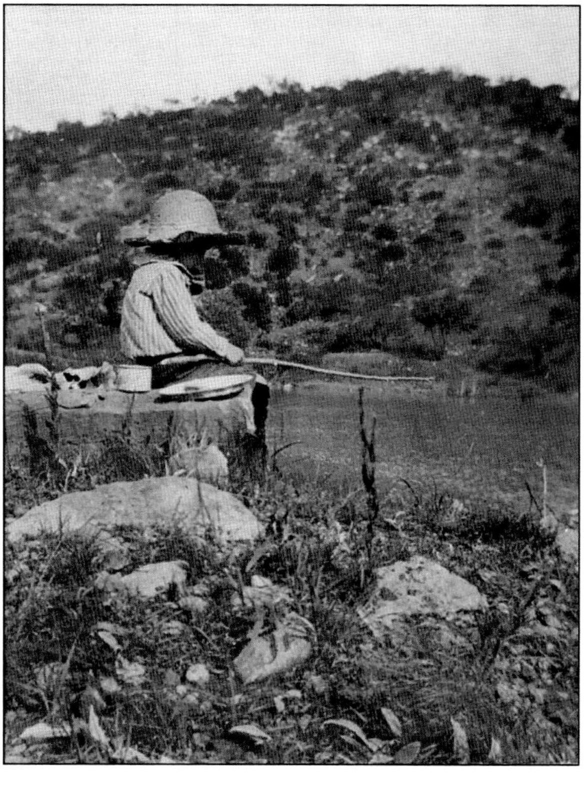

Shown fishing at the age of six is Watt Matthews (1899–1997). The youngest child of J.A. and Sallie Reynolds Matthews, Watt became co-manager of the historic J.A. Matthews Ranch in 1941 and general manager in 1977. A Princeton graduate, he was well known for his preservation of local history and support of education and the *Fort Griffin Fandangle*. (Courtesy of Fort Griffin State Historic Site.)

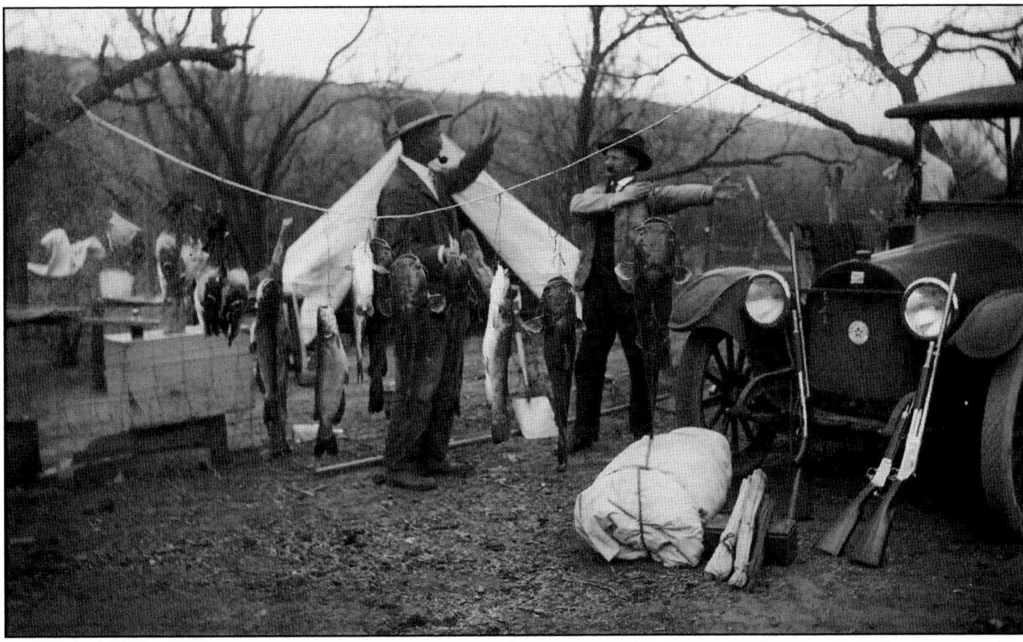

Fishing and hunting parties were common in the early 1900s, just as they are in the area today. These unidentified men, photographed around 1910, have clearly enjoyed a successful day of fishing. If the rifles leaning against the car are any indication, they are planning for a hunting expedition the next day.

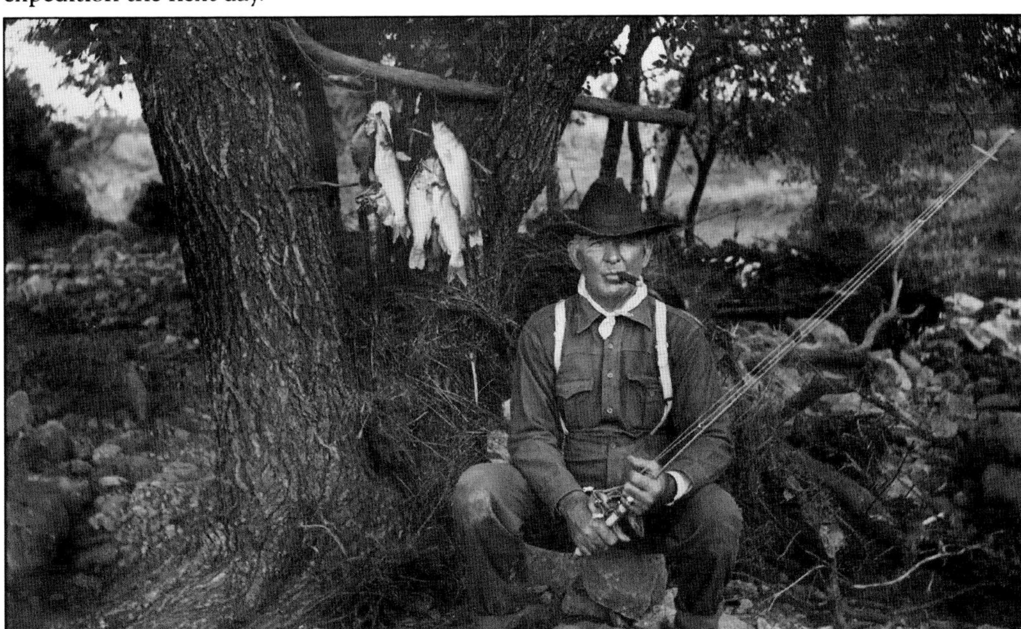

William Ivy Cook (1857–1923) and his wife, Missouri Matilda Nail (1858–1932), moved to Shackelford County in 1885. With brother-in-law J.H. Nail, they purchased a 17,760-acre ranch. The Cooks bought out Nail in 1898. With their oil wealth, Matilda Cook founded the W.I. Cook Memorial Hospital in Fort Worth (now Cook Children's Hospital) in 1929. The Cook Ranch has enriched Albany and its trade area by expanding petroleum-related business activities.

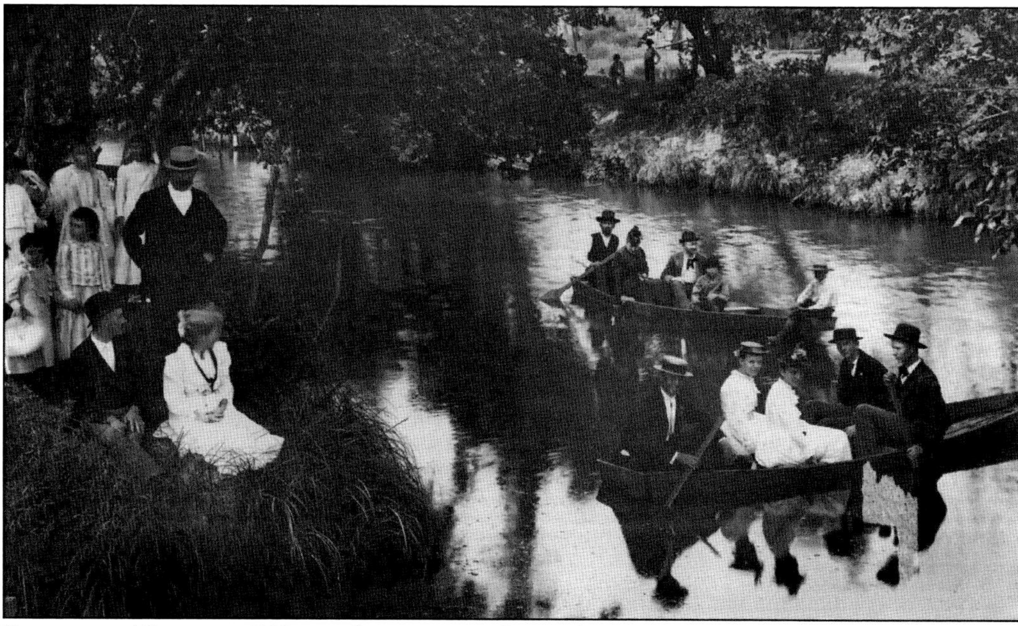

Boating in Albany in 1892 was done wearing hats, gloves, suits, and white dresses. And ladies carried parasols. Seated on the bank wearing a derby hat is Piner Moody. Jim Center stands behind him. Others on the creek bank are not identified. Among those in the far boat are Carpenter Browning and his wife, and Jim Lyons in the middle section. Seated in the front boat are, from left to right, Walter Gulledge, Lula Moody, Annie Zug, Carl Burns, and a Mr. Gilbert.

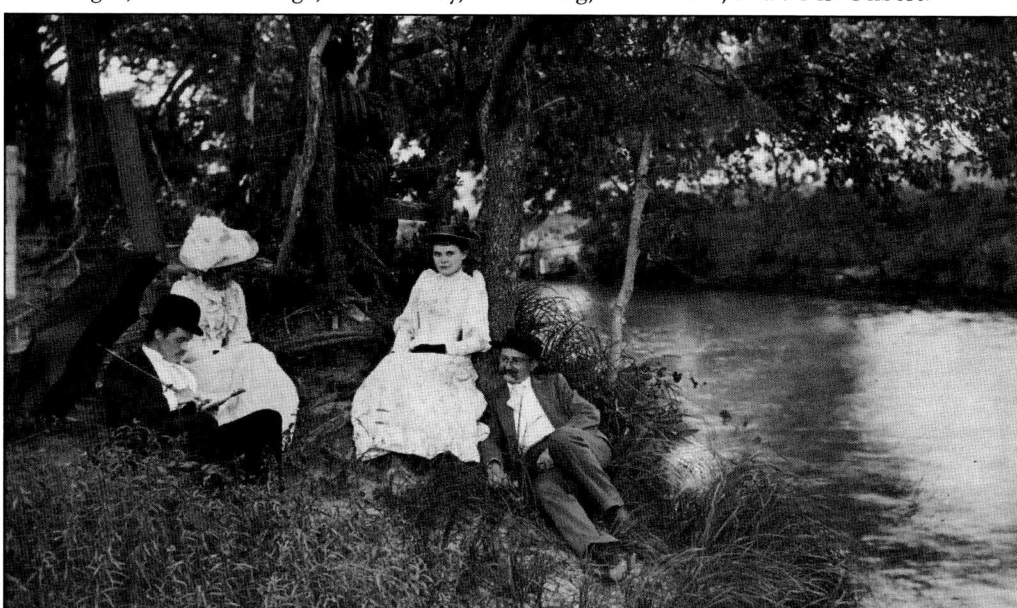

In 1892 Albany, a favorite Victorian pastime was renting boats for 10¢ an hour and floating on the creek in Elm Grove Park, owned by John C. and Albert Jacobs. Located behind the Jim George home, the park also contained a skating rink, tennis court, and croquet grounds. Pictured enjoying the outdoors beside the creek are, from left to right, Howard Edgar, Grace Lee, Gertrude Burns, and John F. Lyons.

Shown here playing with puppies are sisters Sallie Matthews Judd (1893–1985, left) and Lucille Matthews Brittingham (1890–1995), daughters of Sallie Reynolds Matthews and John Alexander Matthews. In 1936, Mrs. Matthews wrote her memoir, *Interwoven*, for the family. It was later published, and the book is now considered a classic pioneer story. (Courtesy John A. Matthews.)

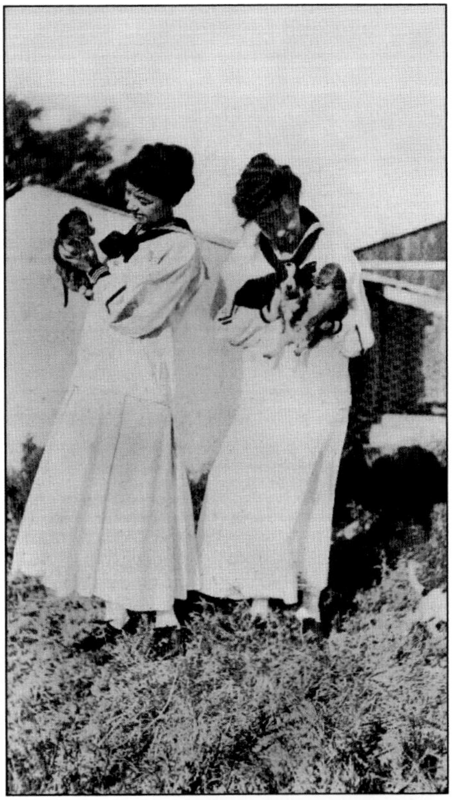

John A. "Bud" Matthews (1853–1941) crosses Foyle Creek with his horses and buggy. Foyle Creek is located about seven miles north of Albany. (Courtesy John A. Matthews.)

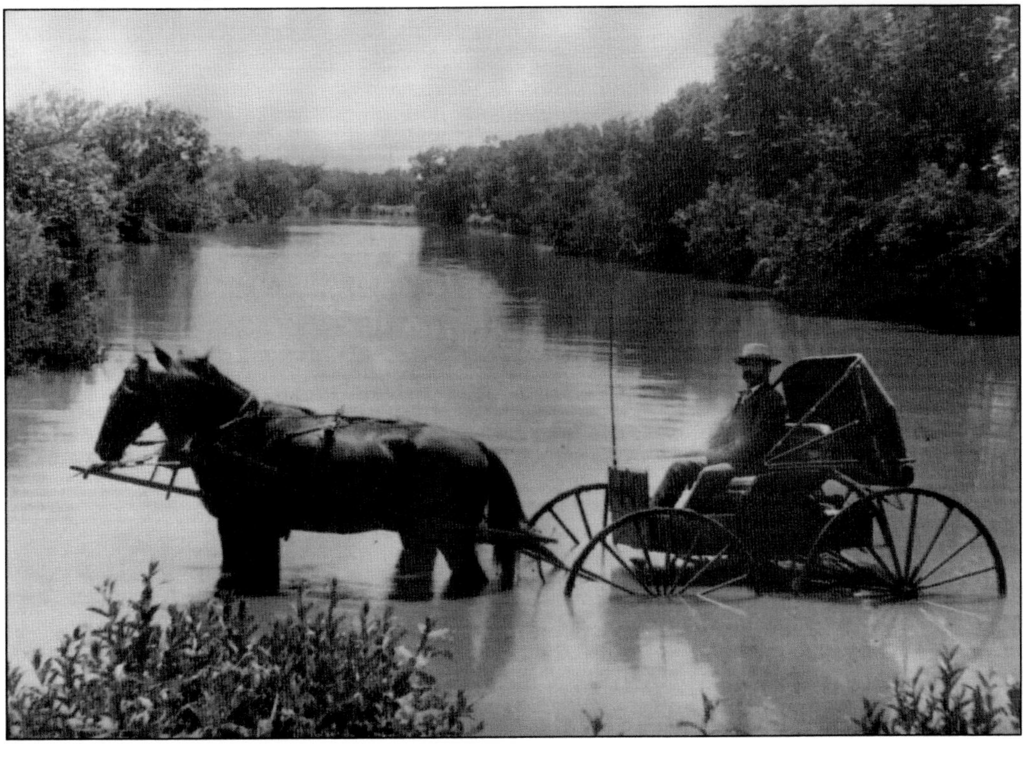

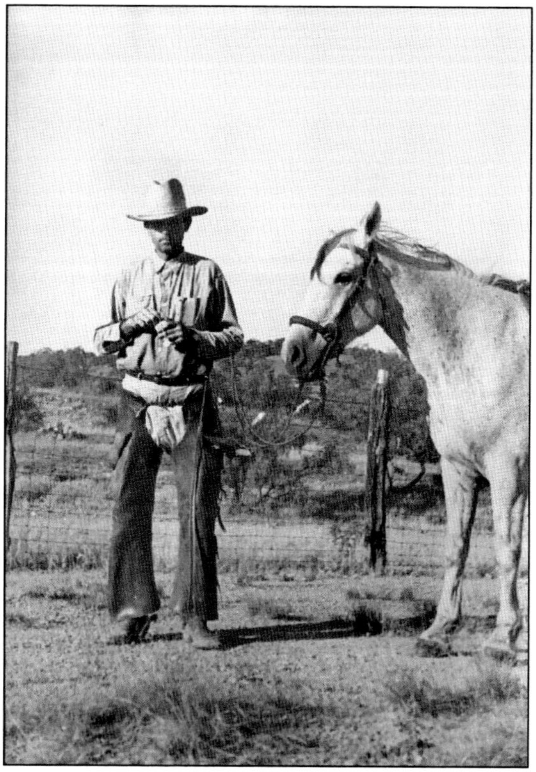

Shown rolling a cigarette is Talmage Palmer, a well-known and respected cowboy. He was an early-day foreman on the Nail, Cook, and Caldwell Ranches. Best known for his hard-work ethics, he survived a broken neck that he received in a horse-dragging accident. He died in 1975 at the age of 90. (Courtesy of Byron and Laura Palmer.)

Bob Green (1924–2009), shown here branding his cattle, was always passionate about the land, and held a keen interest in wildlife and ecological conservation. He was respected not only for his ranching, but for his talents in both writing and public speaking, usually on historical topics. (Courtesy of Nancy Green.)

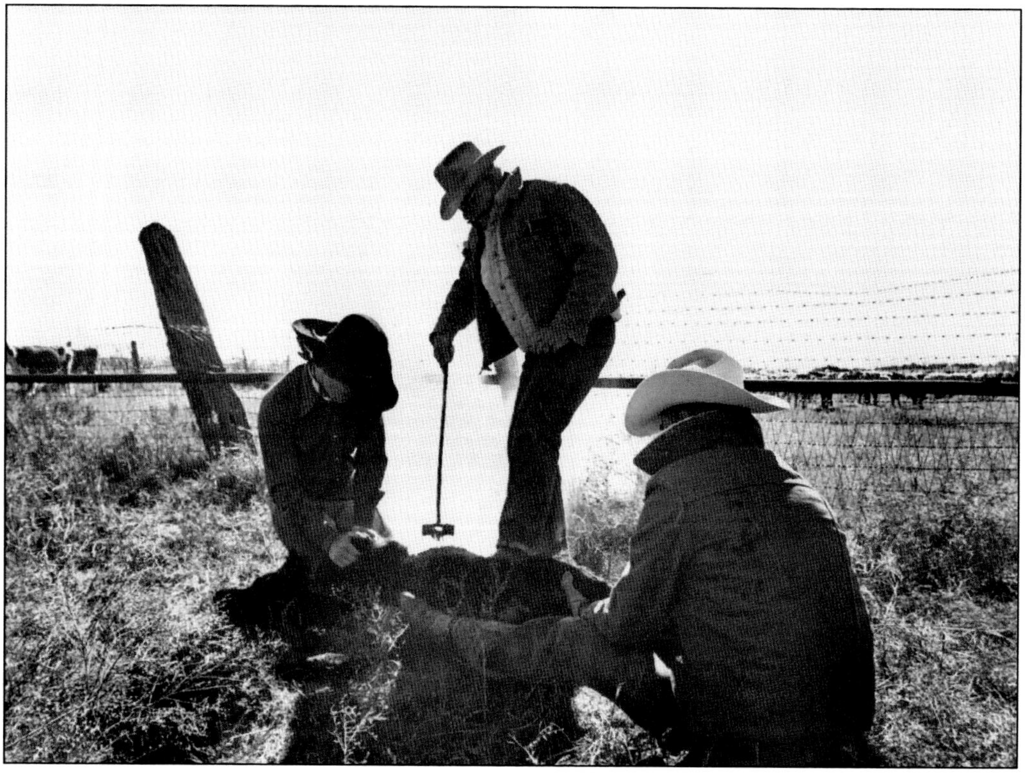

Three

Don't Give Up, Keep Working Down

By A.V. Jones Jr. and Jon Rex Jones

On January 10, 1901, the Spindle Top discovery in Southeast Texas initiated the beginning of the modern oil and gas industry in the state. Major oil companies were born with this discovery and immediately started exploration throughout Texas. There had been a few discovery wells, particularly in the area of Corsicana, but nothing of importance. Most knowledgeable oilmen at the time said they would drink all the oil found in West Texas. Thus begins the story of Shackelford County and the arrival of a sister industry to go along with cattle and farming.

In 1910, the Producers Oil Company (later bought out by Texaco) made a natural-gas discovery on the Cottle Ranch, east of Moran. This led to more drilling in that area, with small discoveries, mostly shallow. In 1915, the Producers Oil Company (Texaco) made another discovery west of Moran on the Tarrant-Cloud farm. One of these wells, according to Texaco records, produced over a million barrels during its life, probably the best well ever found in Shackelford County. The next significant event occurred on the Shackelford/Stephens county line, when a group of investors known as the Ibex Company found a prolific oil and gas field in the Caddo formation on the Poindexter Ranch. This led to an oil boom like that occurring at Breckenridge, and Ranger and Shackelford County showed sudden growth. This field, later purchased by Phillips Petroleum, had two natural-gas plants, and the town called Ibex at one time had 3,000 people. In 1926, the defining factor for Shackelford County came to pass.

Mrs. W.I. Cook leased the Cook Ranch to Tol Pendleton and Charlie Roeser. These two young promoters sold an interest in the lease to the Marland Oil Company, and the fabled broken-down truck location and the well, drilled by mistake, led to the discovery of the Cook Field. The discovery well flowed 1,000 barrels per day from 1,200 feet and led to a continuous exploration effort for the prolific shallow sands that existed all over Shackelford County. After the discovery of the East Texas Field and a disastrous reduction in the price of oil, Roeser and Pendleton were willing to shut down the field and wait for better days. The Cook Field is noted by many as a good example of a field that was operated properly. Gas injection resulted in a great recovery. Marshall R. Young later purchased the Roeser and Pendleton interest and became the dominant oil operator in the county.

During the years of World War II, drilling slowed in the county. Oilfield equipment and pipes were very scarce, and care had to be taken in selecting drill sites. Immediately after the war, a new boom started for Shackelford County. Until World War II, most of the drilling in the area was done by cable-tool rigs. Immediately after the war, major oil companies and big independents leased the county. Spurred on by a discovery by Allied Oil Company on the L.A. Sanders property just east of Albany, the Allied No. 1 produced from the Ellenberger formation, and it was hoped that it would rival the prolific production in West Texas.

During the 1950s, there was an increase in activity in the county, as many of the small operators were using portable, small rigs to search for the shallow Cisco Sands, while modern seismic methods were paying off not only in the deep structures, but also in Mississippian reefs. In the late 1950s, the fact that oil had stayed at about $3 per barrel for 10 years and that natural gas was almost worthless led to drilling activities falling off, and the production mirrored this trend. The early 1960s saw oil prices about the same as they had been since 1948. By the late 1960s a rebound occurred, caused not by price increases, but by a new play, the Mississippian Reef in Northeast Shackelford County.

The 1973 Arab oil embargo gave Shackelford County a shot in the arm, and prices rose to $12 per barrel. This was followed by the new Delhi Gas Pipeline in 1974, which crossed the county from north to south. Gas prices immediately increased from 12¢ to $1 per thousand, and soon rose to $3. Most of the county was leased, and royalty owners and businesses alike benefited. The Iranian Revolution of 1979 brought oil prices above $40/bbl. and were believed to be heading for $100. Activity in Shackelford County responded. The population in Albany increased from a low of 1,800 to 2,400 people; not boomtown numbers, but just about right for the infrastructure in place. It is said that Cotter & Neff, a local accounting firm, filed more forms with the state than any other establishment working in the area. There was an active atmosphere, with people borrowing money to drill wildcats all over the country, and banks were eager to make the loans. Among the active drillers in the deeper play (4,500 feet) were MP&L of Austin (Johnny Musselman), Jones Company Ltd., C.E. Jacobs Company, H.R. Stasney & Sons Company Ltd., and many others. During this frenzied time, the Jones Company was drilling about 100 deeper wells per year, and C.E. Jacobs Company actually drilled over 1,000 shallow wells north of Albany.

All of this activity came to a halt with the price decline of 1986, caused by Saudi Arabia opening the oil flow at the insistence of the Reagan administration. It achieved the goal of breaking the back of the Soviet Union. It also broke many oil companies and most large banks in Texas. Since that low of $10/bbl., oil prices have increased through the years, to $100/bbl. in 2008. Natural-gas prices have fluctuated and are in the $3 range now, the same as in the 1970s. Drilling activity in this mature area has never gotten back to the 1980s level. Smalley Drilling, Jamie Nail, and H.R. Stasney & Sons Company Ltd. remain active.

It is encouraging that there has been increased activity in the last two years. Nonresident operators have drilled wells based on new technology, such as horizontal drilling and fracking. This new play has people excited. Most of the county is leased or at least in play again. And shallow operators are still producing old leases. In addition to the companies mentioned above, current operators in Albany include Momentum Operating Company Inc. with beautiful offices on Main Street. Others active in the business are Herb Hawkins, Kelly Scott, David Schkade, the Ruffs, the Grothes, Ross Balliew, Eddie Edington, Randy Hudson, Jackie Snyder, Lynn and Cliff Teinert, the Whitts, the Neffs, George Hayes, and others. These firms comprise the modern industry in Albany and are important to the viability of the community. With prices at $90 per barrel, they are doing all right. From the earliest days to the stripper operators of today, the oil-and-gas business is a continuing story and is a large part of Albany's history. Who knows? These horizontal drillers may kick it off again. And, it could be big.

In 1909, the Cottle No. 1 was the first gas-producing well drilled in Shackelford County. This began what was, along with ranching, the main economic force driving the growth of the county. The well-drilling equipment shown here was called a standard rig and was powered by a steam engine.

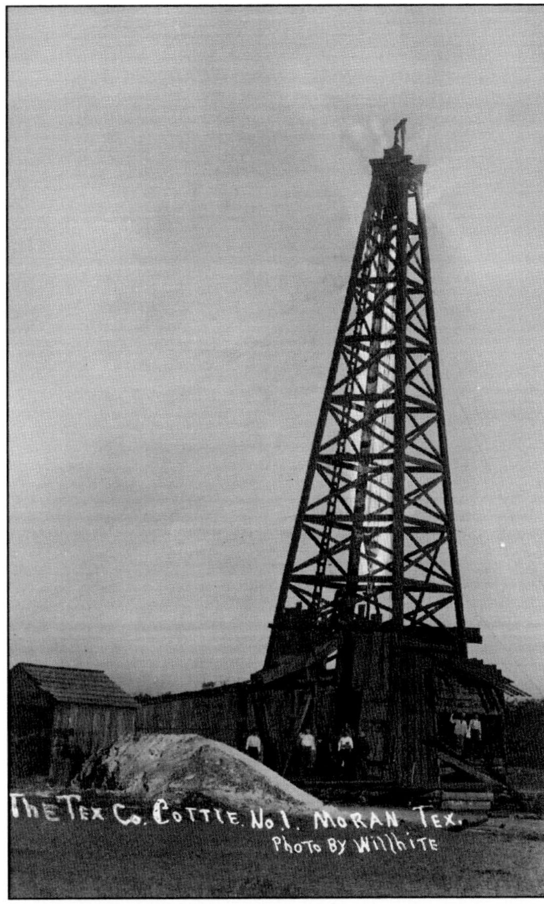

Moran was the first town in the county to have gas available for public use in lighting and heating. The gas was originally piped in from the Cottle No. 1. The Texas Company, later to be called Texaco, laid a pipeline from the well to the city. (Courtesy of the Moran Historical Museum.)

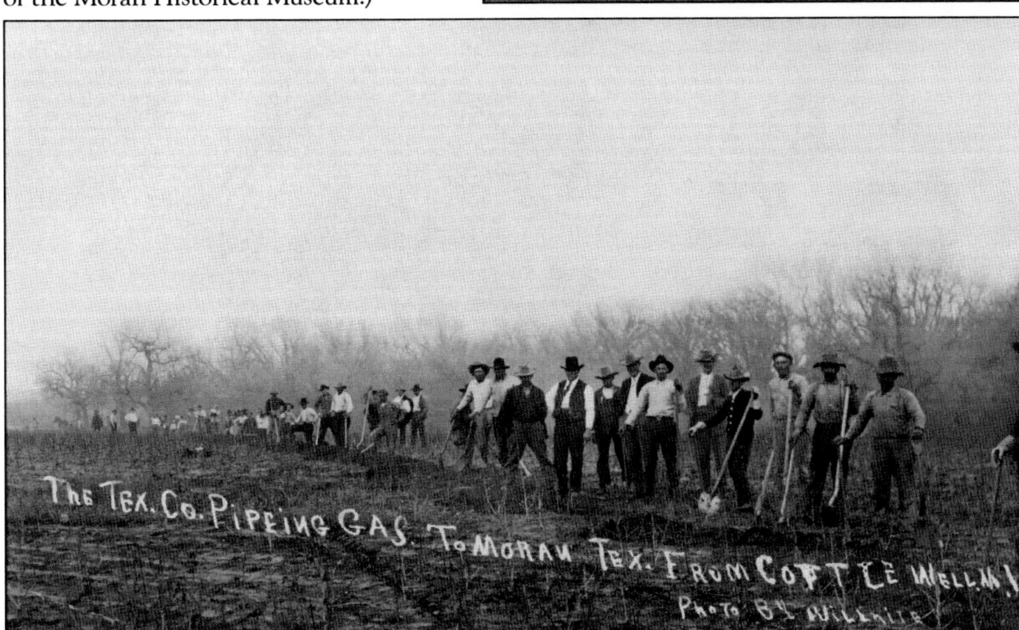

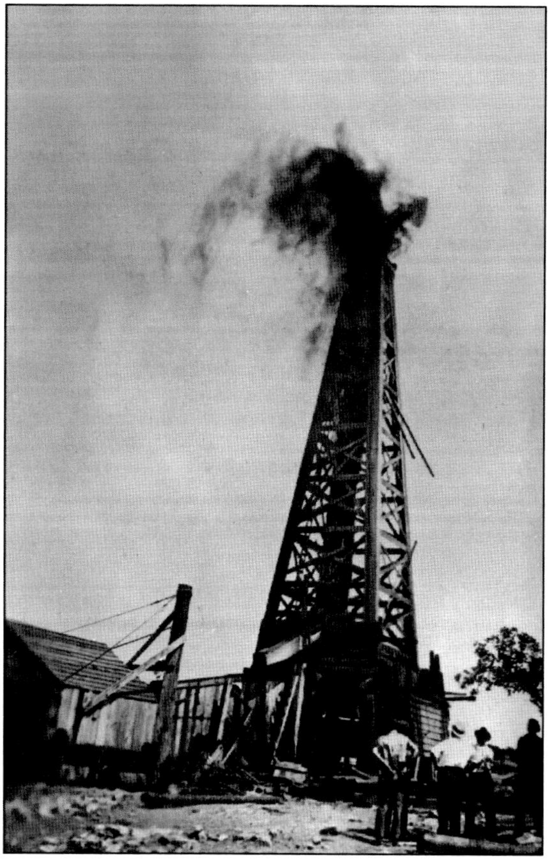

A gushing oil well is a sight to behold. The Madden No. 1 was an oil-producing well with enough gas pressure to cause the oil to flow under the high pressure and go out the top of the derrick. The well was soon capped, and the oil was finally piped into a tank.

Albany was the hub for the distribution of all kinds of oil-field equipment. Goods were delivered to Albany by train or truck and stored in local wagon yards, then delivered by trucks to the sites. The size of the Cook Field called for thousands of feet of pipe. Each well used hundreds of feet of pipe to case the well down to the play.

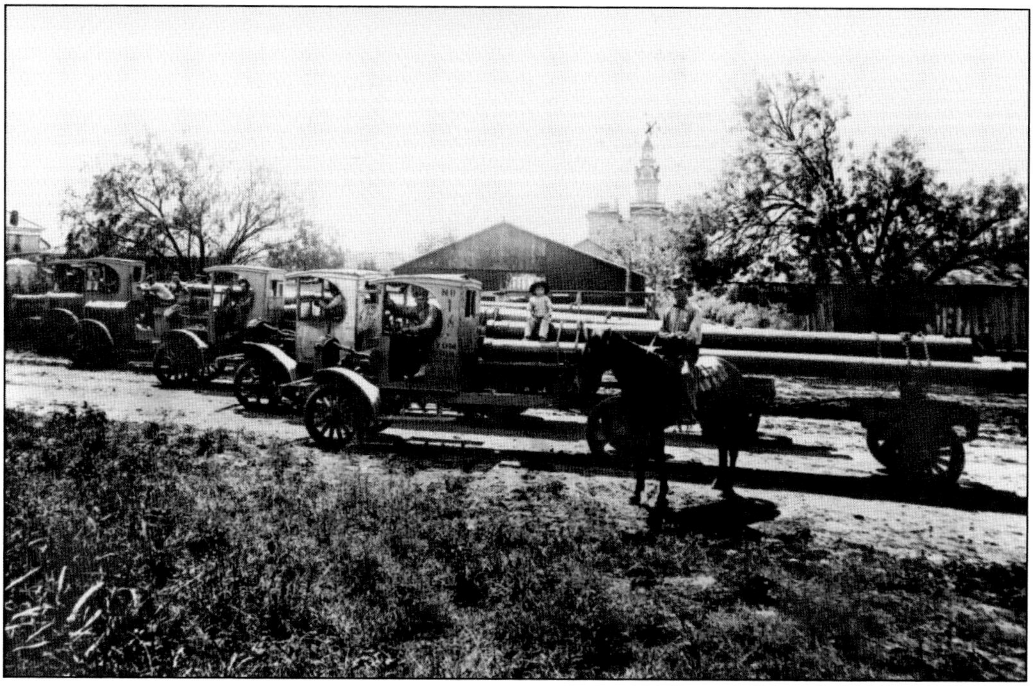

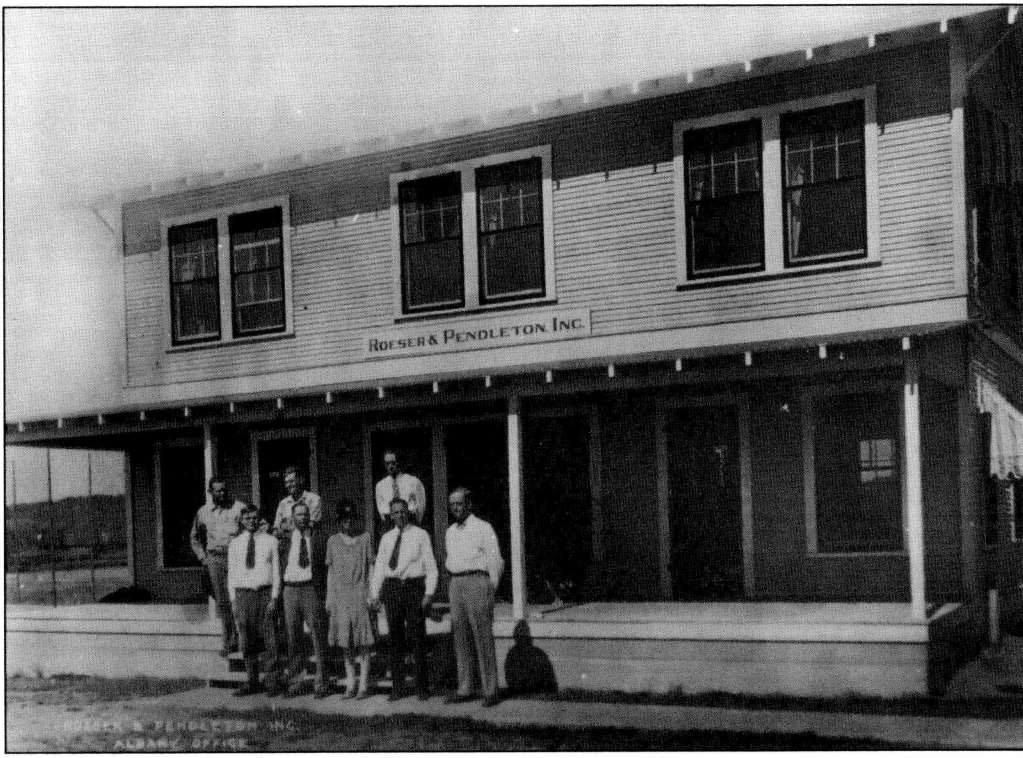

Shown here in October 1927 is the building of Roeser & Pendleton Inc., operators of the Cook Field in its early years. Posing in front of the building is the office staff. G.P. Crutchfield is on the far right. He is known in the area for his later work on the equipment for the *Fort Griffin Fandangle*.

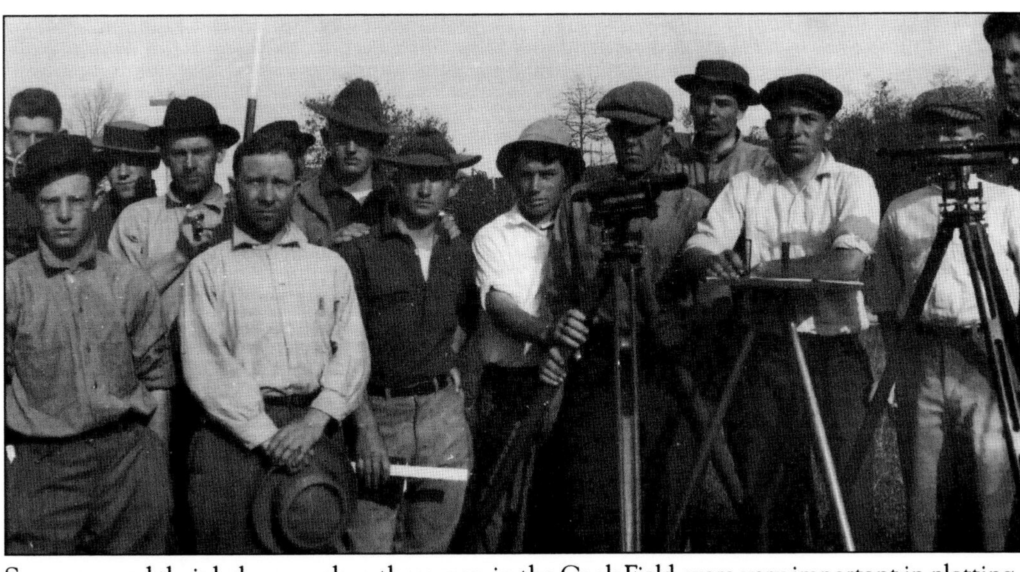

Surveyors and their helpers, such as these men in the Cook Field, were very important in plotting a field. They surveyed the area, locating all natural features. When well sites were selected, each site had to be exactly located on the map. On the far right is a transit instrument, and the man behind it is Vaughan Moore, probably the leader of the team. (Courtesy of Kristen Landry Guerin.)

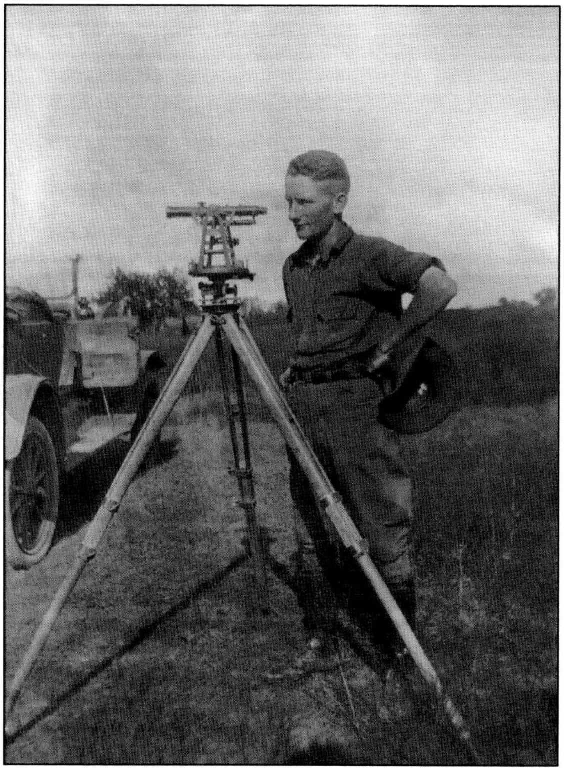

Vaughan Moore works in the field. He has an unseen crew with him, possibly establishing a site for a new well. Considering the large number of wells (1,087) drilled on the Cook Ranch, there was constant work for a large number of surveyors. Of the wells on the Cook Ranch, 825 yielded oil, and four were gas wells. (Courtesy of Kristen Landry Guerin.)

In 1926, this newly completed Well No. A5 in the Cook Field is spewing its oil into a slush pit at the well site. Soon after, the well will be closed in and piped into lines leading to tanks for collection. The large wheels seen on the right, called bull wheels, were used in controlling lines going into the drill hole. (Courtesy of Kristen Landry Guerin.)

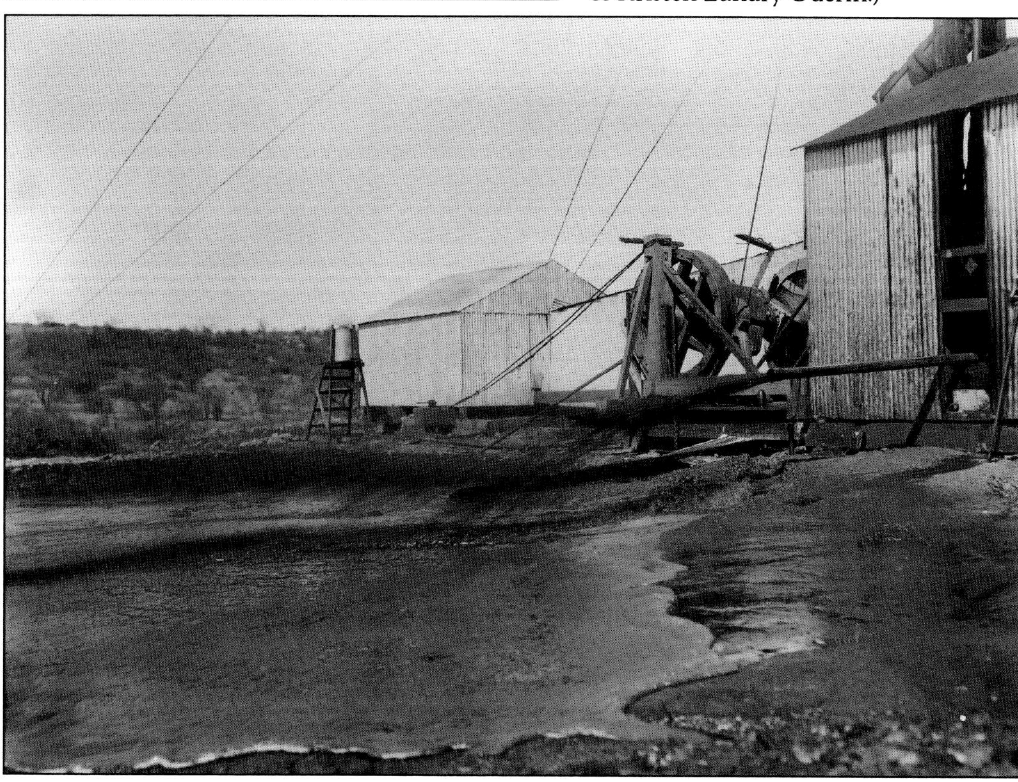

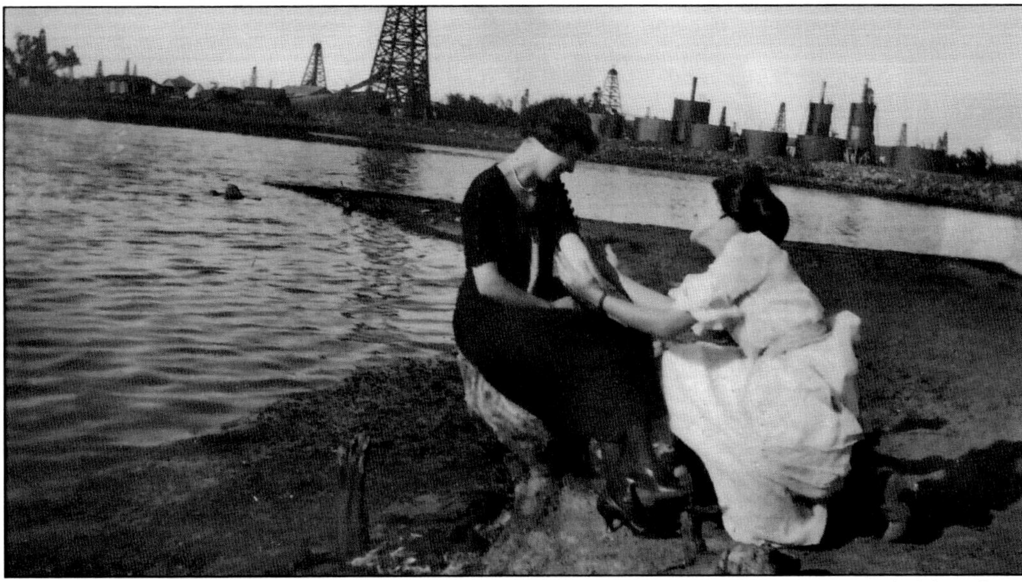

Mary E. Moore (left) and a friend enjoy time together beside a small lake surrounded by a busy, working oil field and refinery. They are fashionably dressed to be in such a place. The scene would have been noisy, with large engines running, metal hitting metal, and a strong smell of oil. Amid all of this, these ladies seem to take it all in stride. (Courtesy of Kristen Landry Guerin.)

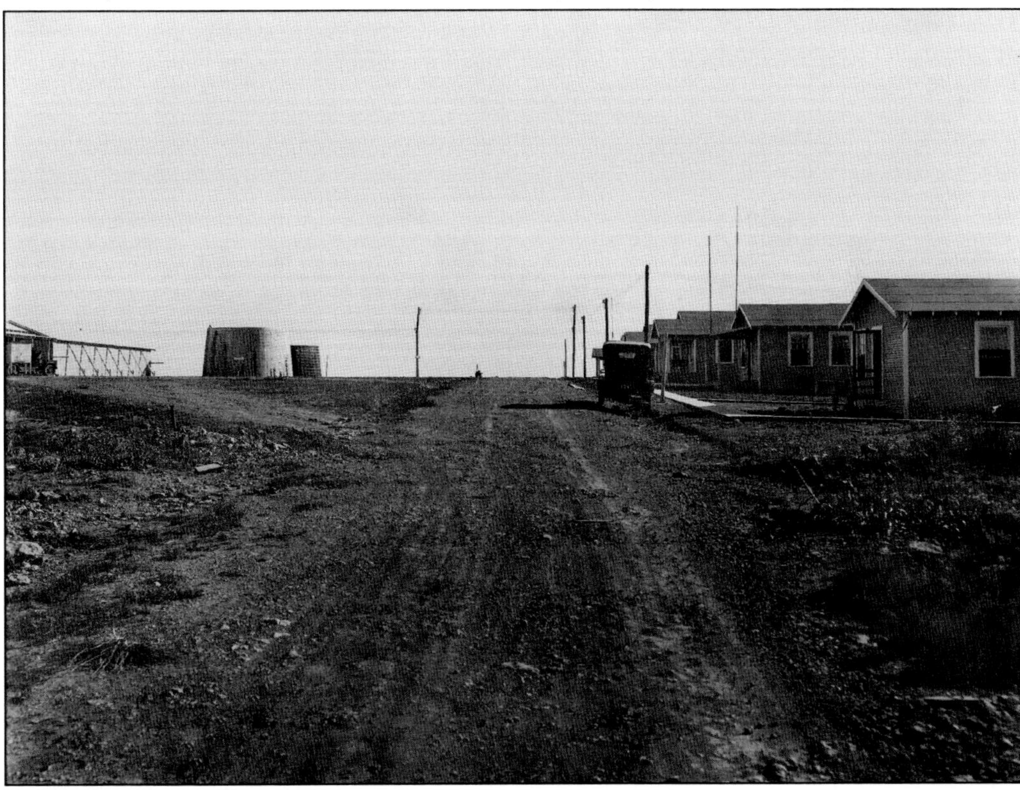

Employees were provided with housing close to their work. Families lived amid the hustle and bustle of a very busy, sometimes dangerous, working environment. (Courtesy of Kristen Landry Guerin.)

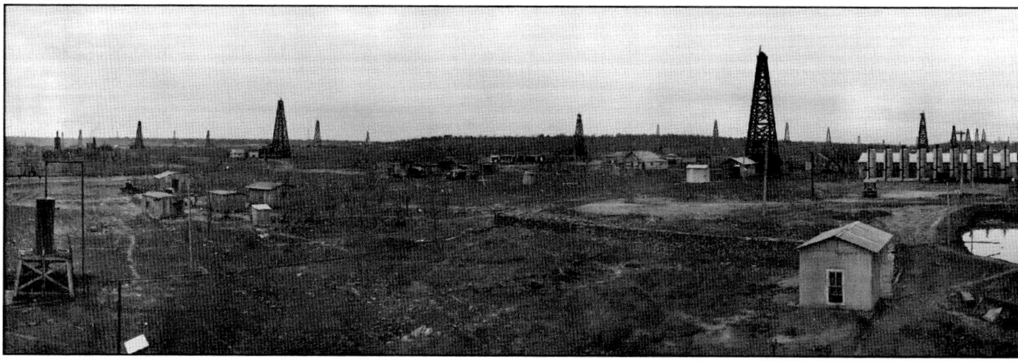

The Cook Field, drilled in 1926, was the first major field established in the county. Roeser & Pendleton Inc. leased the land west of Albany from the Cook family. The field was well planned, and the area contained drilling wells, a producing well, a gasoline plant, offices, and homes for the workers. These developments caused Albany to grow rapidly. The Cook Children's Hospital in Fort Worth was built with money from this high-producing field. (Courtesy of H.R. Stasney & Sons Ltd.)

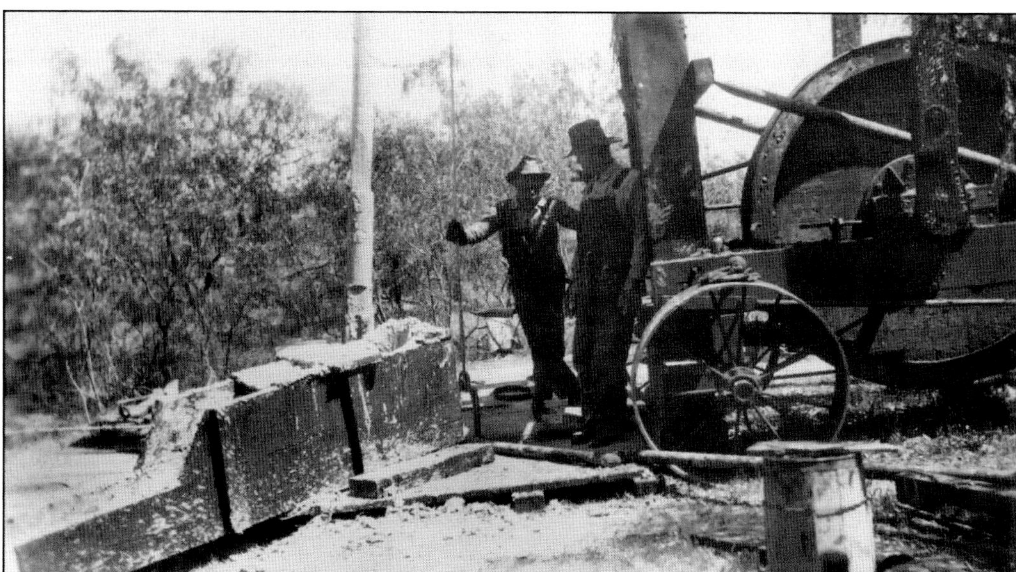

There were always independent oilmen drilling on the edges of the big fields. Here, a spudder, a movable drilling rig, is being operated by a driller and a tool dresser. John Grothe (left) is pictured with an unidentified man. (Courtesy of Mary Kay O'Connor.)

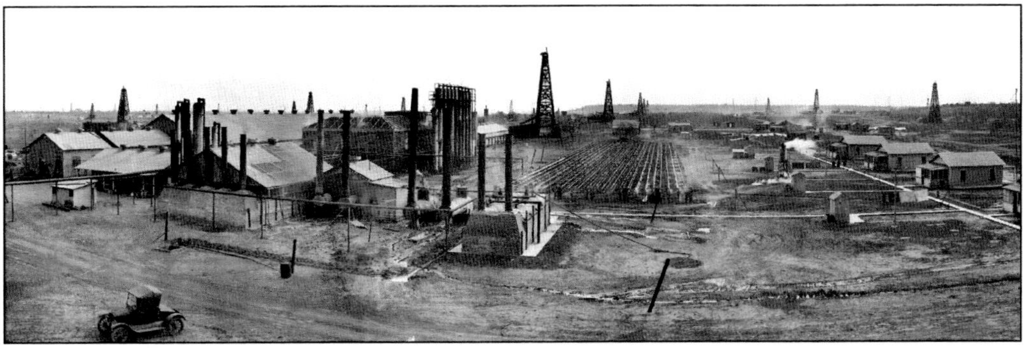

The Cook Field gasoline plant is on the left of this photograph. At right are homes for the workers. The wooden derricks were left after the wells were completed. When the price of oil dropped in the early 1950s, the field was closed down for a time. When prices rose and the field opened again, it was one of the first to use low-pressure gas injection to bring the wells back to a good production level. (Courtesy of H.R. Stasney & Sons Ltd.)

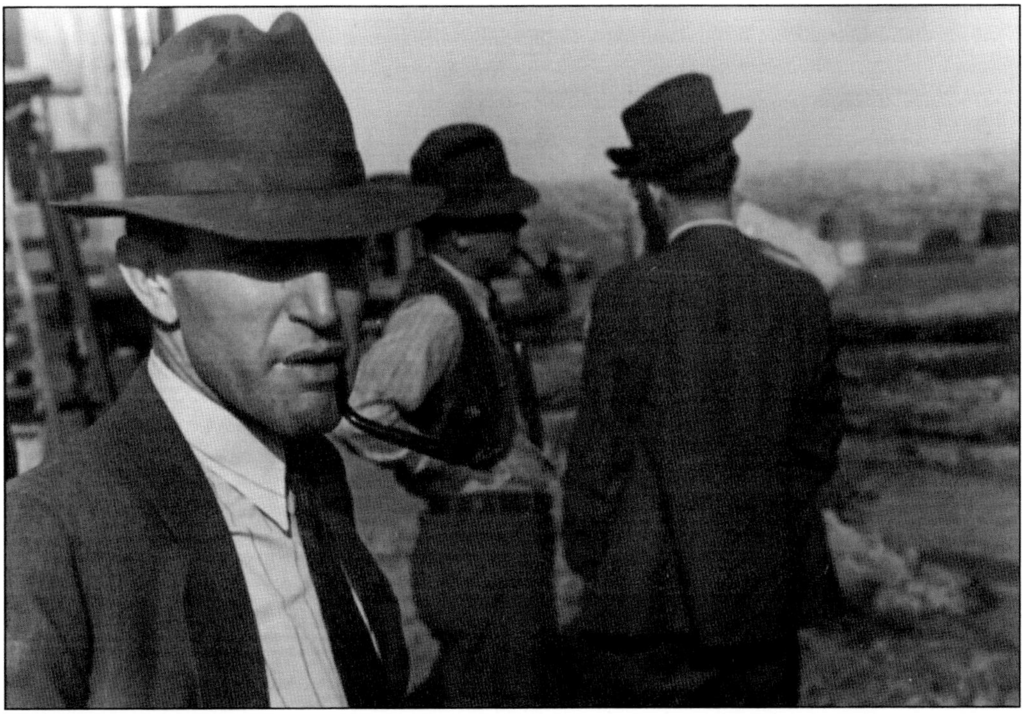

The Albany area was inundated with oil people from all over the Southwest when news broke of the Cook Field discovery. Among the newcomers was A.V. Jones Sr. (shown here). A graduate of the University of Oklahoma, he earned a degree in the new field of petroleum geology. Jones was with Marland Oil Company, which later became Conoco. His sons, A.V. Jr. and Jon Rex, followed in their father's footsteps, making their homes in Albany and continuing in the oil and gas business. (Courtesy of the Jones family.)

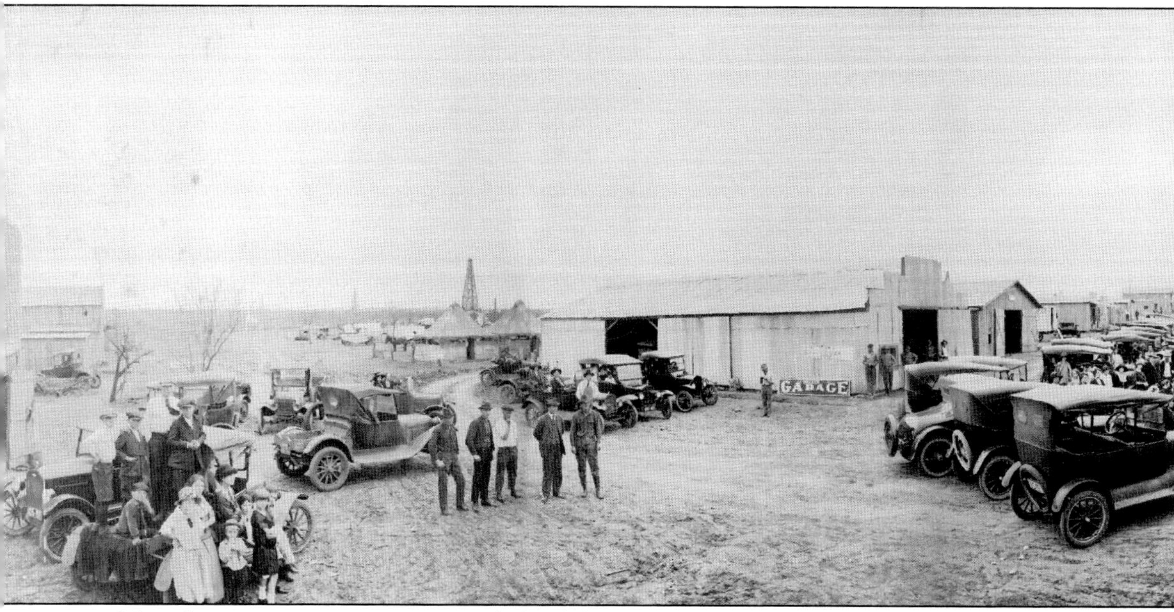

Many boomtowns sprang up in rural Shackelford County. By 1923, the growing town of Ibex was strung out for many miles along the dirt roads. Men came from all over the country to work in the oil fields, some bringing their families. Temporary housing was often tents, but some attempts were

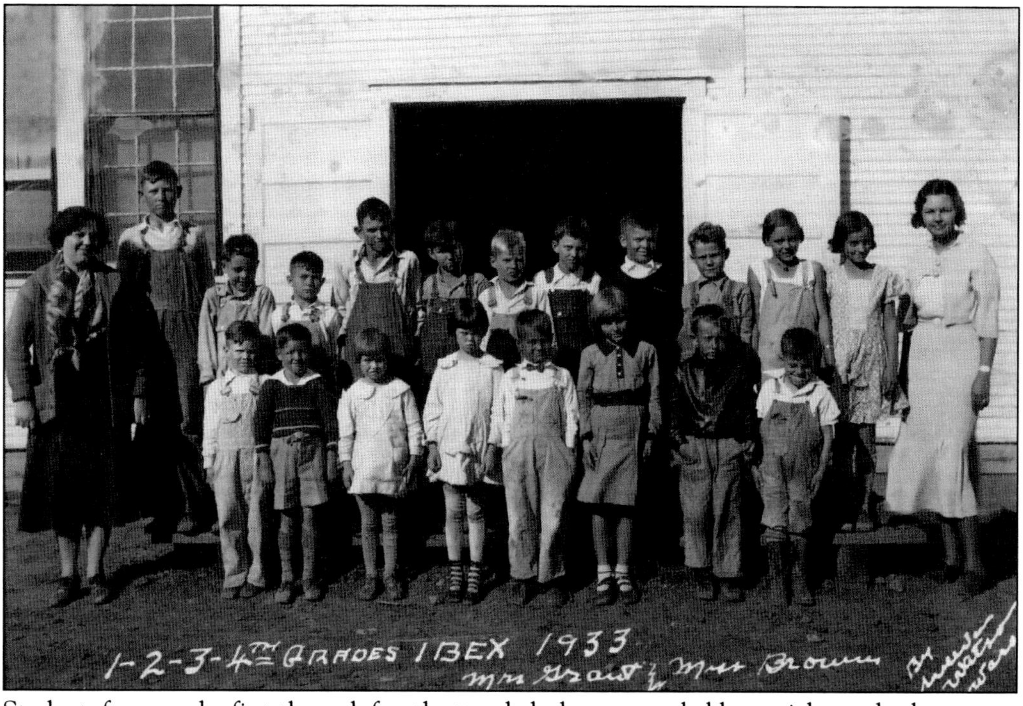

Students from grades first through fourth attended what was probably an eight-grade elementary school in Ibex. Usually, there were two rooms in these rural schools. By the time of this 1933 photograph, Ibex was at the height of its population. (Courtesy of Sandy Conway.)

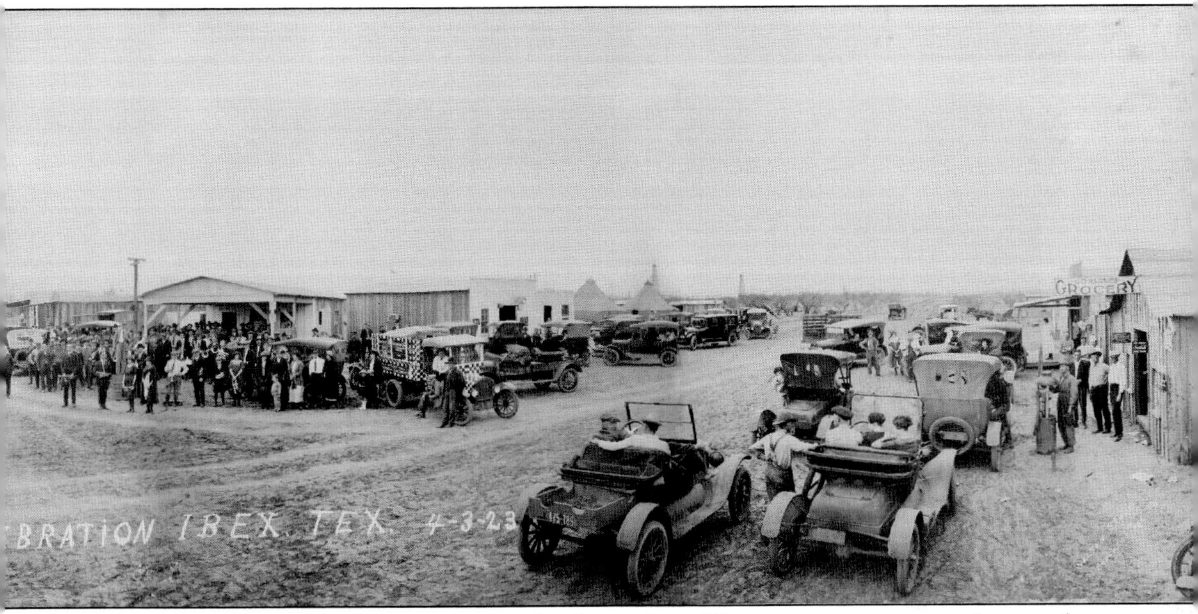

made to create more stable accommodations for the workers. The new towns attempted to supply the sleeping accommodations, restaurants, and stores necessary for everyday living. These small boomtowns disappeared after the initial oil plays were drilled out. (Courtesy of *Albany News*.)

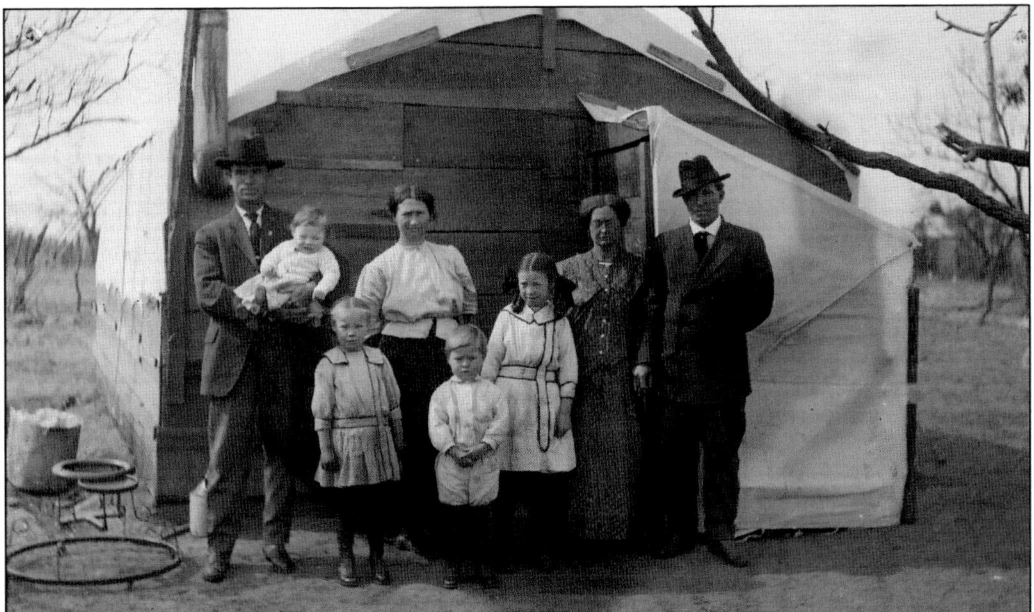

Some of the men coming to work in the oil fields in the early days brought their families along. This multigenerational group is living in a small tent-wood home. Even with the hard conditions, appearances are important. (Courtesy of the Moran Historical Museum.)

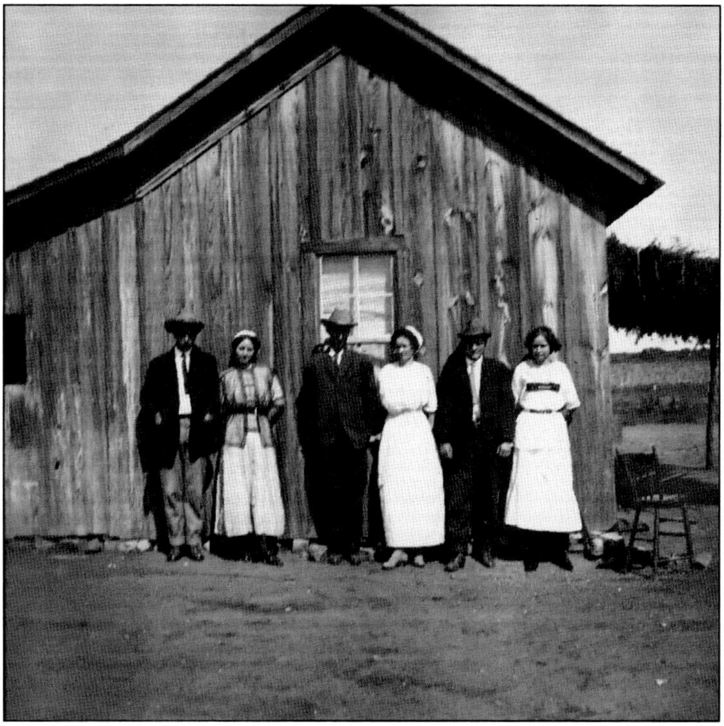

Three couples dressed in their Sunday best pose in front of one of the fairly well-built wooden structures in Ibex. (Courtesy of Sandy Conway.)

It was not all work in an oil and gas boomtown. This dressed-up group poses with a 1923 automobile. (Courtesy of Sandy Conway.)

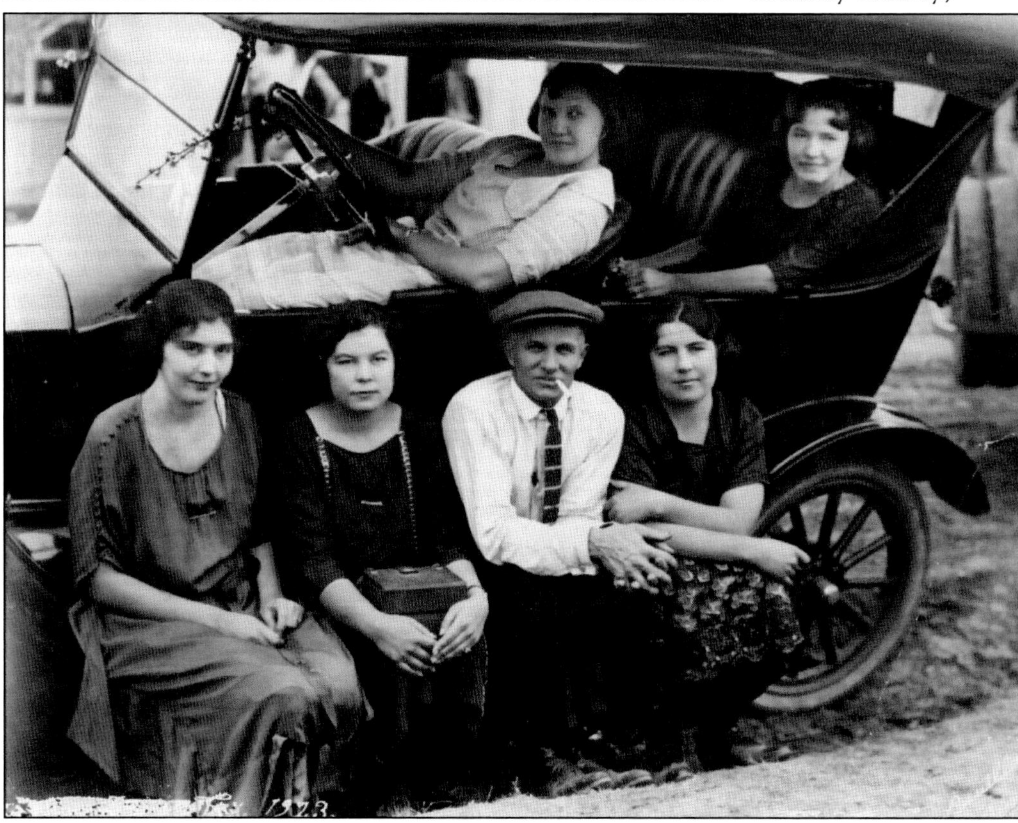

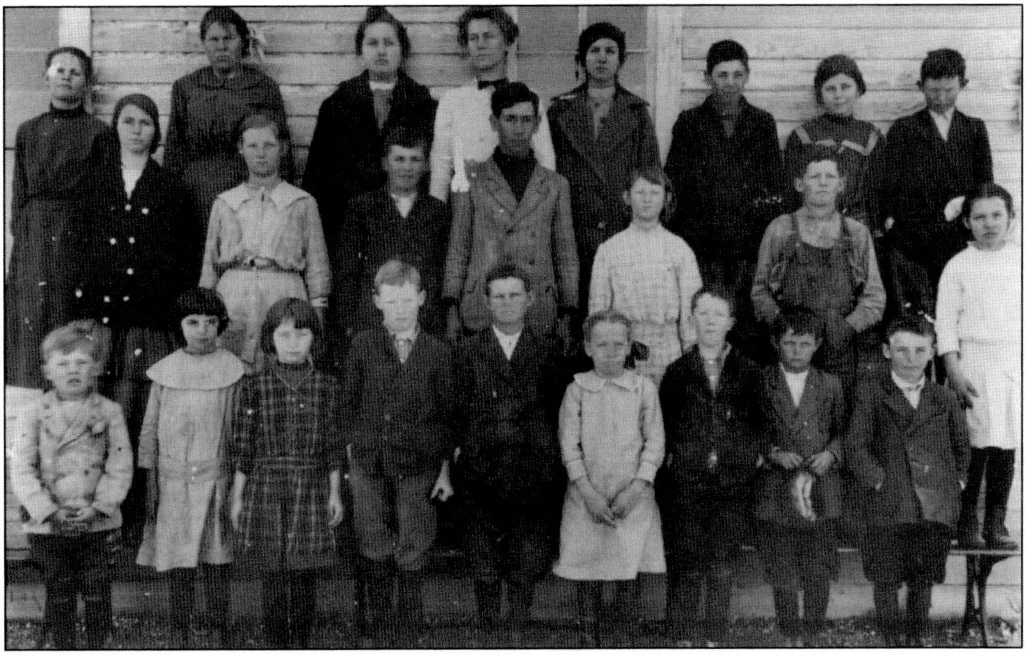

Snalum is another example of an oil boomtown that came and went during the peak years. The school was established in 1906, about 10 miles east of Albany. In 1908, it moved about a mile farther east. The building also served once a month as a church for the Baptist congregation. The school closed its doors in 1920. (Courtesy of Dee Balliew.)

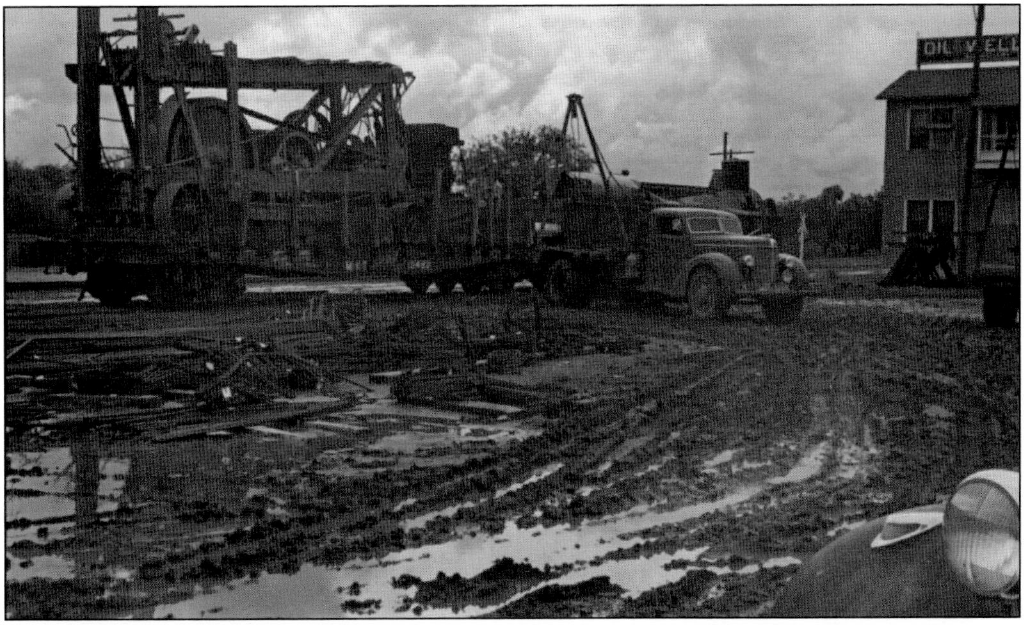

One of George Callihan's Fort Worth Spudder drilling machines is loaded for shipment to Cuba, where Callihan had taken a contract to drill a well. The spudder, with its accompaniment of other drilling equipment, occupied two flatcars, which went by rail to New Orleans, then by train boat to Havana. This photograph was taken by Virginia Clarke at the Albany Katy station in the summer of 1940.

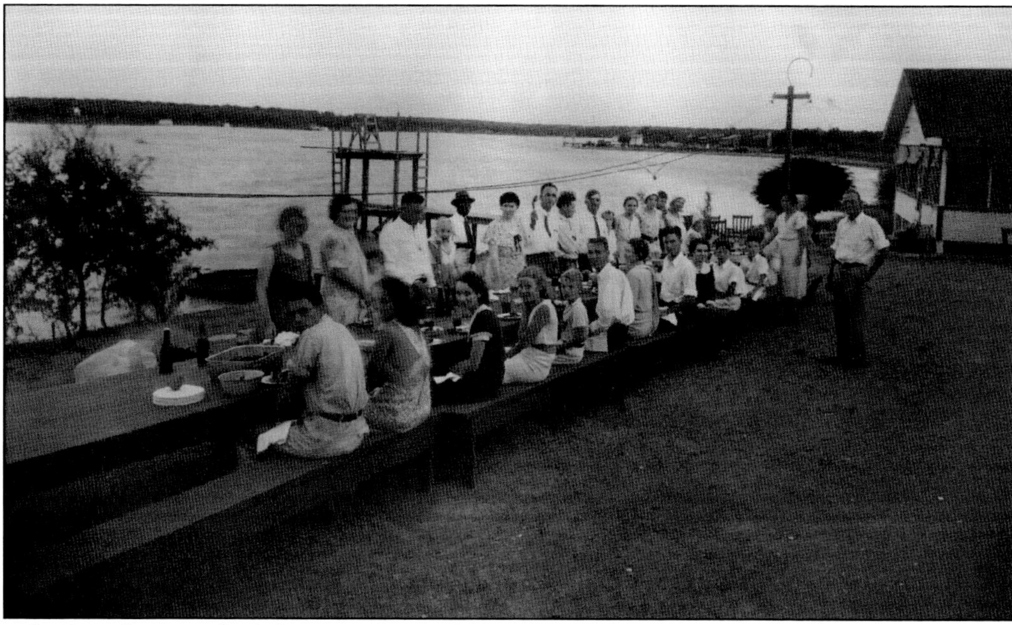

Lake DeLafosse was built by George DeLafosse to supply water for the growing town of Ibex and all the nearby oil and gas production facilities. It was north of the town, near the Stephens County line. By 1931, it not only supplied water, but served as a recreation area in an arid county. This 1931 photograph of a Labor Day party includes George DeLafosse, in the center of the back row. (Courtesy of the Jones family.)

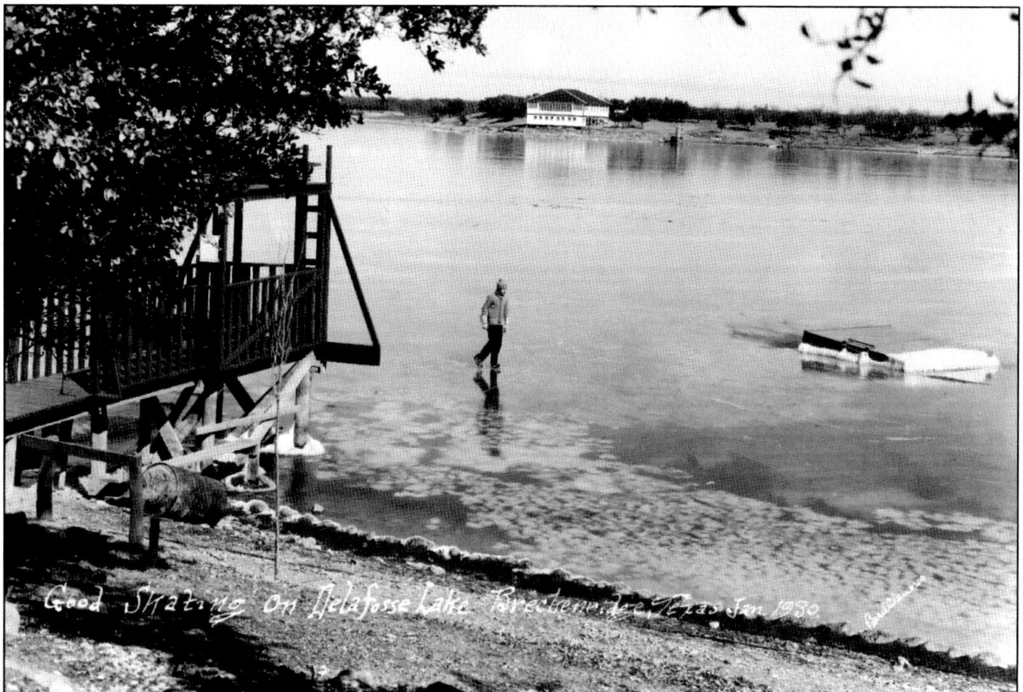

It does get cold in Shackelford County, cold enough for ice skating in 1931 on Lake DeLafosse. Across the lake is the Breckenridge Country Club building. (Courtesy of the Jones family.)

Four

There's a Little Town Called Albany

By Wilma Jo Tucker Mitchell

Although the first white man settled in Shackelford County in the 1850s, it was not until 1874, when Albany was chosen as the county seat, that development began. Albany was named by W.R. Cruger after his hometown in Georgia. Sheriff Henry Jacobs donated a 43-acre townsite, and a wooden picket courthouse was erected. A post office was opened on August 1, 1876, the first permanent jail of native stone was built, and, by late 1877, there were 16 buildings in the town. D.H. Meyer and Edgar Rye began publishing the *Albany Tomahawk* in 1879. Realizing the importance of a railroad to Albany, the citizens raised $50,000 to entice the railroad, and by 1881, the Houston & Texas Central built a rail line to Albany, and the city expanded as a major shipping point for the area. A permanent courthouse of native stone was built in 1883. That same year, the first public school system for Albany was organized, as well as the Albany Bank (now First National), and the *Albany News* superseded the *Albany Sun*.

In 1886, Albany was ravaged by a severe drought that lasted for 23 months and prompted the Red Cross to send its national president, Clara Barton, to inspect the situation. The Reynolds academy, then a college, was in Albany from 1898 to 1915, and for a short time, it was used as an orphanage. The Reynolds College bulletin of June 1911 described the town: "Albany with her 1400 population, has a salubrious climate, no malaria, no saloons, churches of every denomination, and an altitude of 1500 feet." The building was raised in 1927. In the early 1900s, the local Albany Band was a popular source of entertainment. In 1910, The Moving Picture Co. was organized by three local men, who brought silent movies to town. The first permanent movie theater, Ritz, was built by Frank Whitney in 1926, but was sold and closed in 1929. Whitney then built the Aztec theater, which opened in 1927. In 1929, the first "talking" movie was shown there, which brought Albany "right up now with the big cities," as reported by editor Dick McCarty in the *Albany News*. A new breed of cattle, Hereford, was introduced to the area, and since 1920, Albany has been known as "The Home of the Hereford."

The oil boom from 1910 to 1930 made Albany grow even more, both in population and in wealth, and the cry for a new hotel was made in the newspaper by McCarty. Prior to that time, the main hotel was the Albany House (the old Sackett Hotel), operated by Ada McLemore. In 1926 this hotel was moved off Main Street, and a "modern" brick hotel was built by McLemore. In 1929, a new jail was built on the courthouse square, and the 1877 building was abandoned. Bob Nail purchased the historic building in 1940 to use as his studio. In 1936, Sallie Reynolds

Matthews published *Interwoven*, a book depicting life and customs of the pioneer period. She died two years later, but the book has been published six times, proving its historical value. In 1938, Bob Nail and the senior class presented *Dr. Shackelford's Paradise*, which was the beginning of the *Fort Griffin Fandangle*. The following year, the *Albany Nativity*, written and directed by Nail, was presented.

In the early morning of June 10, 1941, a 10-inch rain caused the dam at the Diller City Lake and one on the Newell Ranch to break, sending a wall of water down the western edge of the city limits of Albany. Among the 12 people killed was a family of seven in one house. A total of 90 houses were damaged or completely destroyed. It was believed that more than 300 people were affected, the larger portion left homeless. During World War II, the historic cannon on the courthouse lawn was donated to the war effort; many of the young men of Albany were killed, and some were taken prisoner. As with most West Texas towns, Friday night football played an important part in the lives of Albany citizens. They are proud to point out that the high school teams of 1960–1961 won state championships. During the 1950s and 1960s, the population declined, as especially the younger people moved to larger cities. In 1965, Watt Matthews donated land, and the Prairie Theater was built for the *Fort Griffin Fandangle*. Bob Nail died suddenly at his home three years later. This is only a brief summary of the early history of Albany, a unique town that one writer referred to as "a cut above" other towns its size.

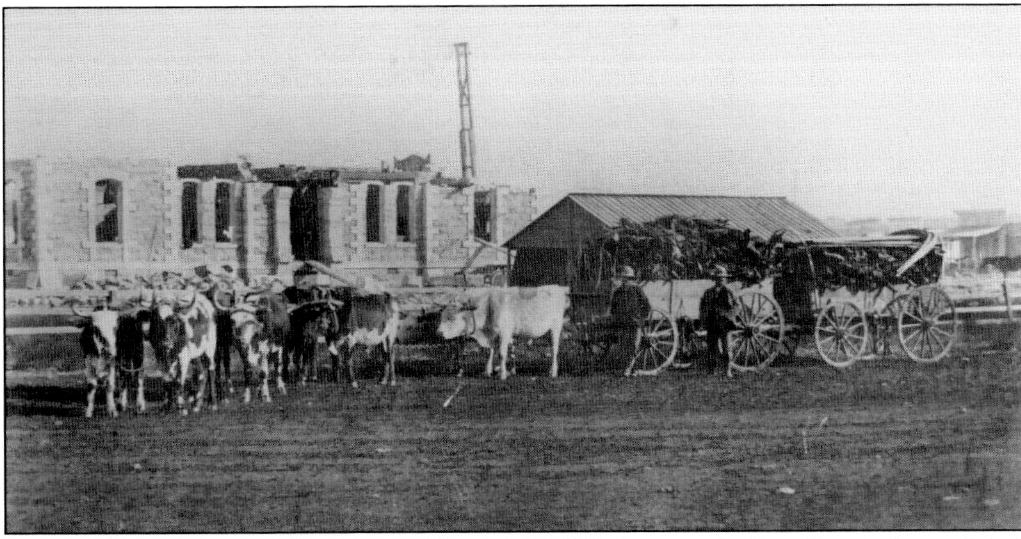

Construction of the courthouse is visible in this 1883 photograph. Standing in front of their wagon are James F. Dennis of Rotan (right) and Will Brooks of Snyder. They hauled firewood to Albany and sold it for $3 a load. They also hauled buffalo bones, which brought $16 per ton. The oxen at the tong are bulls that Dennis and Brooks sold for $50 apiece when they closed their business and quit freighting.

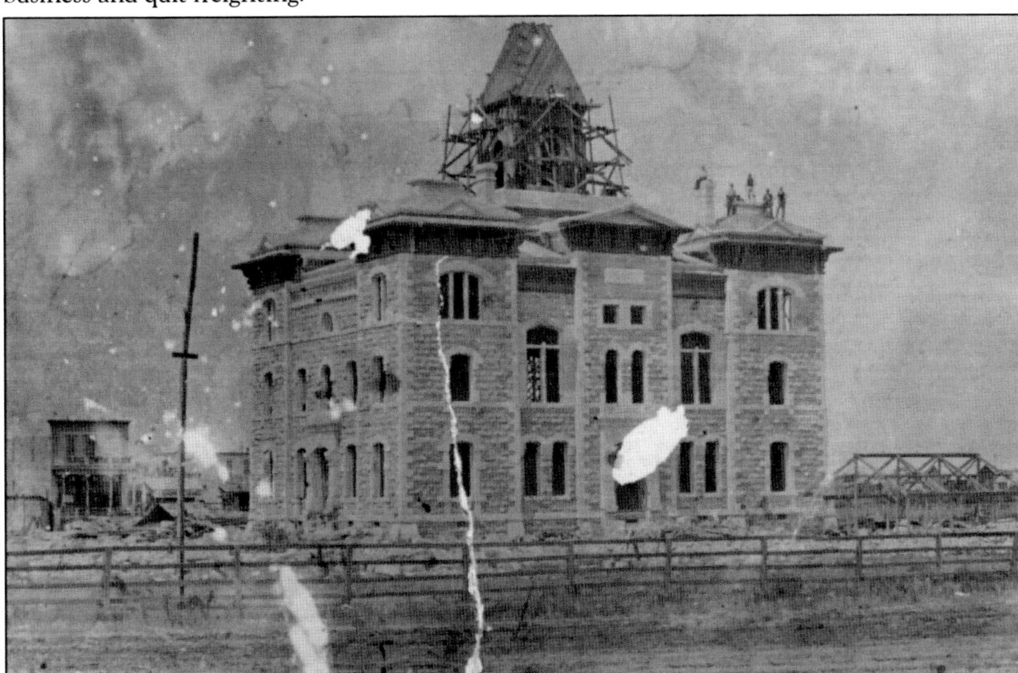

County sheriff H.C. Jacobs donated the land for the first courthouse in 1875. The building was a picket construction erected in the middle of the courthouse square. That building was removed by restaurant owner Charles Hartfield in 1883. The Second Empire courthouse seen here is the design of architect J.E. Flanders of Dallas. Edgar Rye of Albany was the construction superintendent. Kilted Scottish masons erected the walls, made of stone quarried a few miles southwest of town.

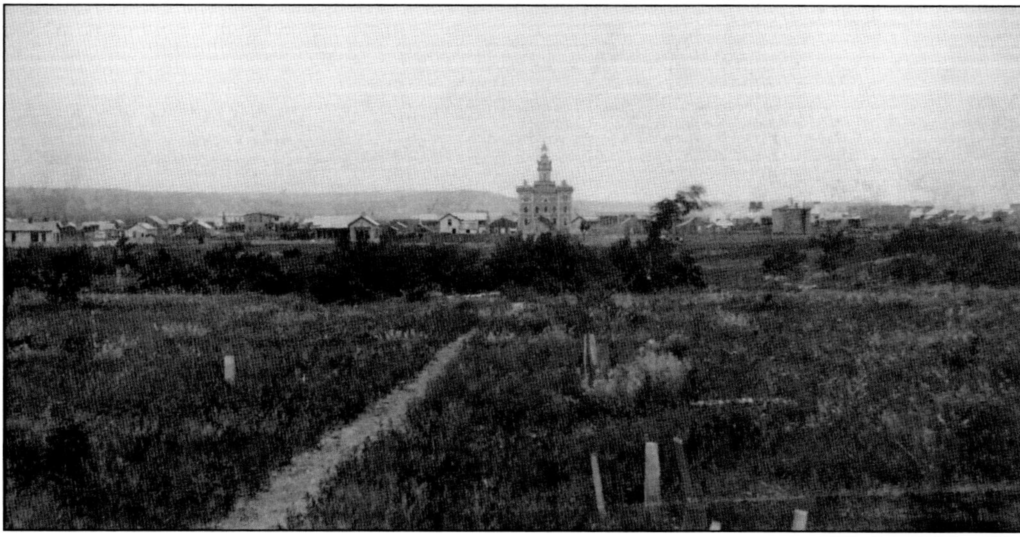

This 1885 photograph of the courthouse and the town of Albany was taken from the A.A. Clarke Place, southeast of town. The stones or posts at the bottom of the photograph are believed to be markers from a now-lost cemetery. The original limestone jail building can be seen on the right.

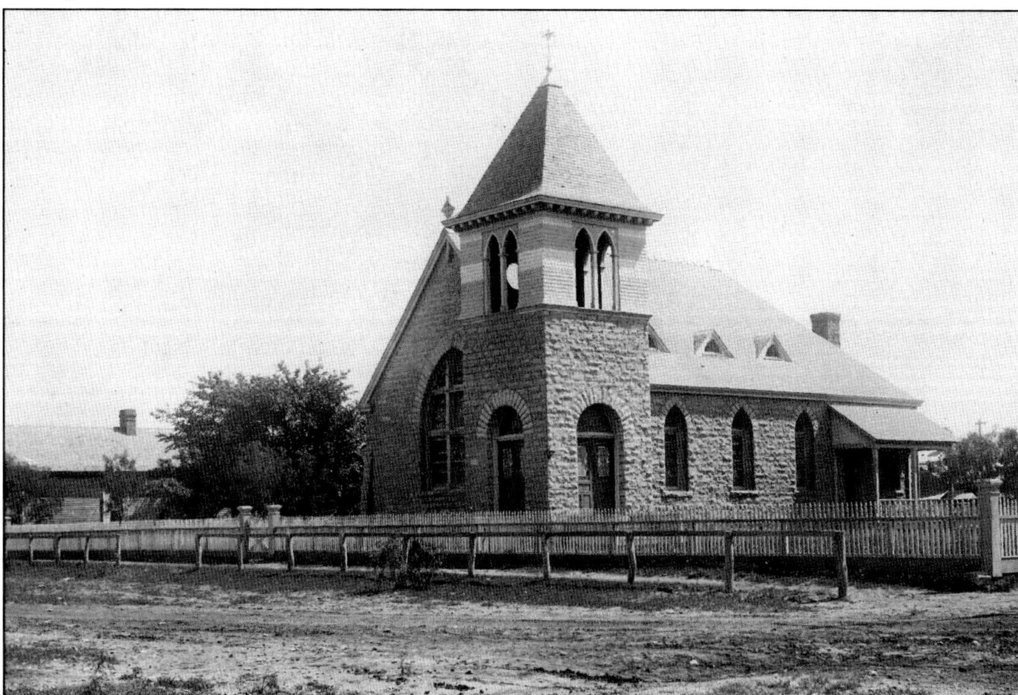

The Presbyterian Church began with only seven members, who met in the first little rock house on Jacobs Street. The first elders of the church, Henry and John Jacobs, gave the lot for the first church building. It was a small frame structure, situated on the corner across the street, west of the present building. When the congregation outgrew the little church, the present stone structure (shown here) was erected in 1898, in memory of one of Shackelford County's first cattlemen and one of the early elders of the congregation, Joseph Beck Matthews (1824–1895).

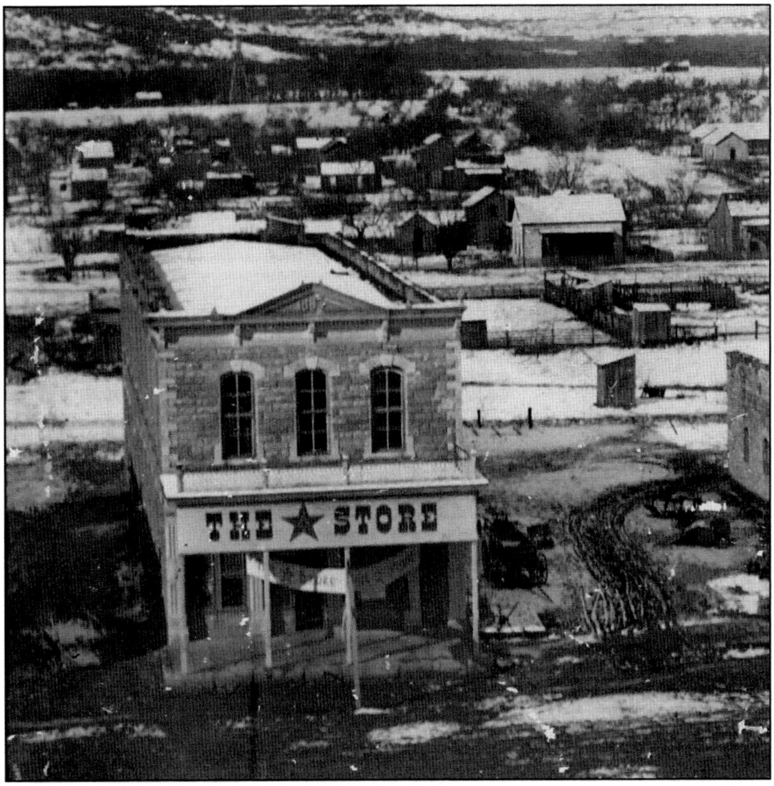

The Star Store was the first business operated in what is now the Hartfield Building. The structure was built in 1884, just after the courthouse, by the same workmen. It is one of the finest old rock buildings in the city. Over the years, it was used for different businesses and also as the Masonic lodge. It finally fell into disrepair and was sold to a new owner, who restored the building to its original beauty.

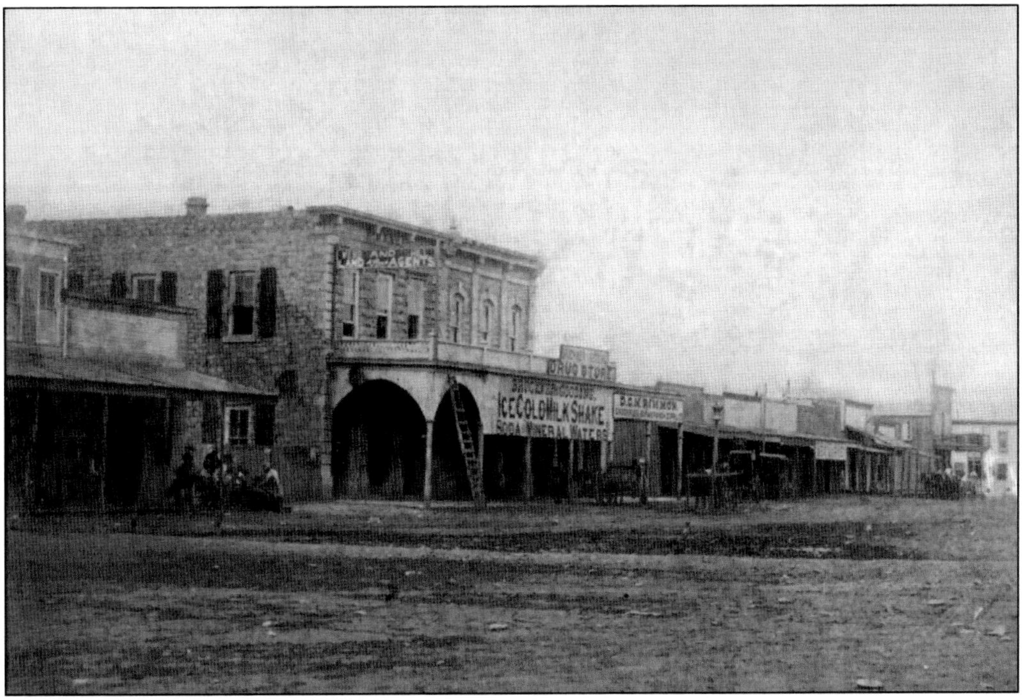

This is the west side of Main Street, between South First and Second Streets. The sign on the right of the ladder reads "Ice Cold Milk Shake, Soda and Mineral Waters."

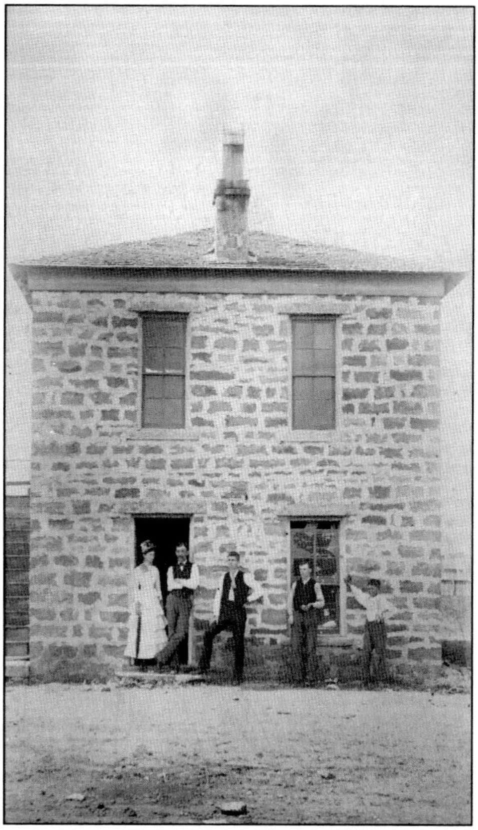

This native limestone building, photographed in 1883, probably housed the *Albany Echo*, an Albany newspaper owned and edited by George W. Robson. Previously, Robson lived in the town of Fort Griffin, where he published the *Fort Griffin Echo* at a time when the buffalo hunts and cattle drives were at their height. After four years there, he moved to Albany, where he published the *Albany Echo* from 1883 to 1884.

The *Albany Echo* and *Albany Star* newspapers merged in 1884 to become the *Albany News* when *Echo* editor George W. Robson sold out his interest in the newspaper to his rival, Edgar Rye, due to poor health. The first issue of the *Albany News* went to print on February 20, 1884.

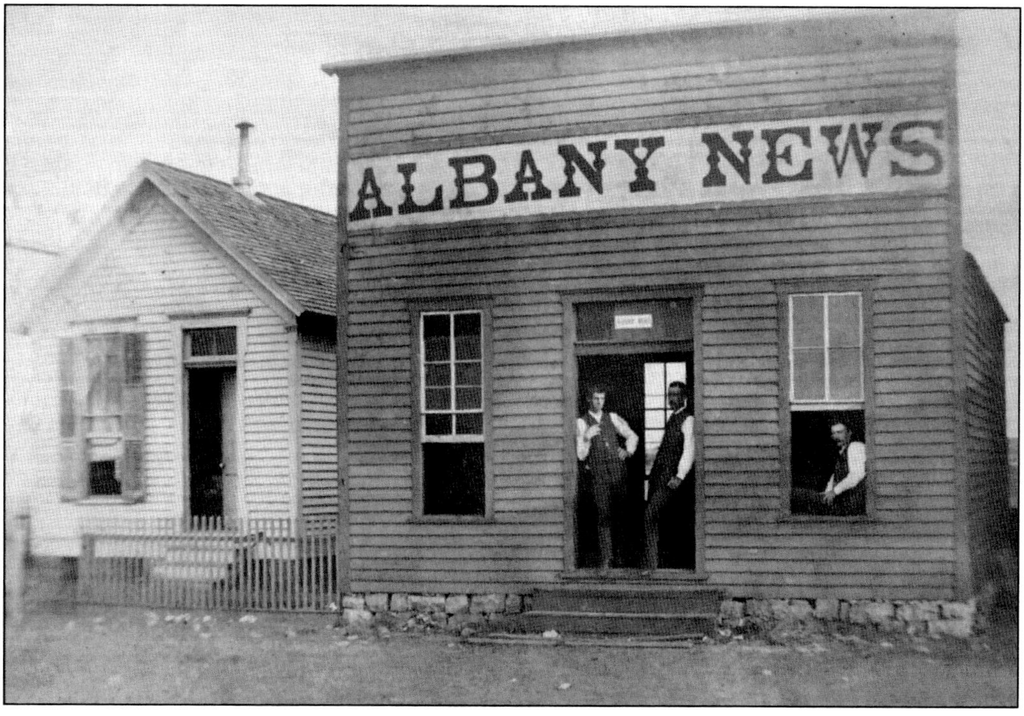

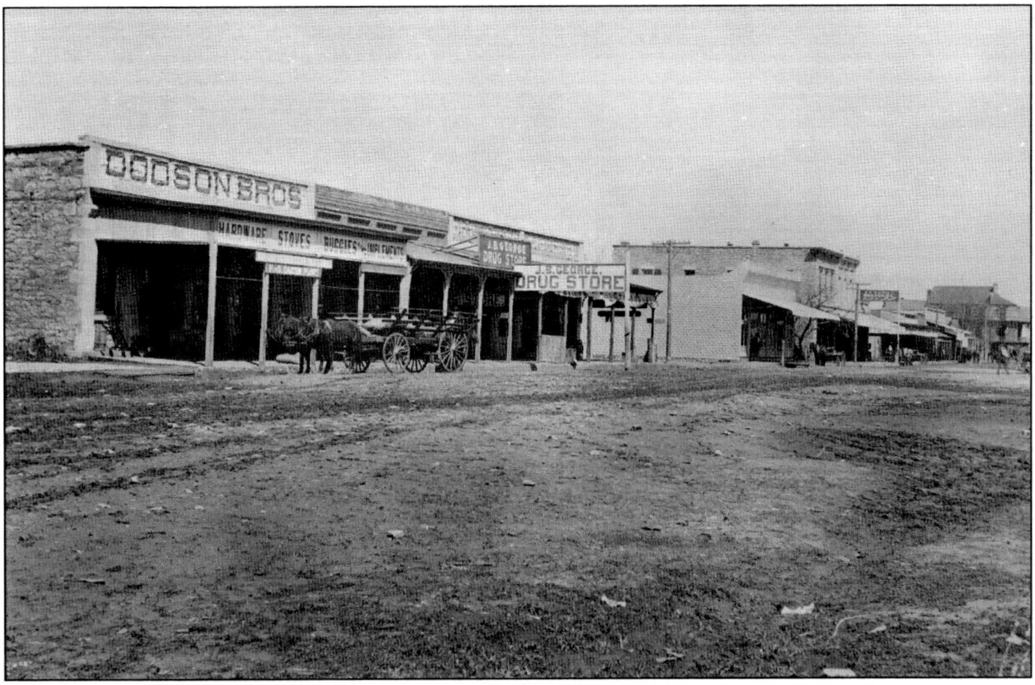

Those who appreciate historical preservation know that one of the things that make a small town great is its Main Street, which provides a vibrant, and often historic, backdrop for all manner of community activities. This 1903 photograph offers a wide view of the west side of Main Street, looking north.

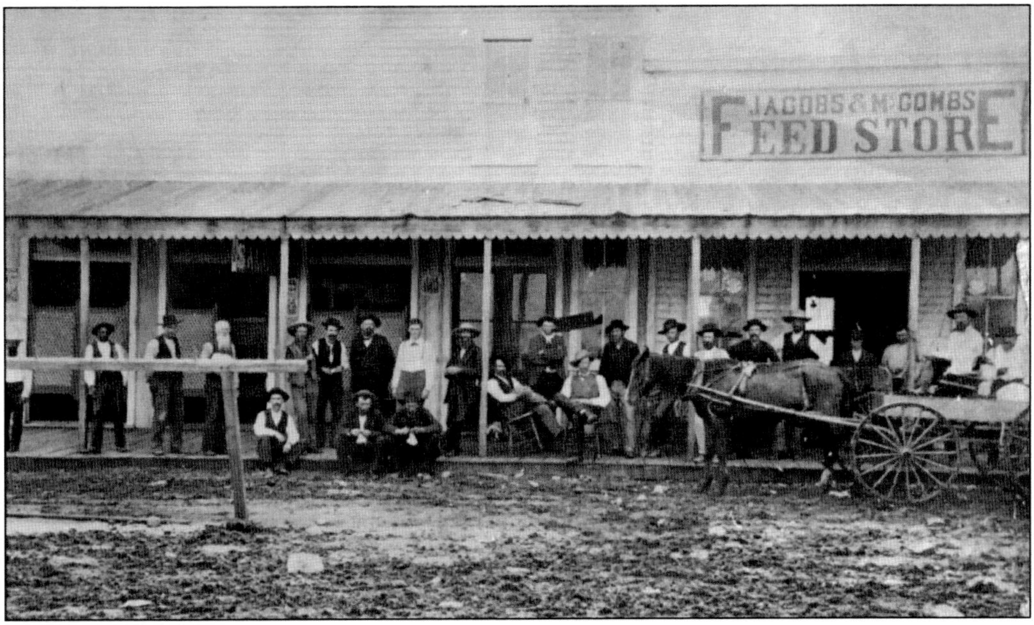

In the late 1880s, noted buffalo hunter Joe S. McCombs put in a feed store two doors down from the Biggs Saloon. A barbershop was located between the two stores. Located on the corner of South Second and Main Streets, these businesses preceded W.C. Moody's 1893 drugstore (Cotter Neff & Co. today). A barbershop occupied the same building from 1885 to 1896.

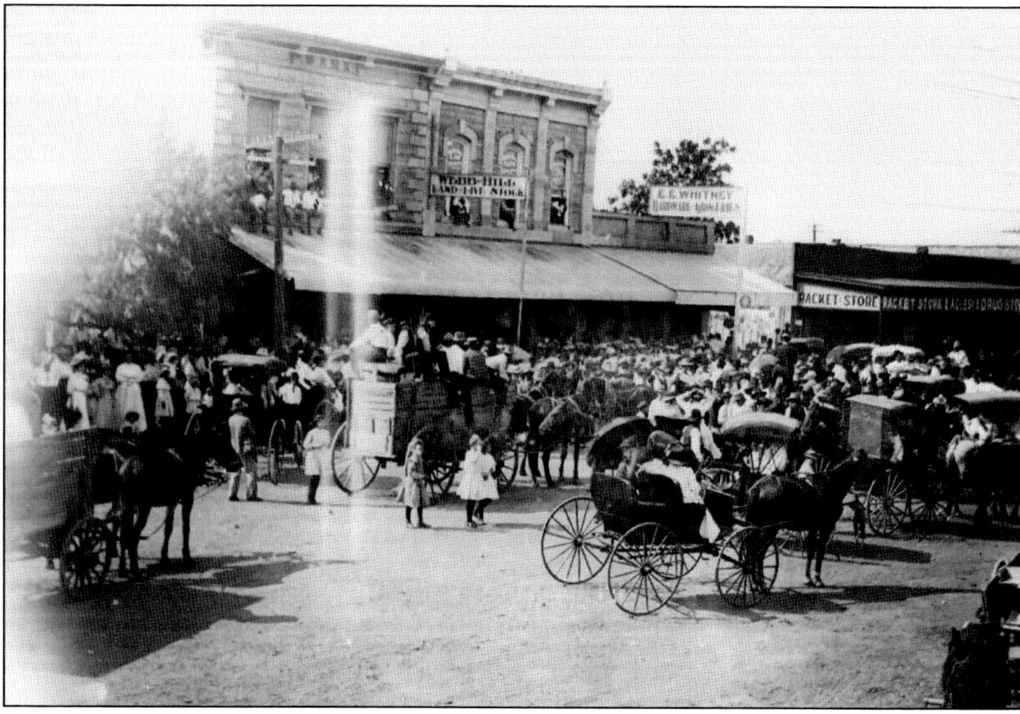

A large crowd congregates along the west side of Main Street for an unknown event. The limestone buildings, still standing today, here house the Webb-Hill offices and the E.E. Whitney Hardware and Grocery store. The Racket Store and a drugstore sit farther north.

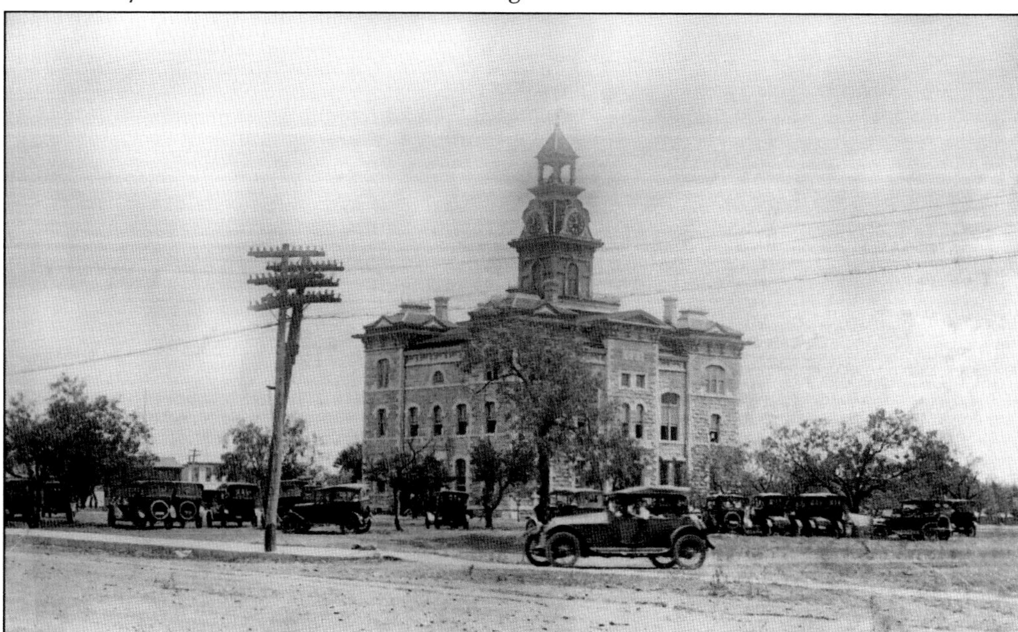

The courthouse lawn was not always the nice grassy area that it is today. It appears to have served as something of a parking lot in this photograph from the 1920s. The roads are still unpaved, although a curb and possibly a sidewalk seem to be in place.

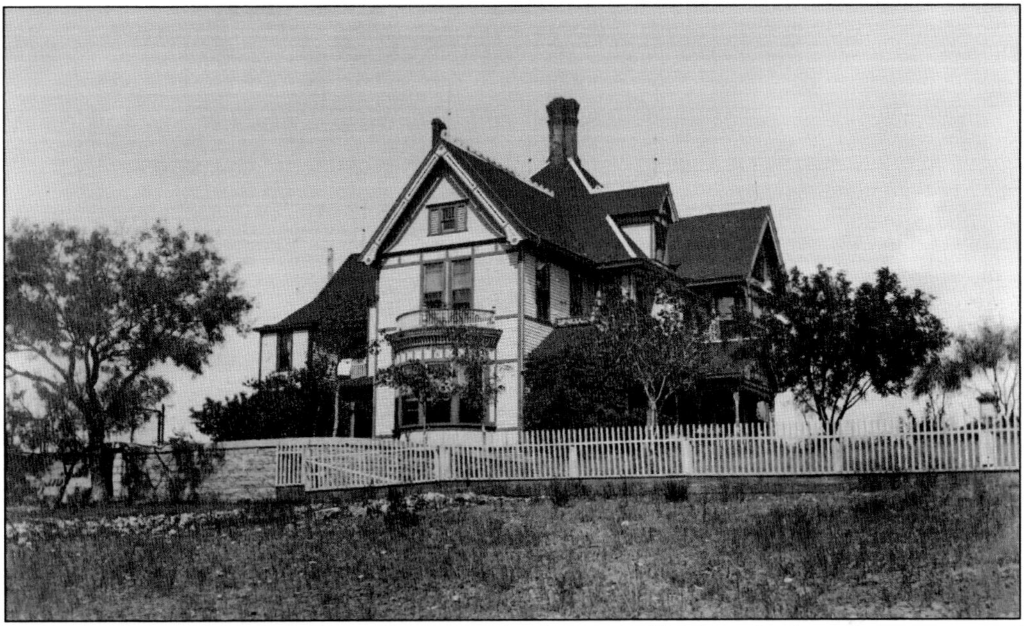

Sam and Ella Webb built this large home on a high point of land overlooking the new town of Albany in 1883. Located just a bit northeast of downtown, it stood out for all to see. After Sam and Ella passed away, one of the grandsons, another Sam Webb, bought the property. When a fire destroyed the garage and apartment, there was concern about the large house also burning. It was torn down, and a new home was built on the site, using bricks from the chimneys of the original house. Sam and Ellen Webb lived there from 1957 until 1999. (Courtesy of John A. Matthews.)

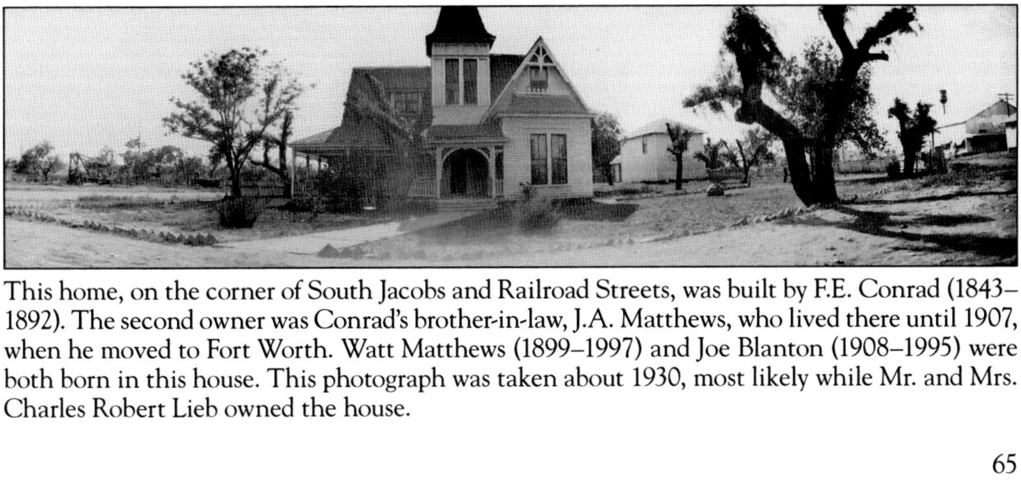

This home, on the corner of South Jacobs and Railroad Streets, was built by F.E. Conrad (1843–1892). The second owner was Conrad's brother-in-law, J.A. Matthews, who lived there until 1907, when he moved to Fort Worth. Watt Matthews (1899–1997) and Joe Blanton (1908–1995) were both born in this house. This photograph was taken about 1930, most likely while Mr. and Mrs. Charles Robert Lieb owned the house.

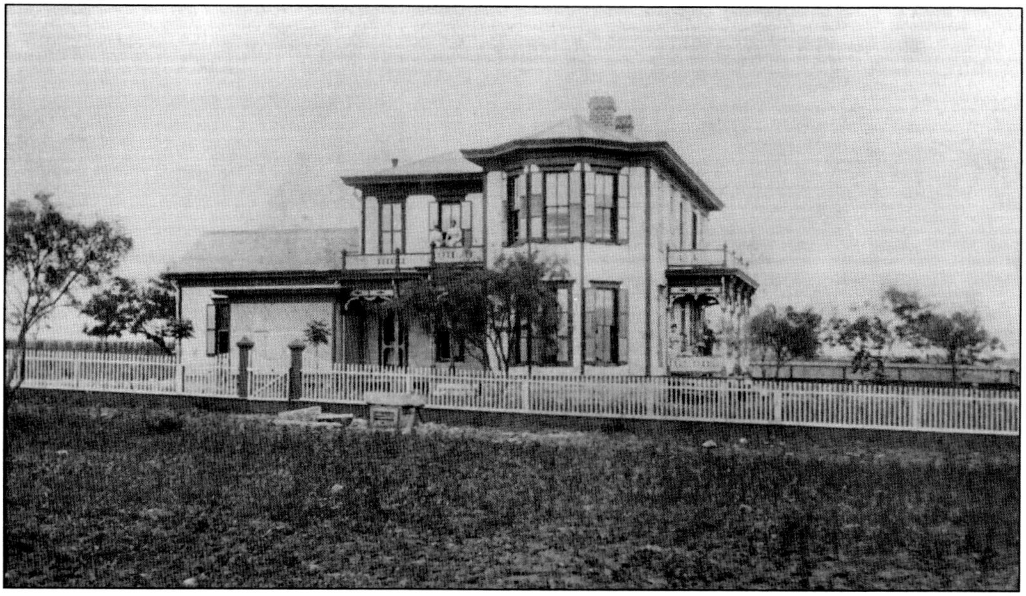

The home of William David Reynolds was built in the mid-1880s and was located on the corner of North Avenue B and North Second Street. Unfortunately, the home burned down around 1901. W.D. Reynolds married Susan Matthews. He was a cowboy for the Goodnight-Loving cattle drives of 1866–1867.

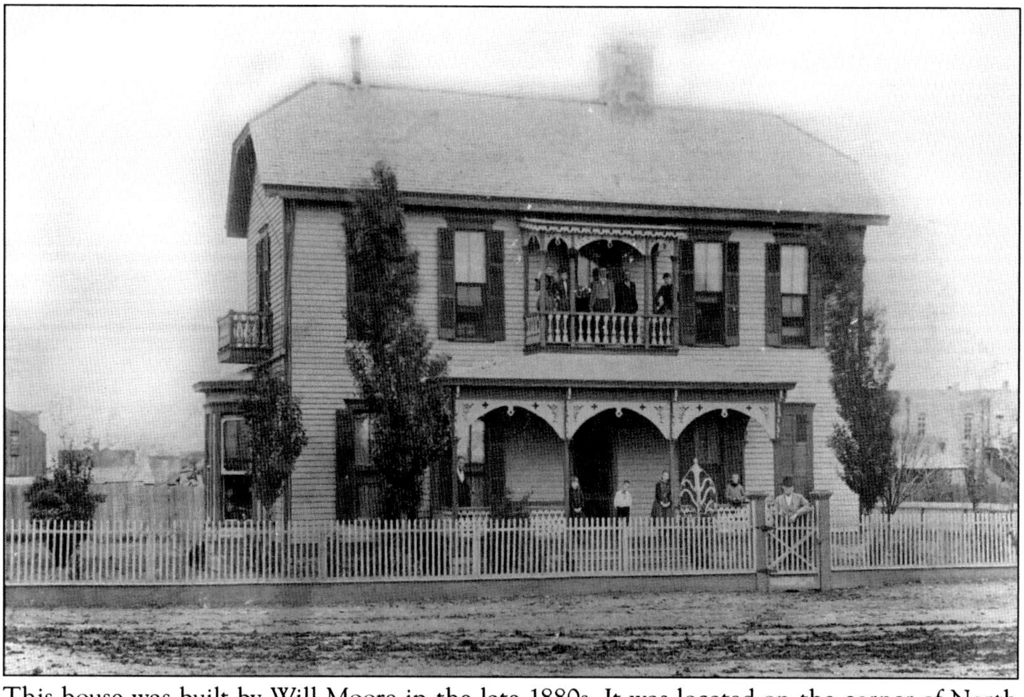

This house was built by Will Moore in the late 1880s. It was located on the corner of North First and South Jacobs Streets, where the present-day AEP Utilities and Masonic Lodge are located. Moore later sold the home to Alfred Merriweather George, an artist, pastor, and Civil War veteran who lost an arm at the Battle of Antietam. Descendants living in Albany include Louann, Whitby, and Jim Tom George.

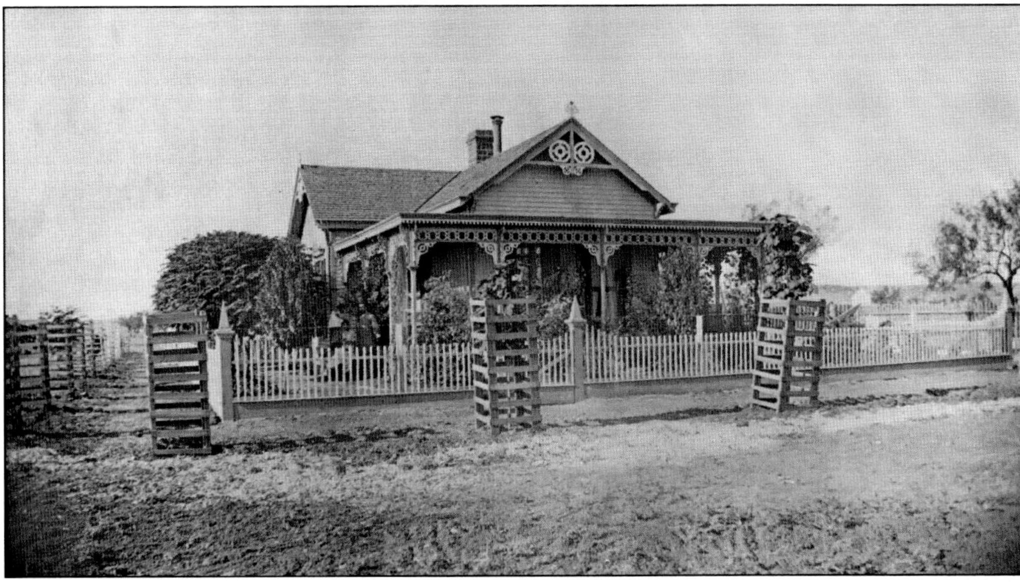

This photograph shows the north side of the L.H. Hill residence, which still stands today on the courthouse square. A.W. Duffy, an Albany contractor, built the Hill house in 1883. Hill first came to this West Texas area in 1879, when he took a job at the B.F. York Company in Fort Griffin. When the railway came to Albany in 1882, Hill moved to Albany.

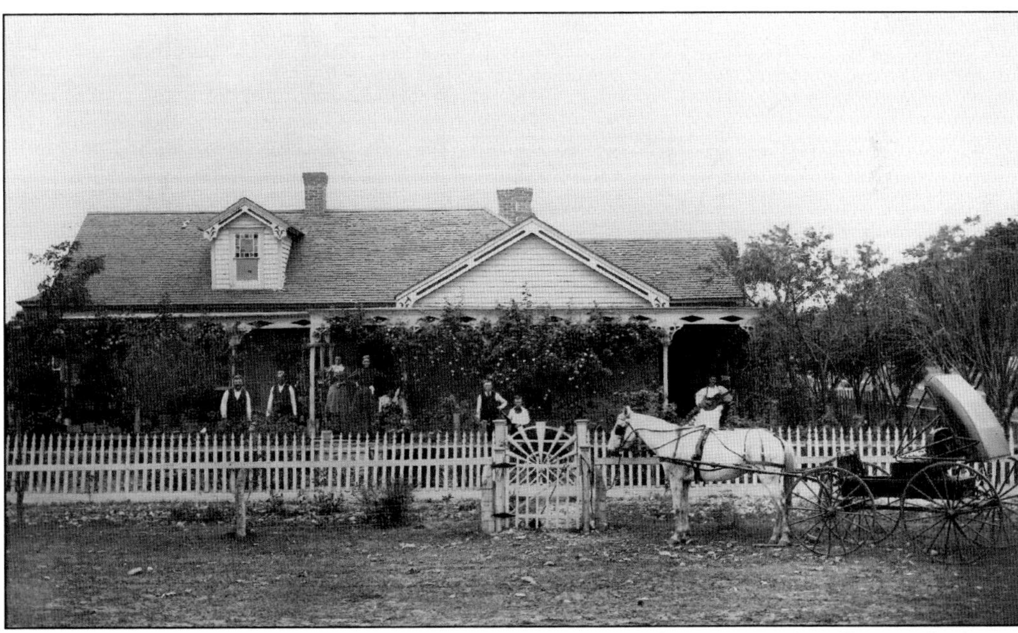

The Tom Hazlewood family poses in front of their spacious home in early Albany. The house, probably built just before 1900, was later occupied by the Stover family. The city had many such large frame homes, some of which were lost over the years to fire, including this one, which burned in 1956.

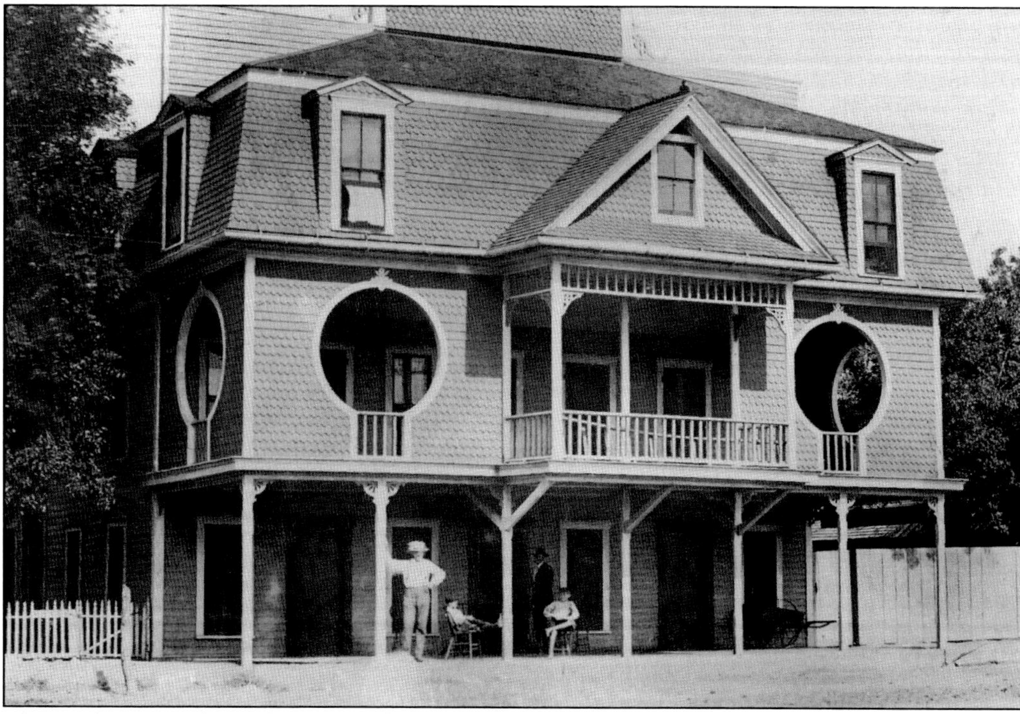

The Sackett Hotel was first located on the corner of Main and First Streets. Mrs. McLemore bought the building in 1926 and operated it under the name of Albany House. In 1926, she moved it just west and built a large, modern three-story brick hotel on the Main Street lot. Both structures are now gone.

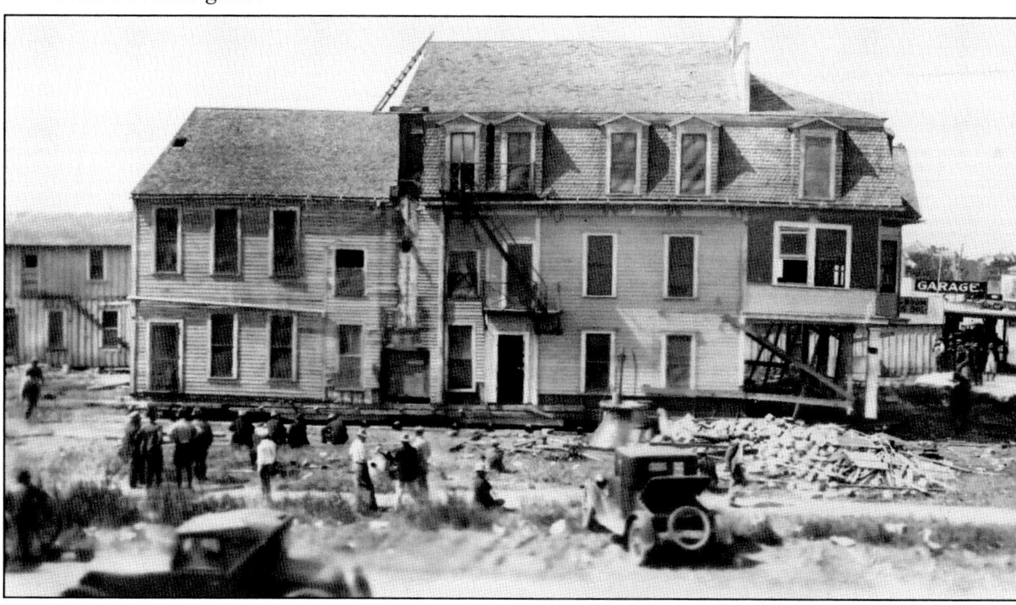

This 1925 photograph shows the Sackett Hotel being prepared for moving, to make way for the McLemore Hotel. Located on the southwest corner of the current Bank Park, it was moved across the back alley and repositioned to face South First Street. Referred to as a bowl-and-pitcher hotel, it remained in operation until 1931, when it was destroyed by fire.

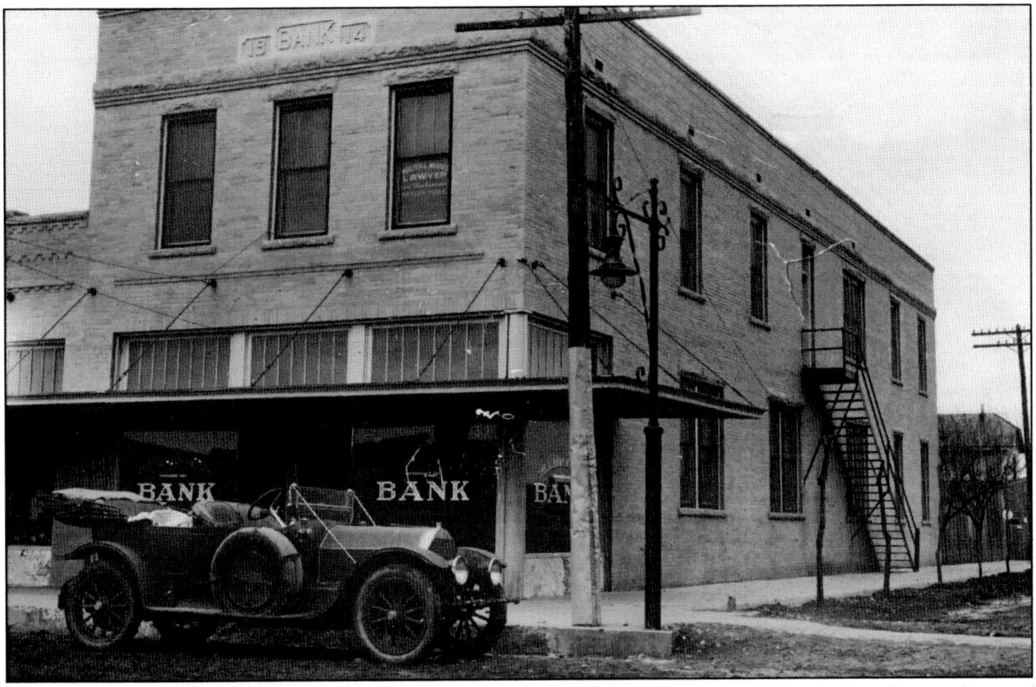

The Albany Bank was organized in the summer of 1883 by private individuals, all members of prominent Shackelford County families. A year later, the bank was granted a national charter, and it officially became known as the First National Bank of Albany, Texas. This brick building, the bank's second and current location, was completed not long before the photograph was taken in 1915. Note the gaslight pole on the corner.

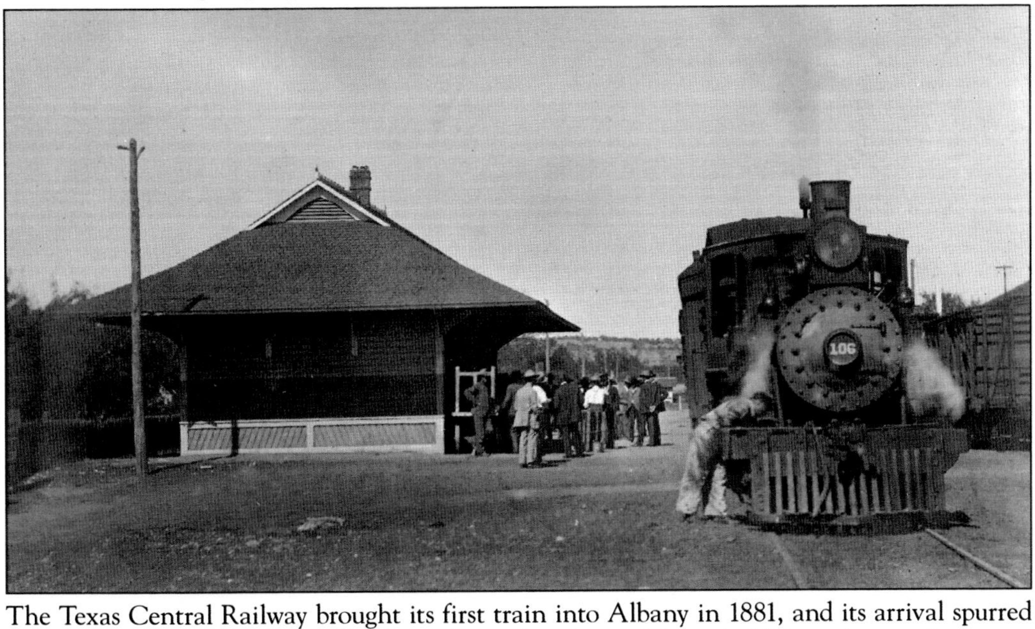

The Texas Central Railway brought its first train into Albany in 1881, and its arrival spurred economic growth in the area. The depot shown here burned down in 1920, and a new, larger one replaced it. The railroad has been gone for a long time, but remnants of the train bed remain. The new station now houses the chamber of commerce and the ticket office for *Fandangle*.

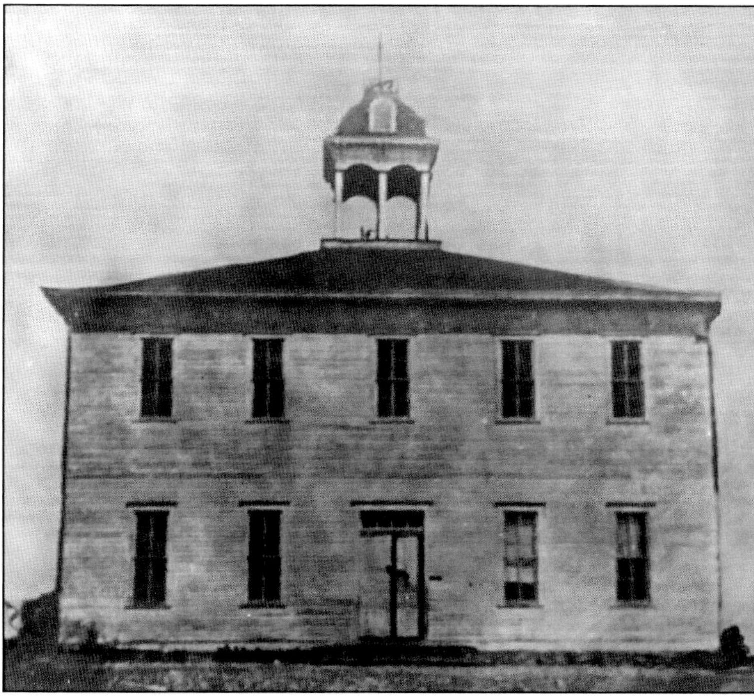

Albany's first public school was this two-story frame building constructed on what was later called Schoolhouse Hill. In July 1883, an election was held authorizing a public school system for the immediate area. The Sanborn Insurance maps show the school building in use by 1891, but not in 1885, so it took a while for it to be planned and constructed. The school was no longer in use after 1908, and the building sat empty for many years.

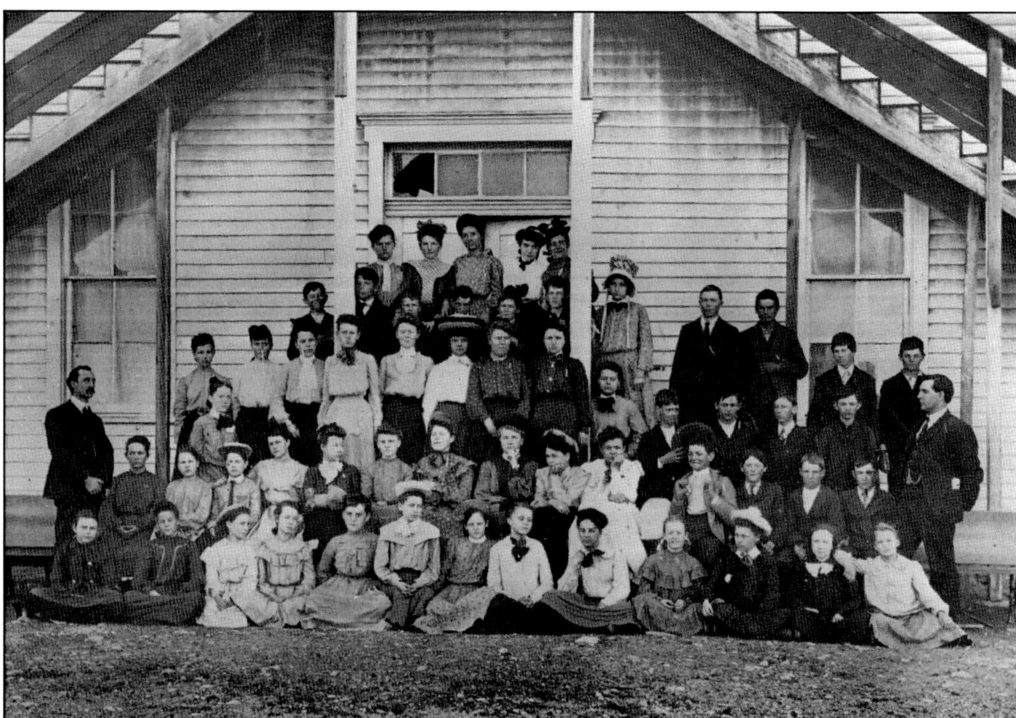

Posing in front of their school building in 1904 are Albany students attending grades seven through eleven. This was the first school building the city constructed with the addition of outside stairs to the upper floor. About four years later, a new school was built.

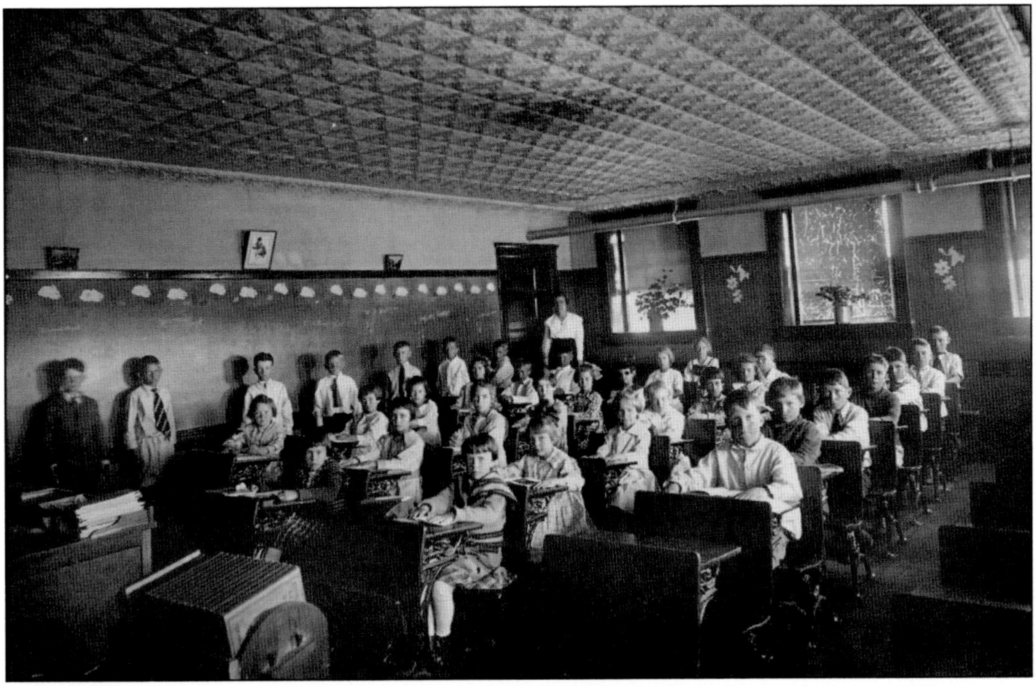

The third-grade class of Nannie Adamson solemnly poses for its school picture. The year is probably 1919, and the photograph shows what the classrooms in the new school building looked like at the time. Note the detail in the ceiling and the large windows in back.

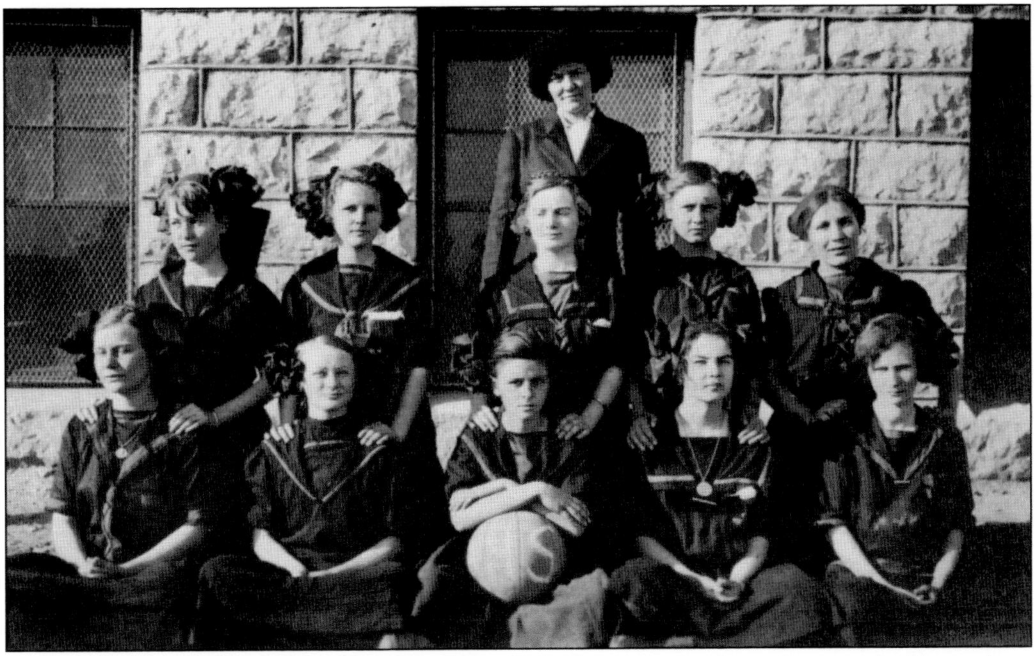

The 1910–1911 Albany Public School girls' basketball team poses for a photograph. Shown here are, from left to right, (first row) Beatrice Adamson, Kate Ivy, Amy Poer, Mary Mums, and Mamie Ward; (second row) Betty Matthews, Lois Poer, Nelly Howsley, Grace Knowles, and unidentified. The teacher in the back is Gertude Holson.

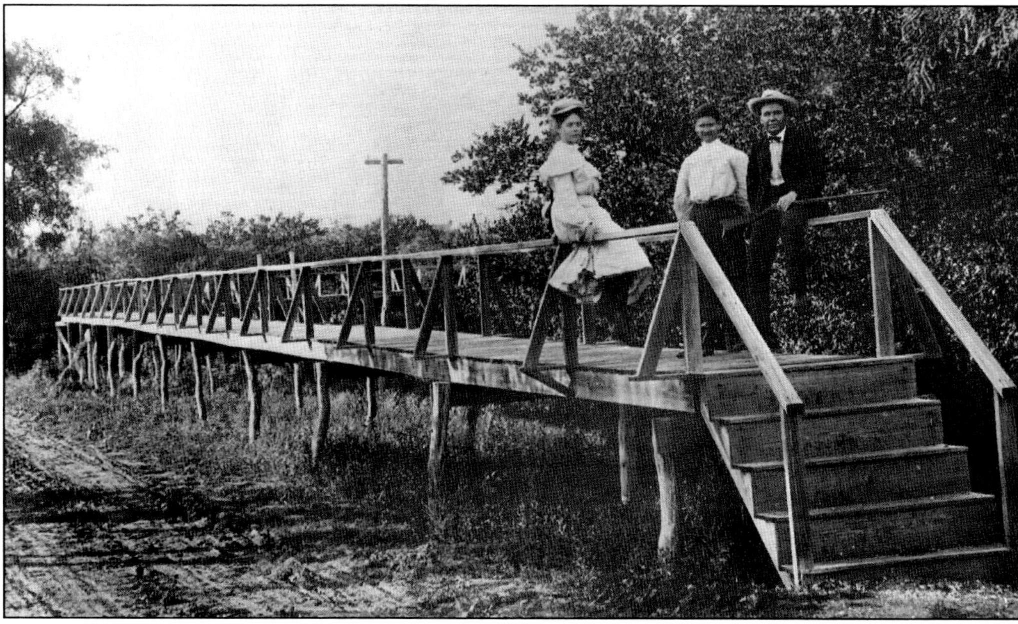

The Bartholomew Bridge, seen in this 1890s photograph, is south of US 180. The bridge spans the North Prong of Hubbard Creek. The telephone pole in the background carried the first wire to the Bartholomew home. Shown here are Laura Reynolds Bishop (left), Fern Newcomb (center), and A.W. "Jack" Reynolds.

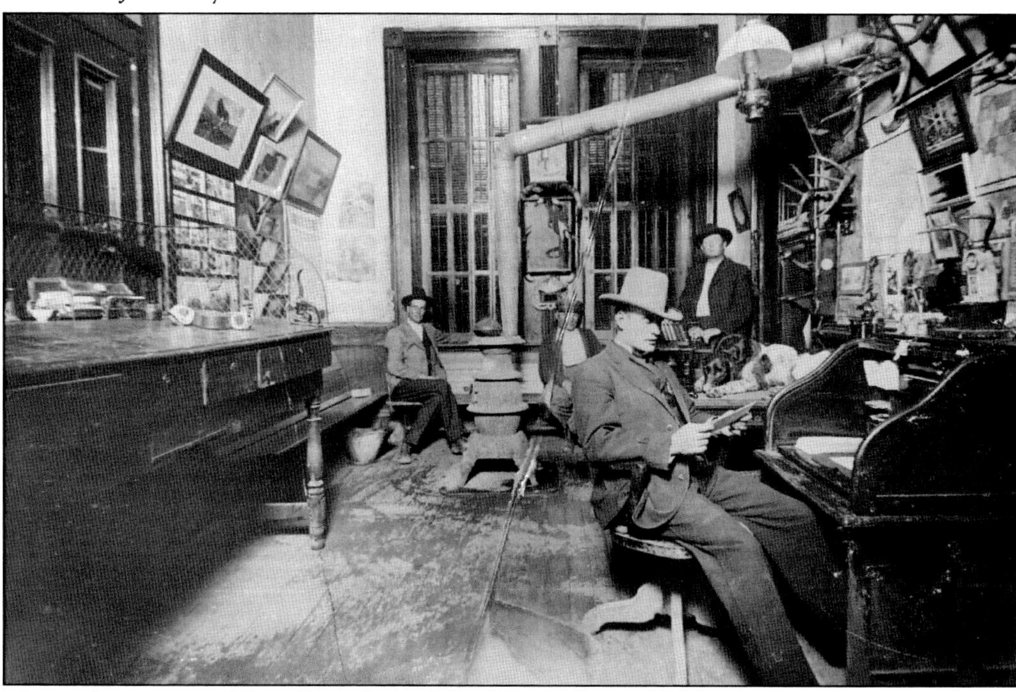

This is the interior of the office of Marshall W.M. Biggs (1870–1922) in the early 1900s. One of the longest-serving sheriffs Shackelford County has ever had, Biggs was first elected in November 1904 and served a total of nine consecutive terms. He had been nominated for a 10th term before his unexpected death from heart failure on October 19, 1922.

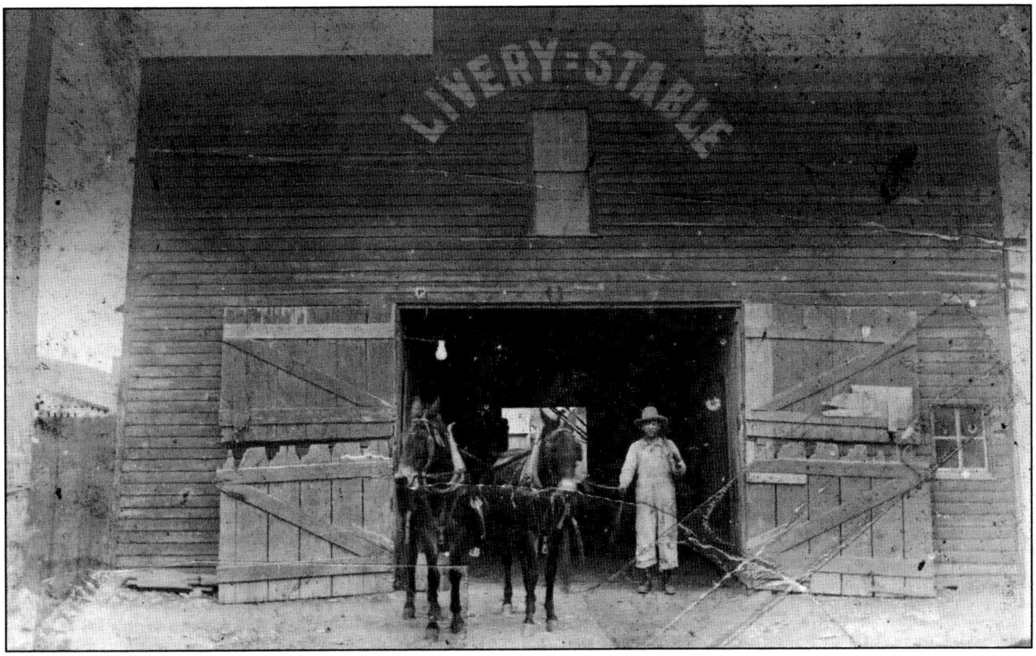

Liveries were short-term boarding stables that cared for horses belonging to people visiting the town. They were a kind of Wild West parking garage or a hotel for four-legged visitors. With the advent of the horseless carriage, the business of short-term boarding declined. The location of this Albany livery, photographed in 1914, is unknown.

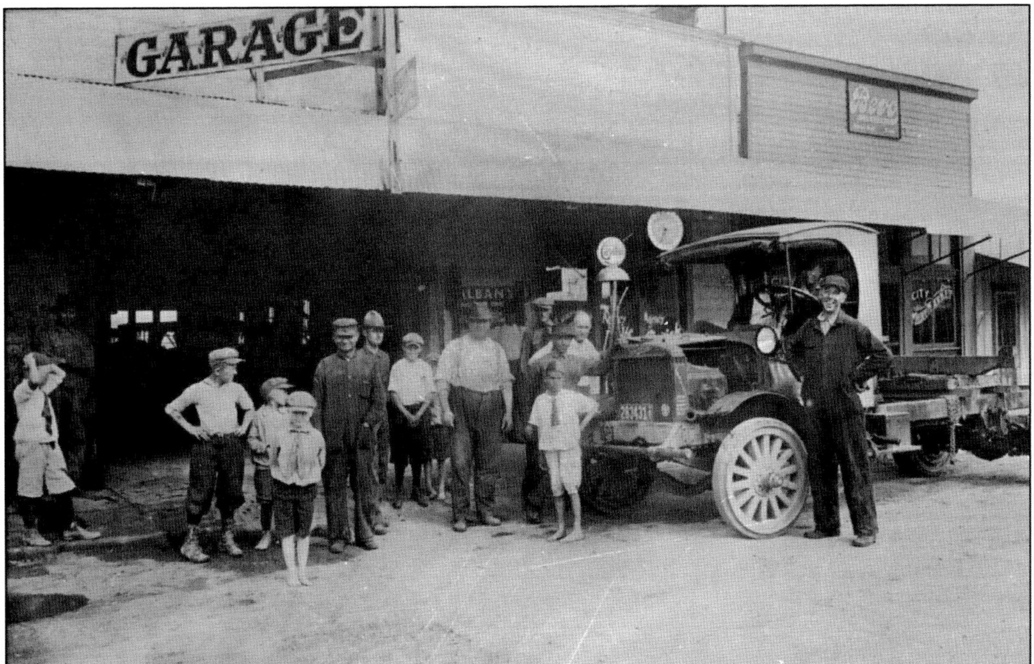

A truck used for hauling large pipe for the oil and gas fields of early Shackelford County sits in front of a garage and gasoline supplier on Main Street. A meat market was located next door. Posing for this 1918 photograph is a group of happy men and boys on a summer's day.

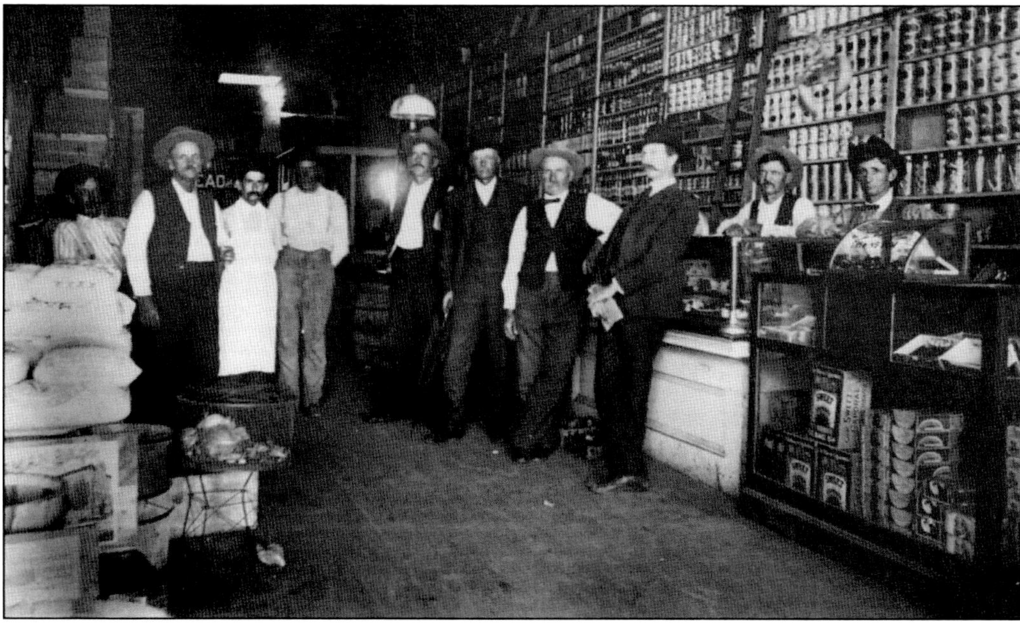

This is the Nance and Meyer Store in 1905. The gentlemen are, from left to right, Eli Meyer (1858–1927), Dutch Nance (1845–1910), Josh Rodriguez (1858–1927), Charlie Poer, Phin Reynolds (1851–1952), Will Manning (1849–1935), R.J. Moberley Sr. (1841–1924), John F. Sedwick (1873–1968), John E. Morgan (1853–1905), and Roy Rodriguez (1886–1945). This building is now the Sanders Drug Store.

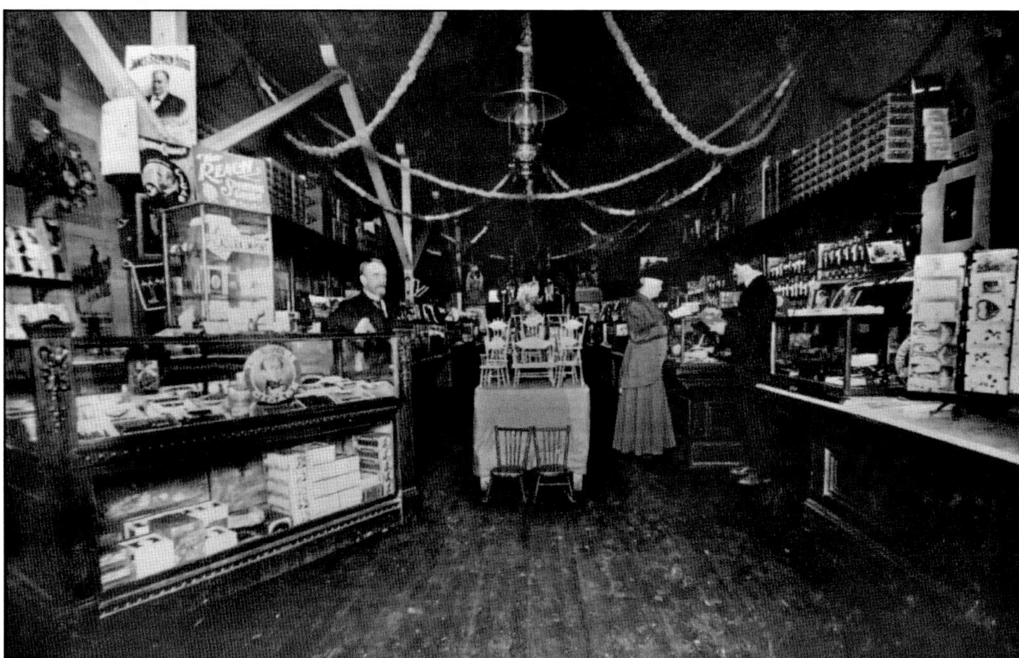

This is the interior of a Main Street store in 1912. Christmas decorations, primarily garland, drape from the ceiling and along the walls. Posing here are, from left to right, a Mr. George (1843–1931), Susan Bartholomew (1848–1821), and A.C. Sneed.

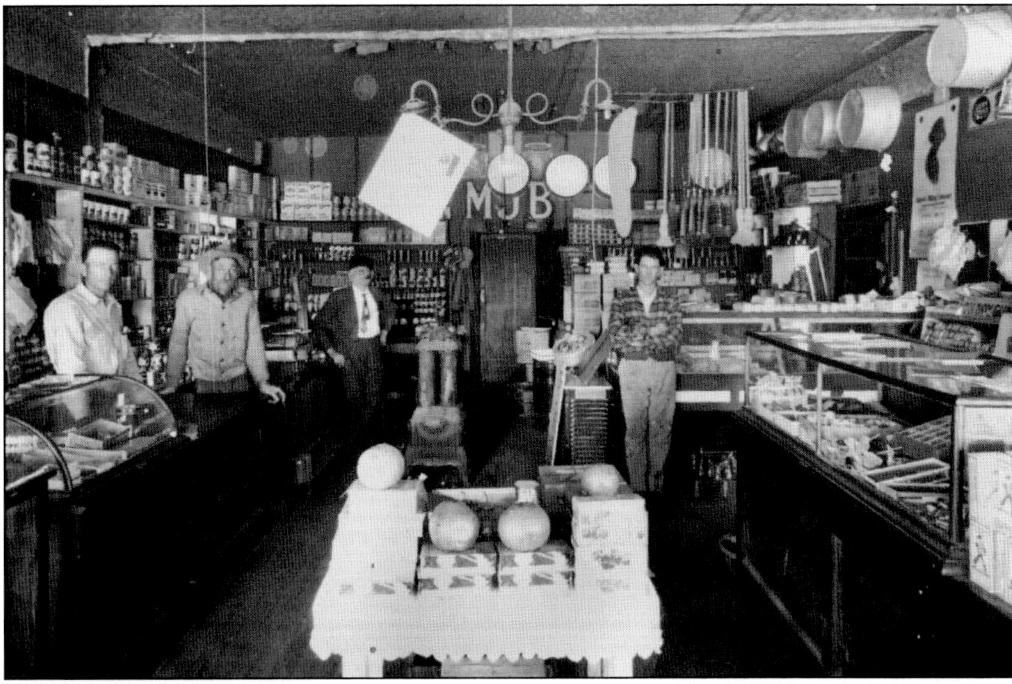

The interior of the J.S. McComb Grocery Store is seen here in the 1920s. It was located on the west side of Main Street, between South Second and South Third Streets. The men shown here are, from left to right, Dennis Tabor, Matt Huber, Joe McComb, and Lee Wayne.

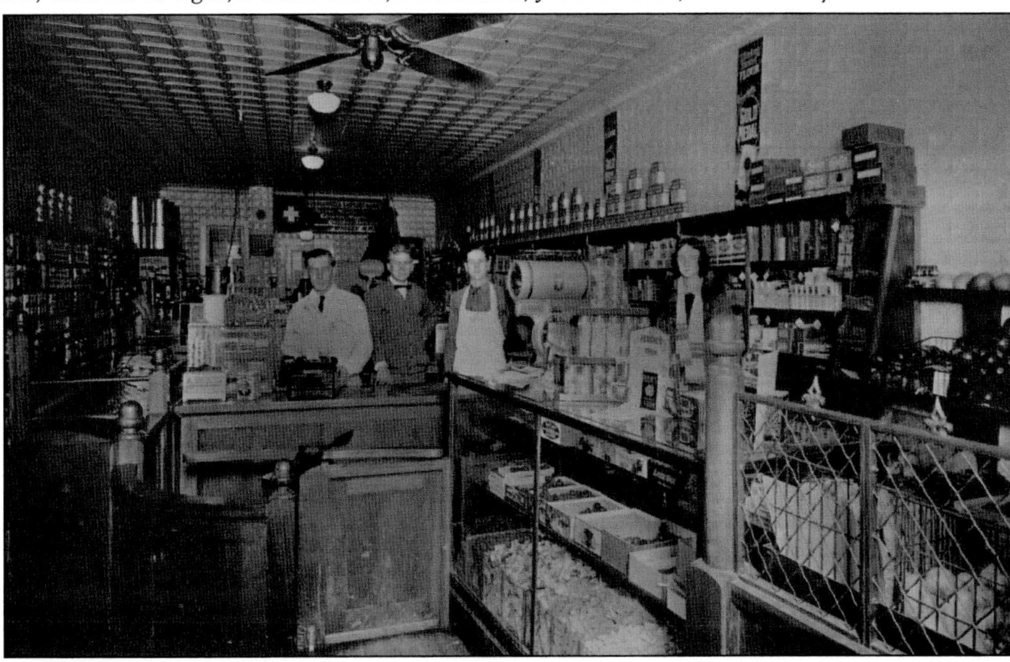

Carter King Grocery was one of a number of grocery stores in Albany. Shoppers gave their orders, and the clerks took items from the shelves and put them in bags or boxes. Often, orders were delivered to the customers' homes. What service! The salespeople in this early 1930s photograph are, from left to right, Arthur Adams, J. Carter King Sr., Bert Cashion, and Dorothy Dee.

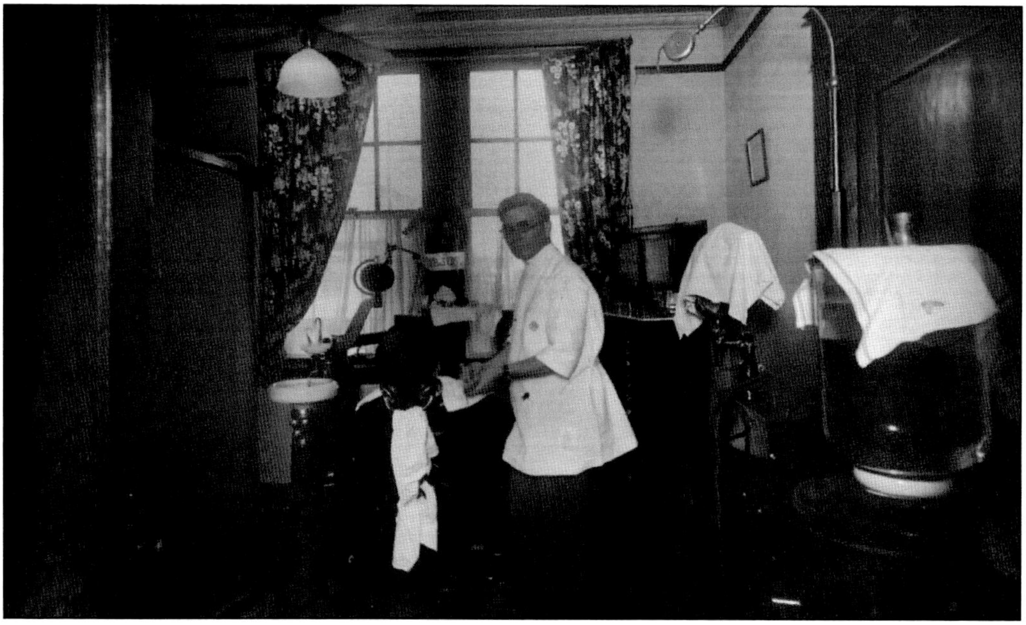

"Hello, my little friend." For 44 years, from 1927 to 1971, Albany children heard these words from Dr. Dewey C. "Doc" McCord as he prepared to work on their teeth. His first office, in the L.H. Hill Building, had no running water. Then he moved to the second floor of the First National Bank. He was a charter member of the Lions Club, a Boy Scout leader, a Mason, and a Presbyterian elder. (Courtesy of Sunday Tidwell.)

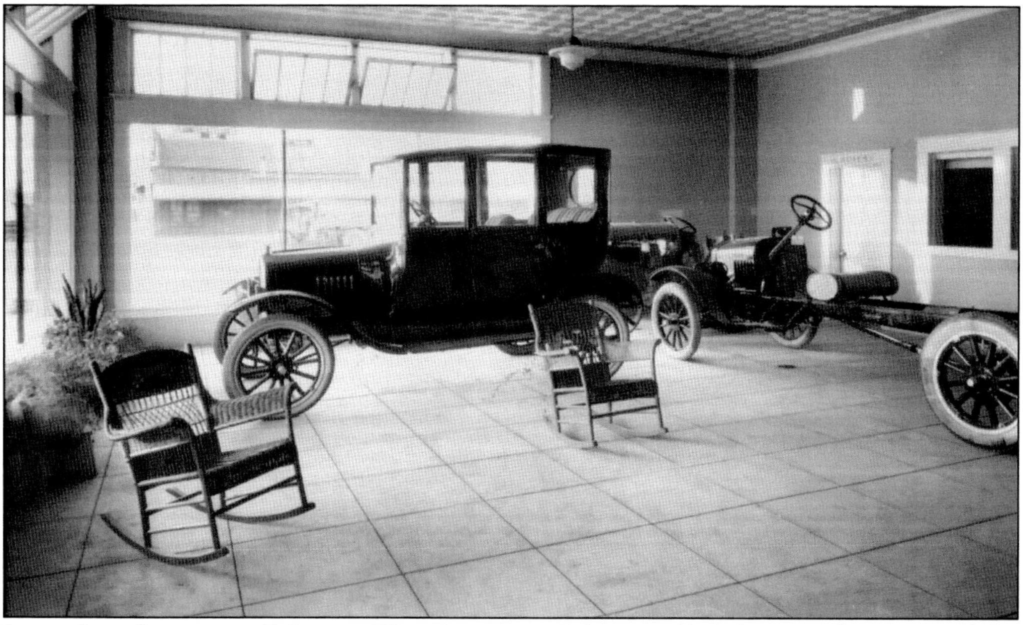

Located on the corner of Main and First Streets was Johnny Miller's Garage, where automobiles were sold and worked on. It would appear that farm tractors were also in the inventory. The automobile industry was still in its infancy in the 1920s, and many people were getting into the new business. Albany soon had many dealerships. The building is now the site of the True Value Hardware Store.

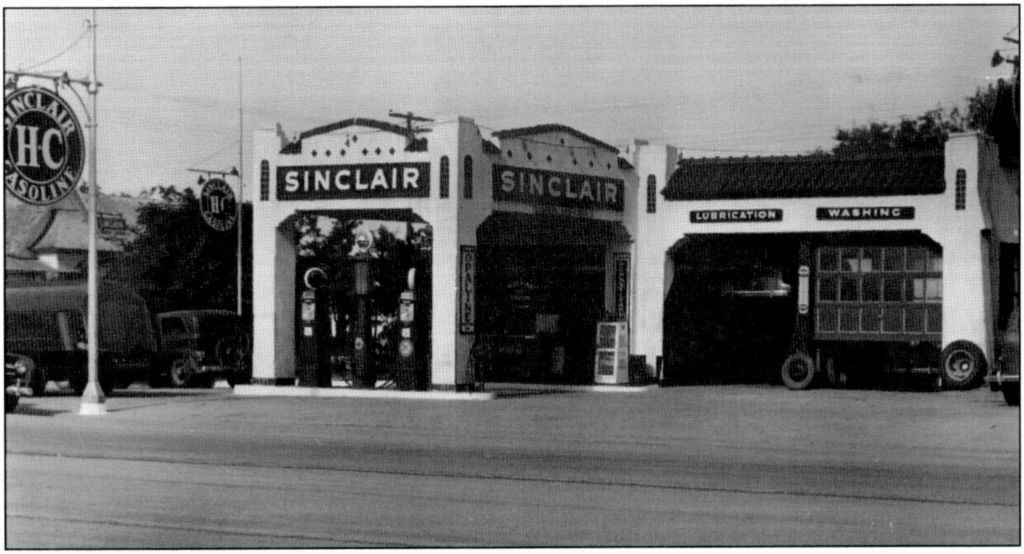

"Fill her up" was heard often at Cecil Hopkins' Sinclair service station on Main Street. For many years, his station filled the gas tank, cleaned the windshield, fixed the flat, and had ice-cold Cokes in the red box. Service stations abounded as automobiles became common. There were a number in town, and everyone had their favorite. This station has been restored and sits across from the courthouse, appearing ready for business. (Courtesy of Jack Hopkins.)

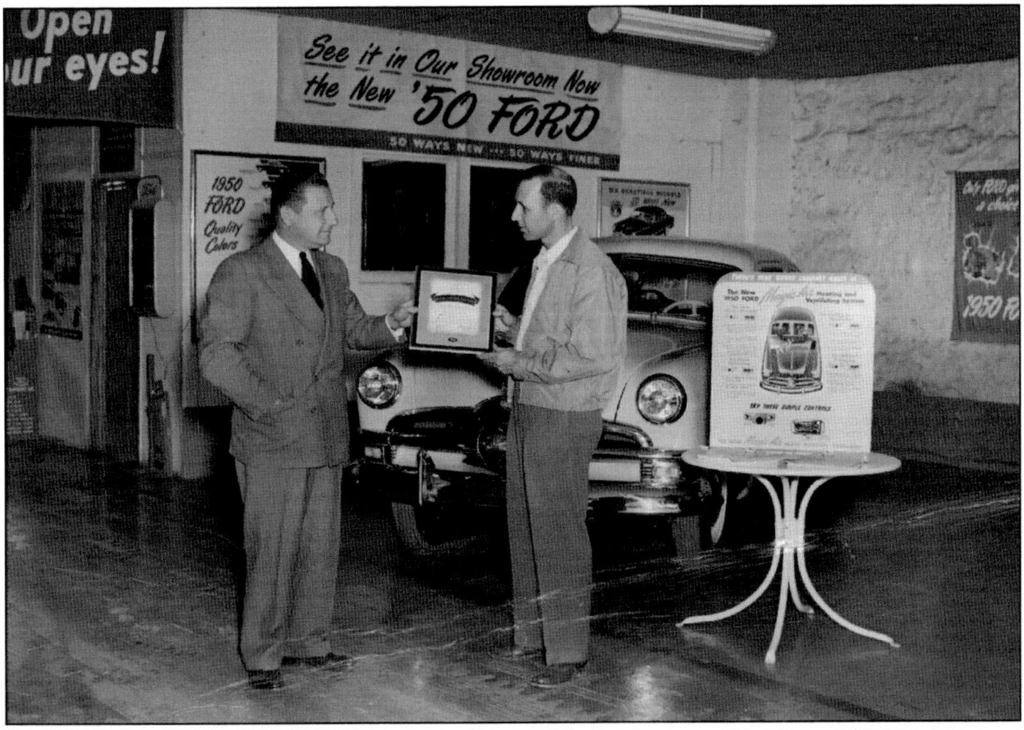

A new car in 1950 at Bill Hill's Ford dealership could cost between $1,339 and $2,262. Pictured holding a certificate are Hill (right) and a suited gentleman, possibly a Ford Company representative. Hill purchased the Ford dealership from Johnny Miller in the 1940s and moved it down the street, next to the current Momentum building. Today, a fitness center occupies the space.

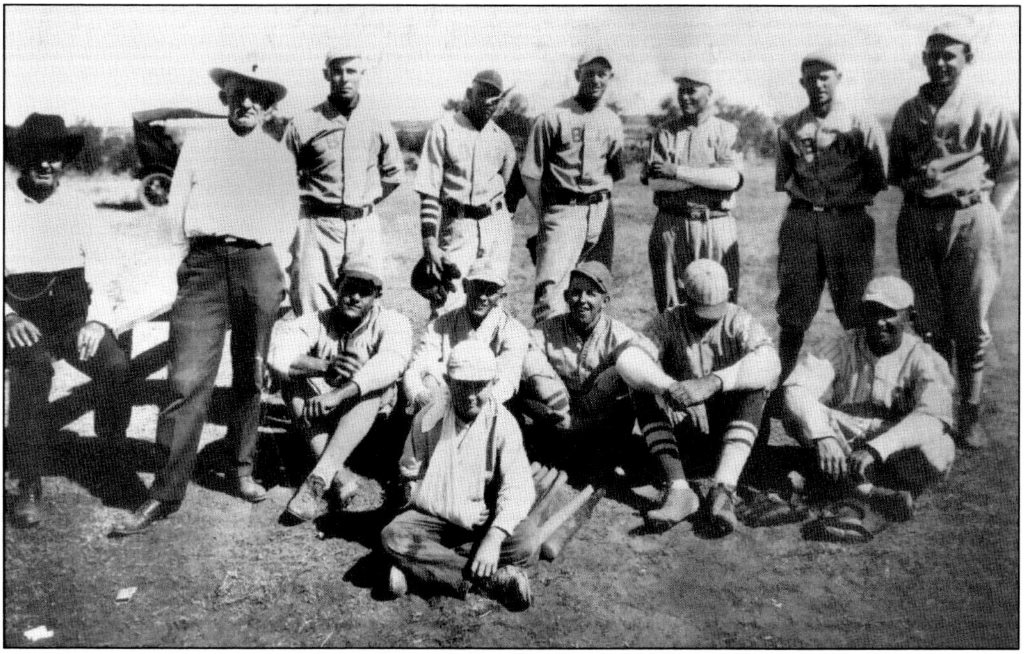

Compared to the other sports in Albany in the early 1900s, baseball truly was in a league of its own. It was America's pastime, and, for the town, it was a matter of pride. Baseball has always been a game that can be played wherever there is an open field or a vacant lot. The only equipment required are a bat, a ball, and something to mark the bases. The object and the rules are relatively simple, and the game itself offers good, healthy exercise for young and old alike. This photograph was taken in 1922–1923.

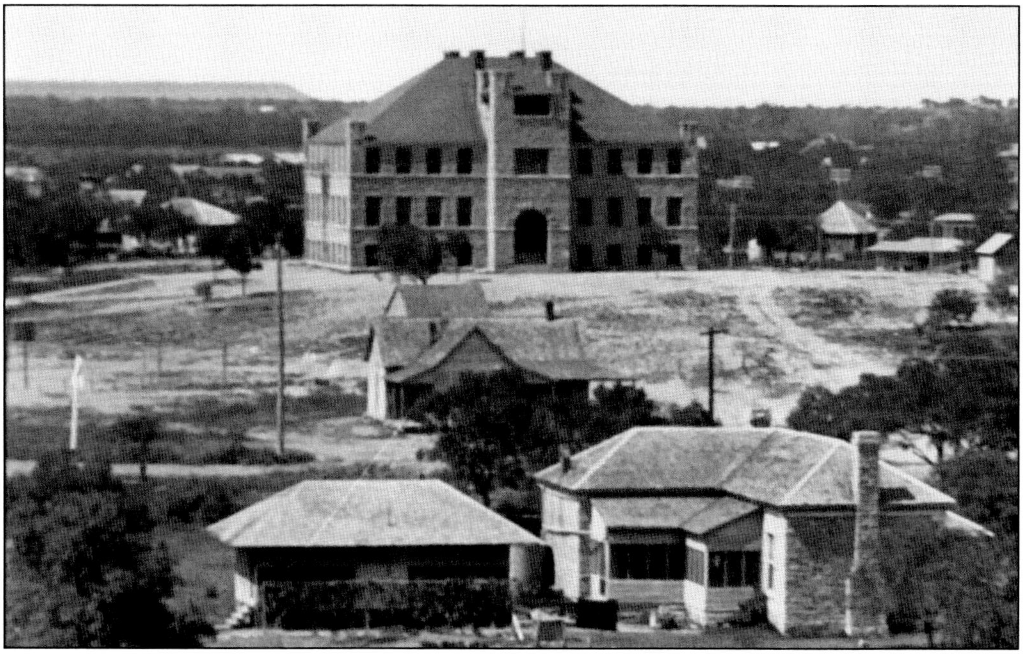

In the summer of 1921, Virginia Clarke climbed to the top of the courthouse and took this picture of the Albany Public School building from the tower.

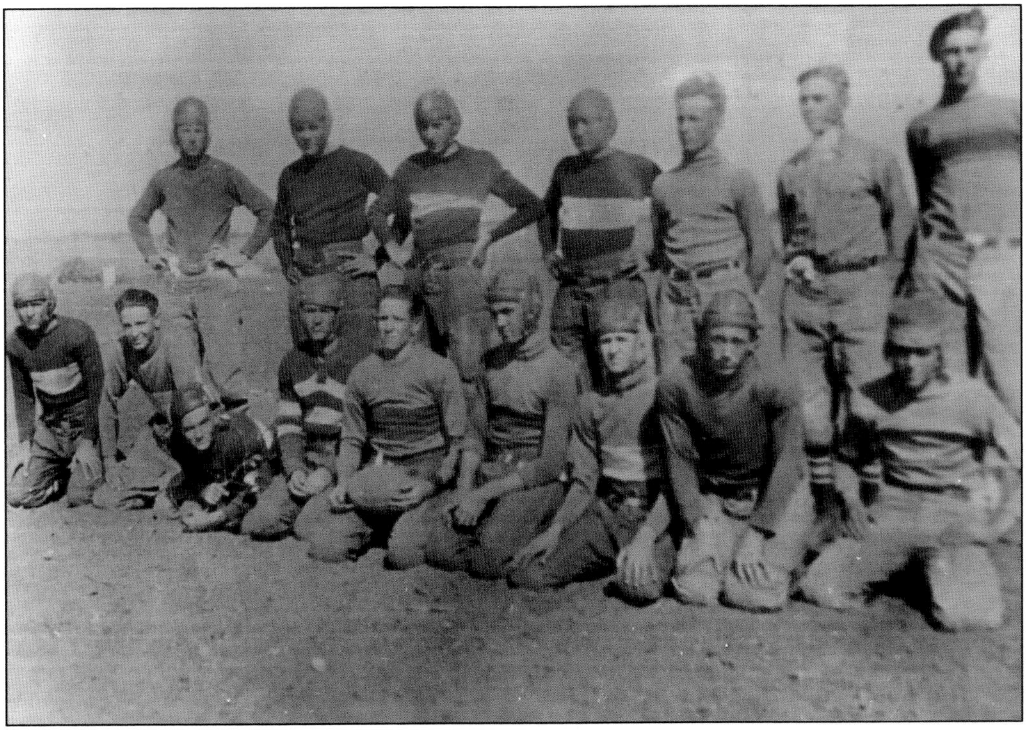

By the 1920s, a new game, football, became the sport of young men. Players had to buy their own equipment, and if they could not afford it, they simply played without. The players shown here are, from left to right, (first row) linemen John Coffee, unidentified, Luther Hollowell, Earl Isbell, Buford Jordan, Melborn Fincher, N.R. Price, Mart Pate, and unidentified; (second row) backfield members Oris Anderson, Jack George, Harvey Palmer, Bob Pate, Glen Gooch, Theron Fincher, and Joe Humble. (Courtesy of John A. Matthews.)

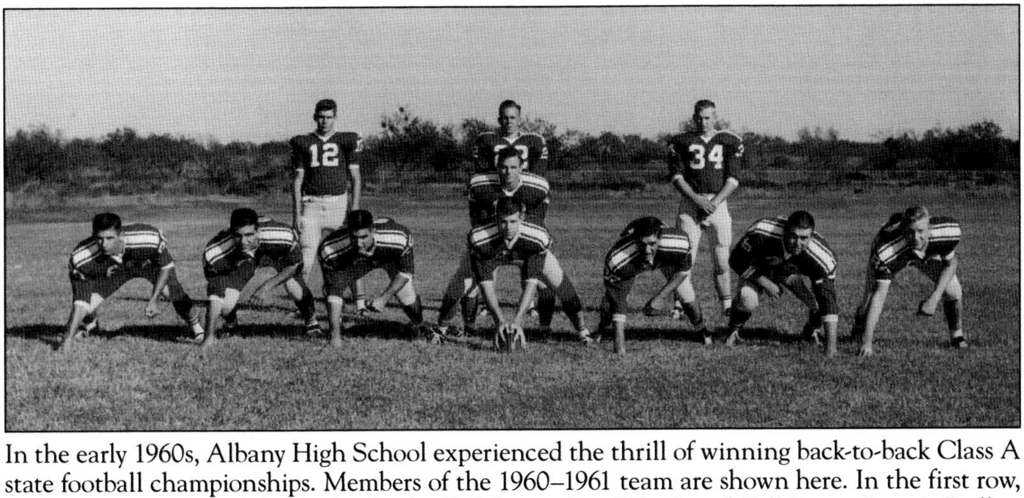

In the early 1960s, Albany High School experienced the thrill of winning back-to-back Class A state football championships. Members of the 1960–1961 team are shown here. In the first row, the linemen are, from left to right, Rocky Hill, Jonnie Ray Woodward, Bill Stapp, Ronnie Badley, Jackie Mitchell, Guy McCain, and Bud Leech. The members of the backfield are, from left to right, Jim Wood, Dennis Tucker, and Johnny Agan. The quarterback is Roy Hogan.

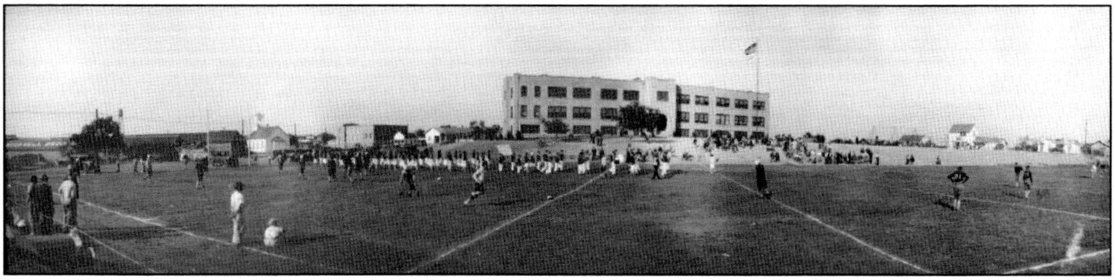

This panoramic photograph provides a wide view of the school building and football field in 1930. The players clear the field to make way for the band at halftime, while the spectators watch from the sidelines. Visible to the left of the school are Trinity Episcopal Church and First Baptist Church. (Courtesy of Cathy Rupp.)

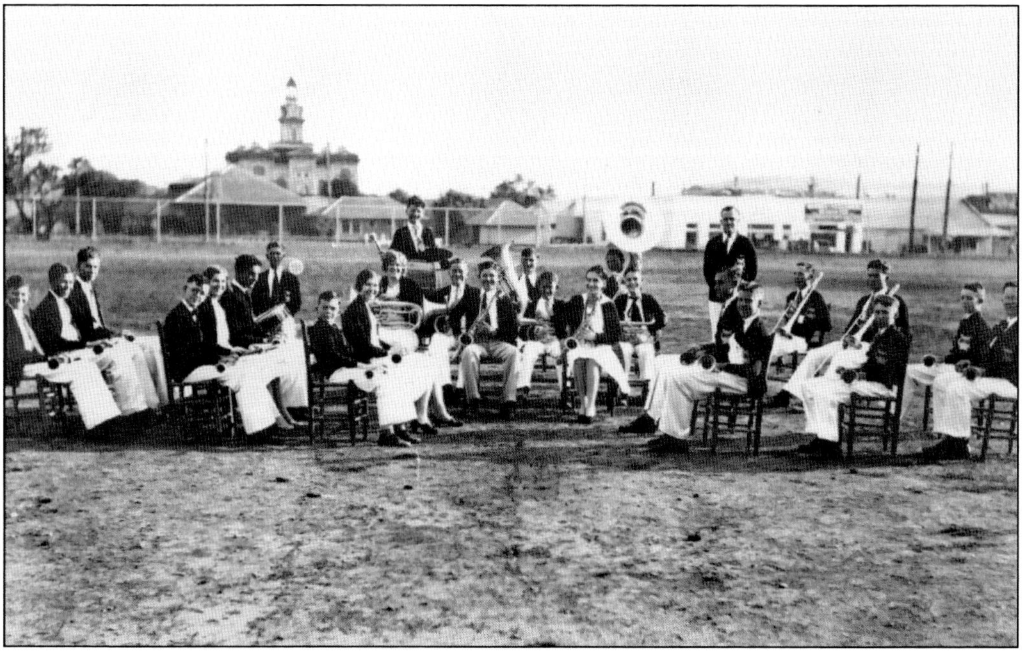

What is a high school without a band? Albany High School has always prided itself on the caliber of its band, and the ensemble shown here in the early 1930s is no exception. The bandleader was W.R. Lennox, and it is apparent that he has formed a band worthy of pride. Director Lennox was hired by the Albany School Board in May 1929 and remained with the school until May 1932.

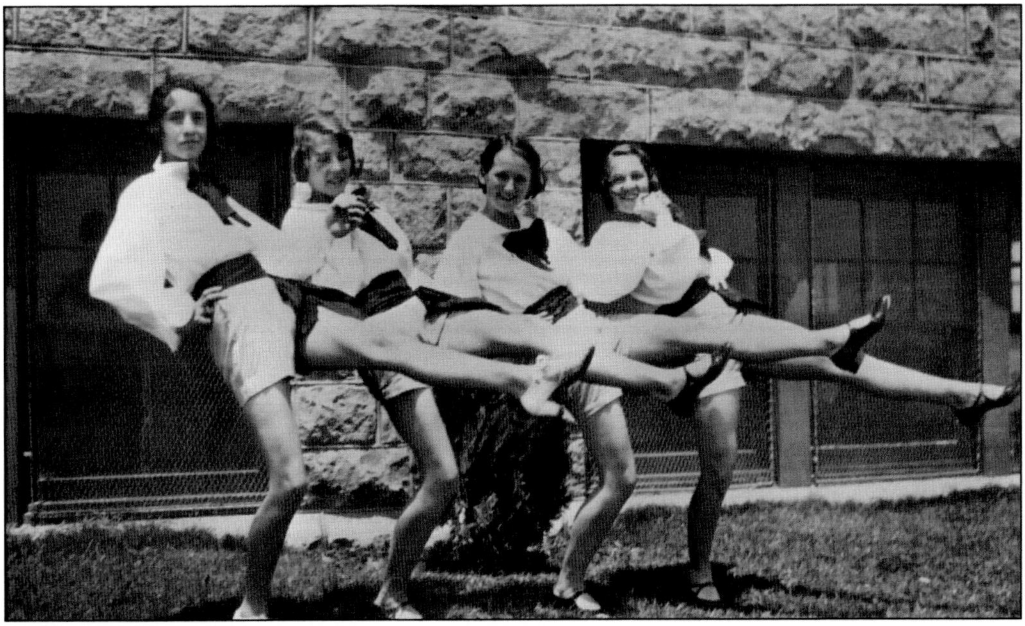

The Yankee Doodle Chorus of the Albany Public School strikes a pose outside the main school building during the 1931–1932 school year. Shown are, from left to right, Ruth Fite, Helen Best, Frances Rowland, and Pauline Dodson.

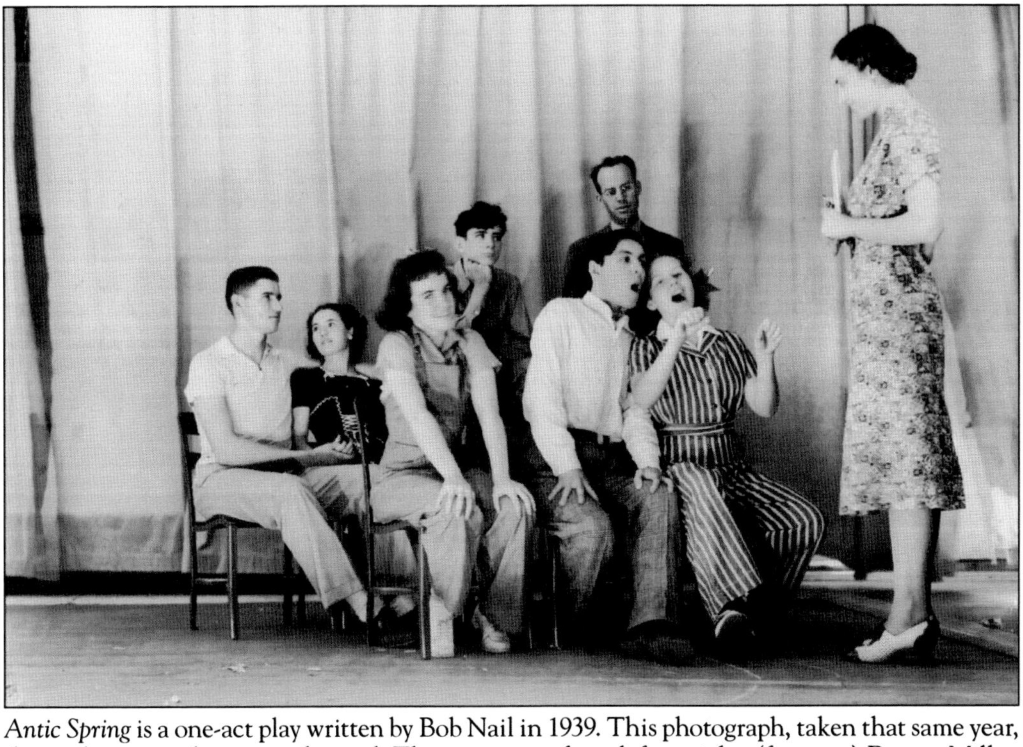

Antic Spring is a one-act play written by Bob Nail in 1939. This photograph, taken that same year, shows the original cast in rehearsal. The actors are, from left to right, (first row) Downs Miller, Lloyd Cete Jr., and Ann Moore; (second row) Joe Blanton, Vernele Grable, Robert Green, and Robert Nail. The woman standing at right is unidentified. (Courtesy of Nancy Green.)

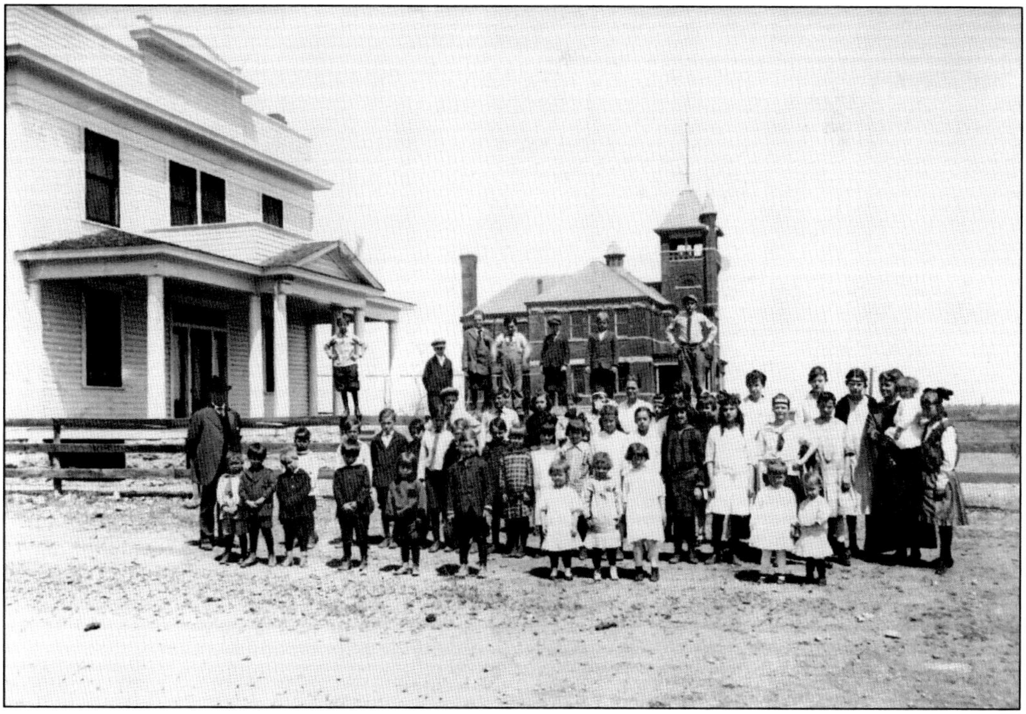

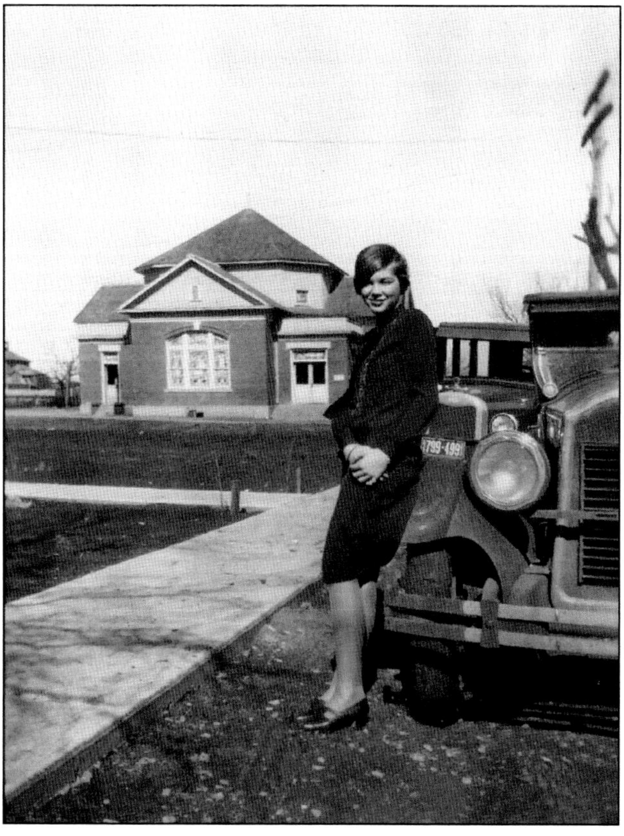

This photograph was taken outside the Reynolds Presbyterian Orphanage. The Reynolds Academy building, in the background, was built in 1899. In 1913, the dormitory (left) became the Reynolds Presbyterian Home, an orphanage under the supervision of J. Gilmor Smith and his wife. The orphanage was later moved to Dallas, and the buildings were razed in 1927.

Albany senior Juanita Durham (class of 1927) strikes a pose for the camera in her Sunday best. In the background is the First Methodist Church, built in 1913 when Rev. O.P. Clark was pastor. Due to issues of space, it was torn down in 1947 and replaced by the present sanctuary and fellowship hall. (Courtesy of Mildred Palmar Diller.)

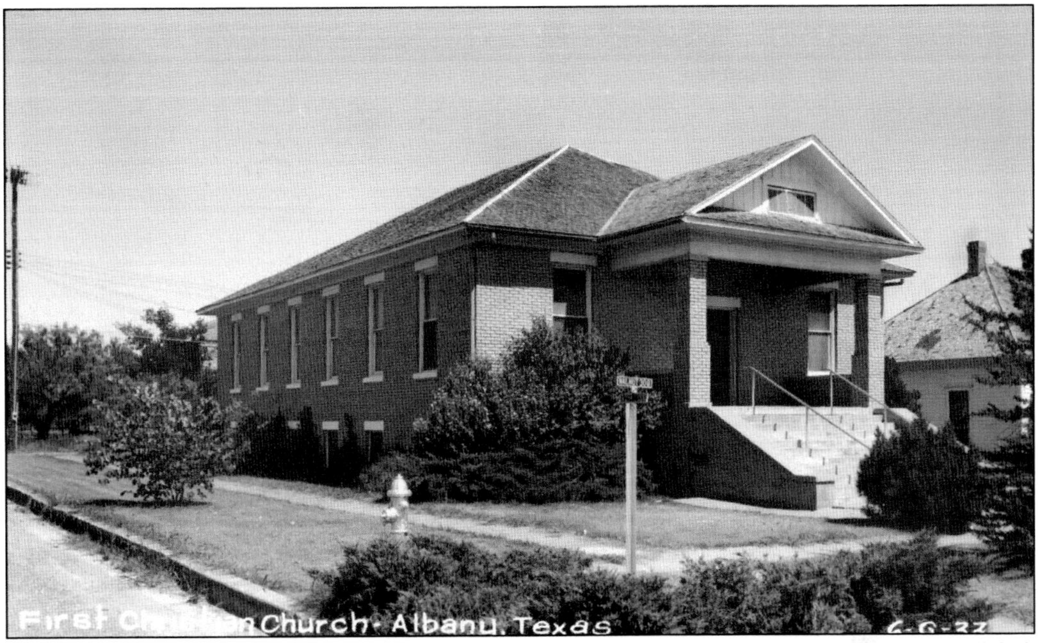

First Christian Church was built in 1921. In 1952, the church building was enlarged and remodeled, and the steeple was added. This photograph was taken in 1933, before those additions had been constructed. (Courtesy of Lea Clayton Hutt.)

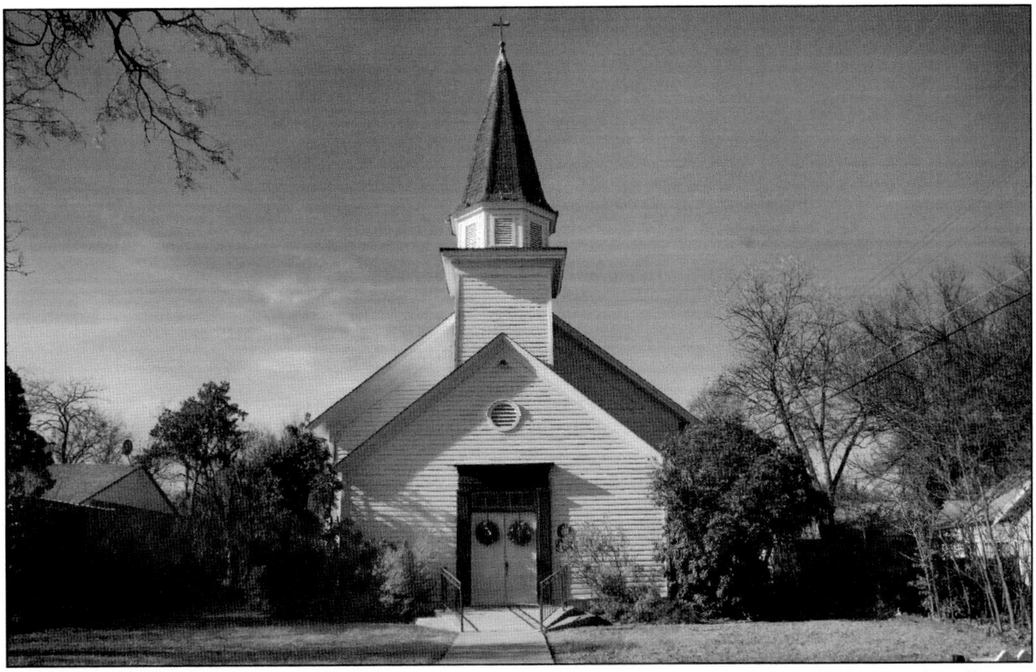

This Trinity Episcopal Church building started as a Methodist church. It was built on Schoolhouse Hill in 1889 and then moved to Main Street in 1909. The Trinity Episcopal congregation bought the building in 1913, remodeled it, and, in 1954, moved it to land given by Watt Matthews. The address is 140 East Avenue B. It was updated inside and out in 2012–2013. The church sits on a slope that shows off the classic beauty of the building. (Courtesy of Watt Casey Jr.)

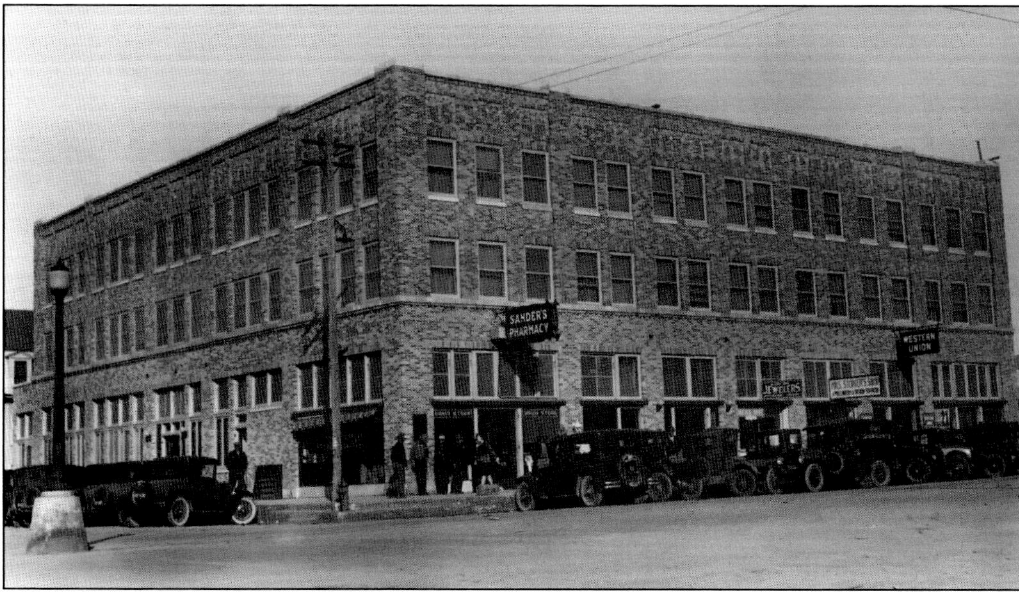

McLemore Hotel was built by Ada McLemore in 1926. The three-story brick building had 48 rooms, private baths, and telephones. In the 1940s, the hotel was sold and renamed the Western Skies Hotel. On August 22, 1974, the building, which had stood for 47 years, was torn down. The shaded, grassy area is now known as the Bank Park. (Courtesy of Special Collections at the University of Texas at Arlington.)

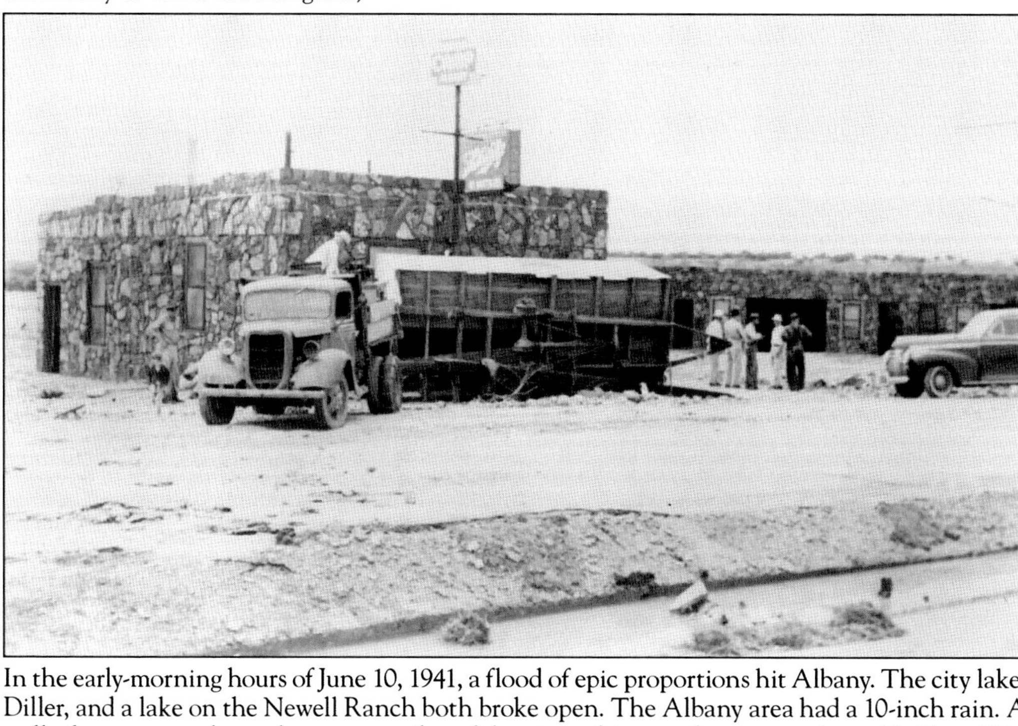

In the early-morning hours of June 10, 1941, a flood of epic proportions hit Albany. The city lake, Diller, and a lake on the Newell Ranch both broke open. The Albany area had a 10-inch rain. A wall of water went down the western edge of the city, taking out homes, roads, and bridges. The flood resulted in 11 deaths, and 90 homes were completely destroyed. This photograph shows the aftermath at the location of the present-day Beehive Restaurant. (Courtesy of R.P. Mitchell.)

Carter's Steak House was one of Edna Carter's restaurants. The steak house was known for its cleanliness, and the waitresses wore snow-white uniforms and hairnets. Shown here is Edna Carter, in the white dress, and Frankie Scott Ayers, her cashier. The building is just north of the railroad right-of-way, on the east side of Main Street. It was originally owned by J. Carter King Sr. and is now the Morehart Mortuary. (Courtesy of Wilma Jo Tucker Mitchell.)

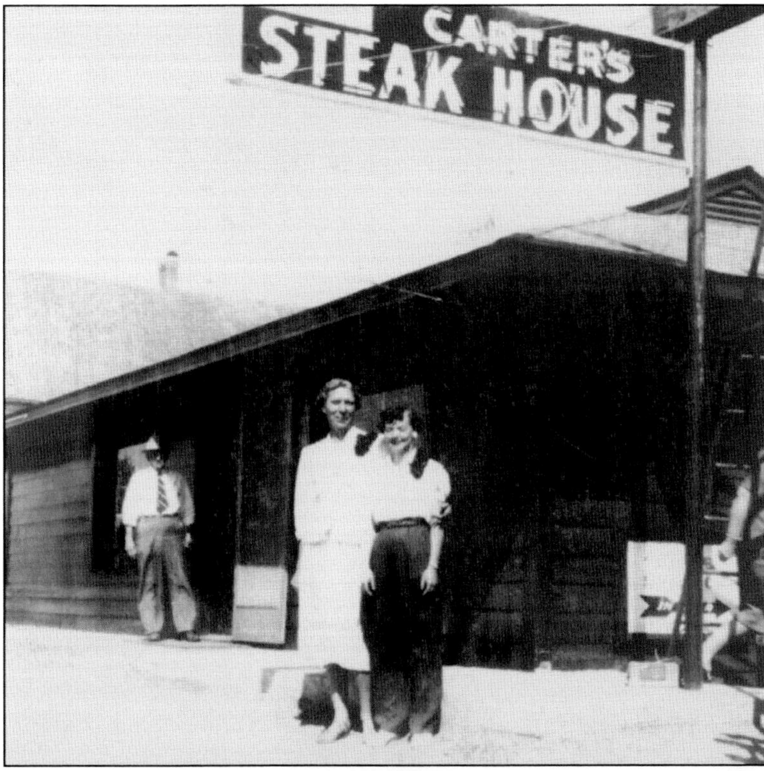

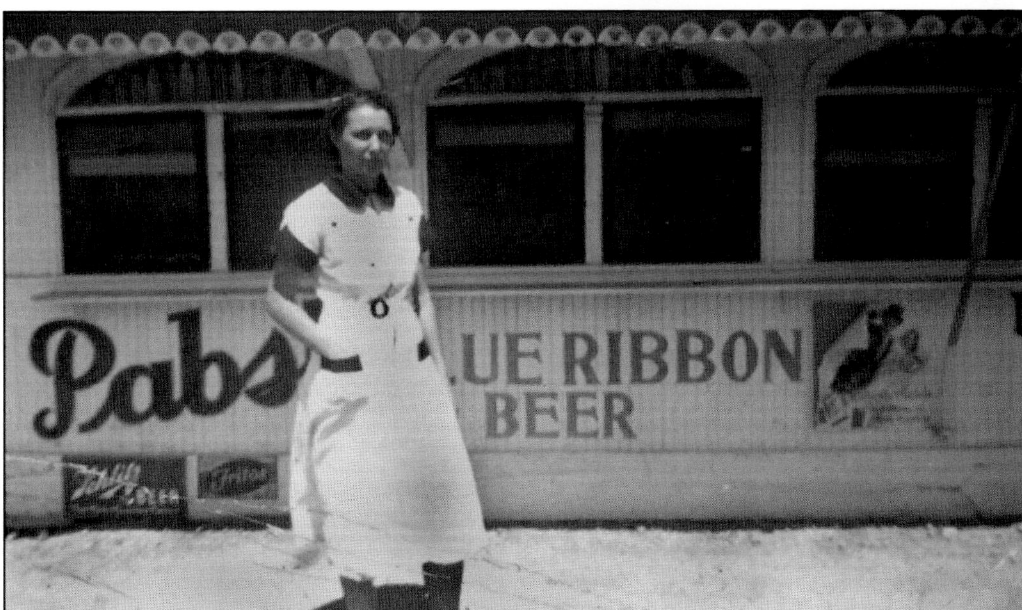

Albany has always been known for its good eating places, and Edna Tucker Carter and her establishments helped to keep this going. In the late 1930s, she managed the Utopian Diner on North Main Street. It was a true diner, having once been a Pullman railroad dining car. The Utopia was located at the corner where Main Street turns and becomes Hill Street. (Courtesy of Wilma Jo Tucker Mitchell.)

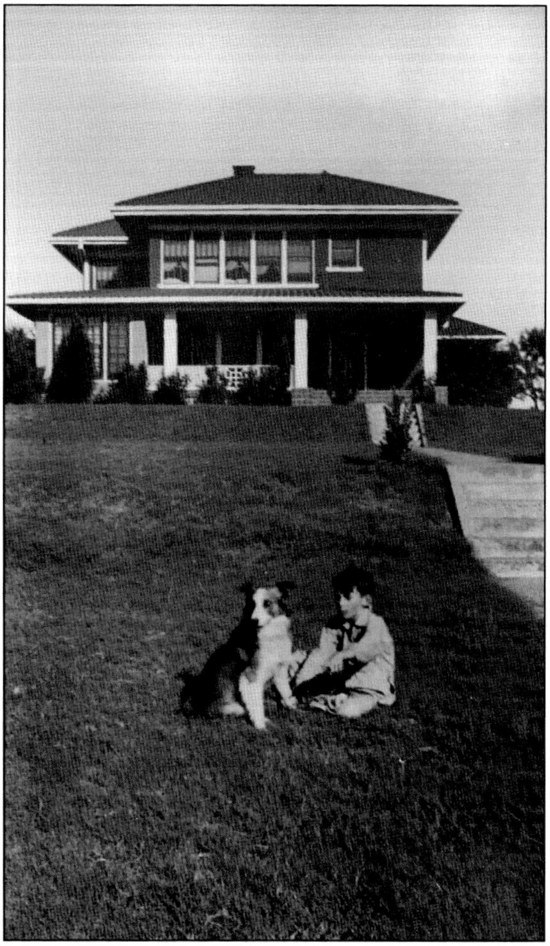

A young Bob Green and his dog play on the large lawn of the Green family "town house." The family lived on a cattle ranch between Breckenridge and Albany, which made it difficult for the children to attend school. Many ranchers had homes in town to make schooling and community participation easier. Bob Green grew up to be one of Albany's favorite sons—a soldier, an author, a rancher, a historian, and much more. (Courtesy of Nancy Green.)

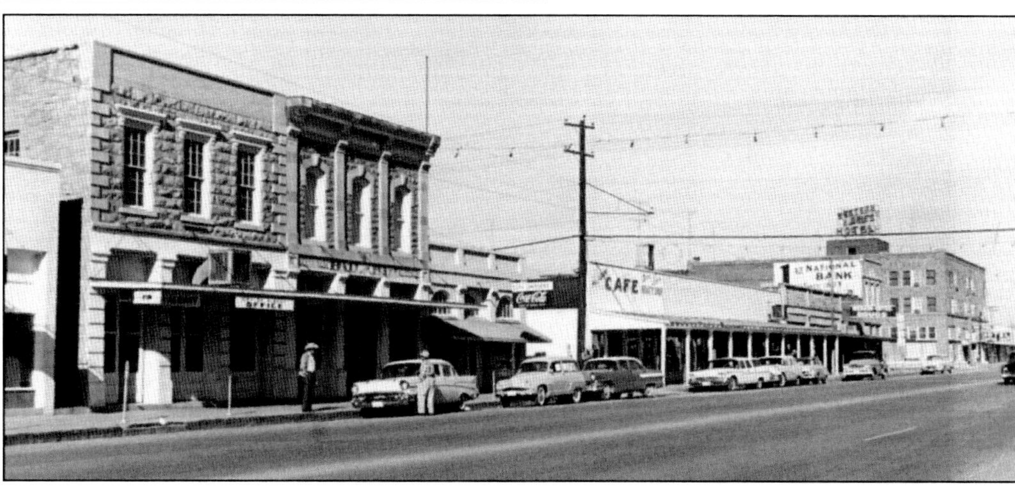

"The more things change, the more they stay the same." In this later picture of the west side of Albany's Main Street, taken in December 1959, the outline of buildings remains much unchanged from earlier photographs. With the exception of the missing hotel building, all of these buildings still stand, though many of the businesses themselves have come and gone over the years.

Five

Money in the Bank

By Duston Brooks

Pioneers came to the rich, fertile lands of southeastern Shackelford County as early as the 1850s. One of the first was George Greer, who operated a way station on Hubbard Creek near a small range of hills that would eventually be called the Greer Mountains. Around 1863, a short-lived family settlement called Fort Mugginsville was built three miles north of the present-day site of Moran, on Simpson Hole along Deep Creek. The fort was built to protect settlers from Indian attacks. After the Civil War, Fort Mugginsville was abandoned. Today, nothing remains of this fort. Only a nearby hill bears the name of Mugginsville Mountain.

The population of the area increased in the late 1870s, as more families arrived in the Deep Creek area. One of the feeder lines of the Great Western Cattle Trail crossed the area for many years, bringing with it thousands of head of cattle moving north to Fort Dodge in Kansas. In 1881, the Texas-Central Railroad, originating at Ross near Waco, was built through the area, terminating in Albany. It was shortly after this that Mary and Swope Hull, a pioneer couple from Virginia, arrived and, seeing the promise of the area, opened a general store near the crossing of the railroad and Deep Creek. On August 29, 1883, Mr. Hull became the first postmaster of the new community, which was called Hulltown. The Hulls bought 160 acres of land between Post Oak and Deep Creeks and platted a townsite on March 1, 1884. Hull began selling lots later that month, most of which were sold to Bem Scott, a Missouri prospector. Scott, who would later be imprisoned for a murder charge in Indiana, sold his remaining interest in the town to prominent local merchant and landowner Matthew D. Bray in 1890.

By this time, the Hull family had relocated to California, and their town was renamed Hicks. The town had grown considerably since 1883, and, by the early 1890s, it had a population of 200 with a school, three church congregations, five business houses, one hotel, another under construction, land office, lumber yard, meat market, barbershop, livery stable, one resident minister, two doctors, and a lawyer. In 1891, citizens requested that the railroad build a proper depot for the town. Railroad officials agreed to fund the construction if the town's name could be changed again, so in 1892, citizens decided on the name Moran, after New York railroad financier Charles Moran. The new name was approved and the depot constructed.

Moran's growth continued through the turn of the century. Moran's first newspaper, the *Moran Argus* (the precursor to the *Moran Tribune* and the *Moran News*), was started. A cotton gin was constructed. The Moran State Bank (later Moran National) was established in 1902. By 1909, the population of the town was over 400, and Moran would soon enter a new era. That year, the Texas Company (later Texaco) began leasing land around Moran based on early discoveries of shallow oil in local water wells. After drilling on the Cottle Ranch two miles east of town, the Texas Company struck natural gas on November 10, 1910. This well, known as Cottle No. 1, was the first commercial natural gas well in the region. Other discoveries quickly followed, and Moran became the first town in West Texas to have its own natural gas for municipal use. The well also supplied the cities of Albany, Cisco, and Abilene with natural gas. The Moran Oil Field, as it became known, made the town famous at the time as "The Center of the World's Greatest Shallow Oil Field" and one of the most important sources of fossil fuels in Texas.

The oil boom, which brought thousands of people and financial prosperity to the town, lasted through the 1920s and 1930s. Moran was incorporated in 1919. A new brick high school was constructed in 1923, a lake was built south of town, and a municipal waterworks system was established. Streets were paved, and a number of businesses and homes were constructed during this period. At its height during the oil boom, Moran's population approached 10,000. After the boom ended, Moran returned to being the small farming and ranching town it had been before oil and gas were discovered. The population began to steadily decline, particularly after World War II. The decade-long drought of the 1950s had a drastic effect on the town's economy. Moran's livelihood was further affected negatively by the rerouting of the main highway, from directly through the town to its eastern edge. Businesses dwindled. In 1968, the railroad line that originally brought the town into existence was discontinued.

There have been positives for the town. In 1967, the Moran Community Center was constructed. In 1979, the Moran Historical Museum was opened. In the late 1980s, the town achieved worldwide fame as the home of the yearly National Fajita Cook-off Championship, which brought thousands of visitors from all over the world. The Moran Independent School District has continued to operate through periods of hard times and low enrollment. First Financial Bank occupies the same building as the original Moran State Bank. The Moran Clean and Proud volunteer organization, established in 1997, has greatly contributed to the beautification of the community by organizing seasonal town cleanups. In 2010, a homegrown gun-stock manufacturing company, Slide Fire Solutions, was established. The company's sales have since exploded, greatly contributing to the local economy. In 2011, the company constructed a multimillion-dollar manufacturing facility two miles east of town, complete with housing units for employees.

Today's Moran is a far cry from its booming past, and many challenges threaten its survival. However, as long as there are residents who still care and want to invest in the town, there is always hope that this rural community, established 130 years ago, will continue to be a part of the Shackelford County landscape for many years to come.

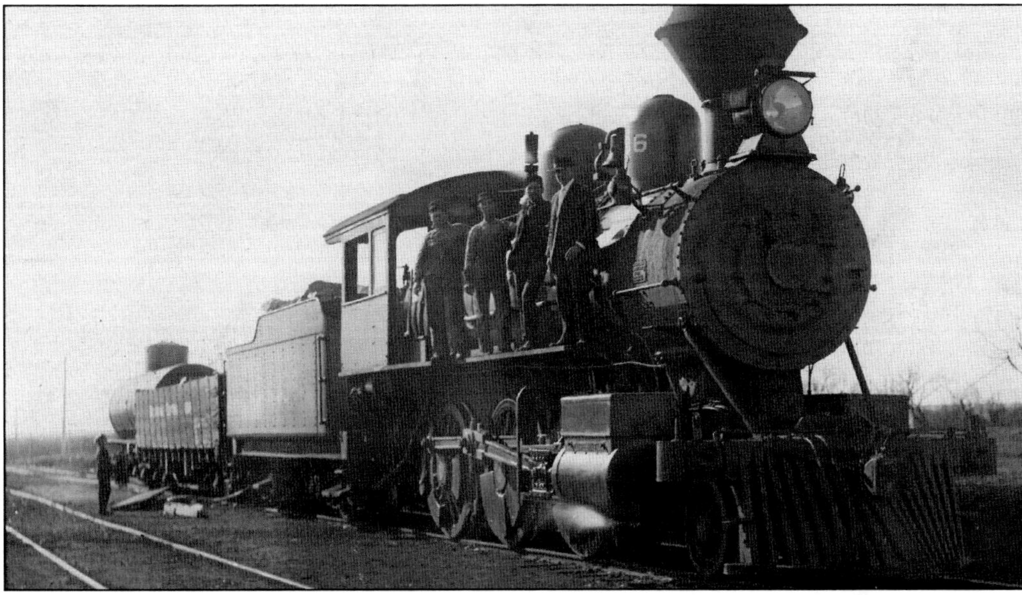

The Texas-Central Railroad line, originating in Ross, near Waco, came through southeast Shackelford County in 1881, terminating for many years in Albany. A number of settlers were already living in the rich farmland along Deep Creek at that time. In the 1850s and 1860s, a short-lived family fort called Mugginsville existed a few miles north of present-day Moran. But it was the railroad that brought Virginians Mary and George W. "Swope" Hull to the area. They established Hulltown in 1883 near the crossing of the railroad and Deep Creek. (Courtesy of the Moran Historical Museum.)

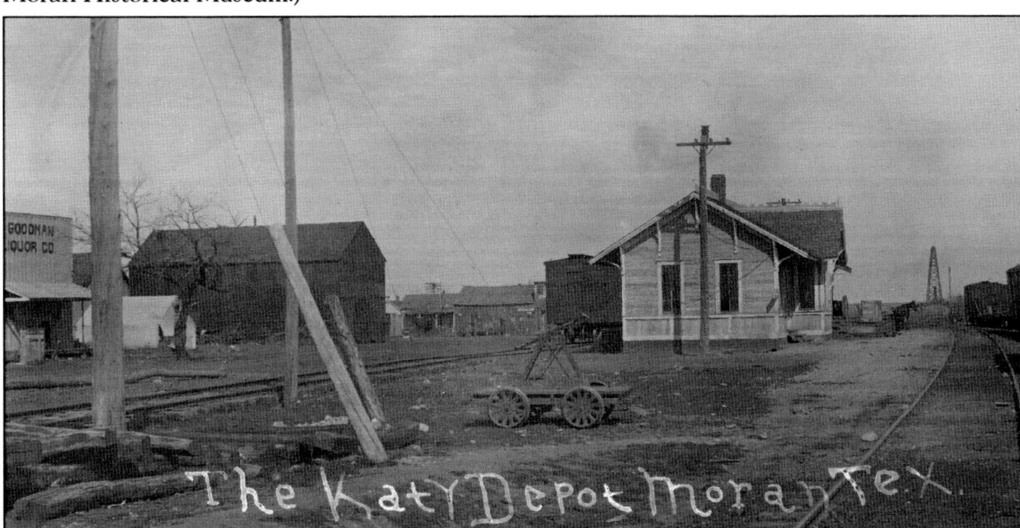

By 1891, citizens of the town wanted a proper railroad depot to replace the existing simple platform. Hulltown's name was changed to Hicks in 1890, but the Texas-Central Railroad agreed to build a depot if the town's name was changed once again. In early 1892, citizens chose the name "Moran," after New York railroad financier Charles Moran. The depot was then constructed. The depot and railroad, later acquired by the Missouri-Kansas-Texas "Katy" Railroad, would remain a vital part of the town for many years, until the line was discontinued in 1968. (Courtesy of the Moran Historical Museum.)

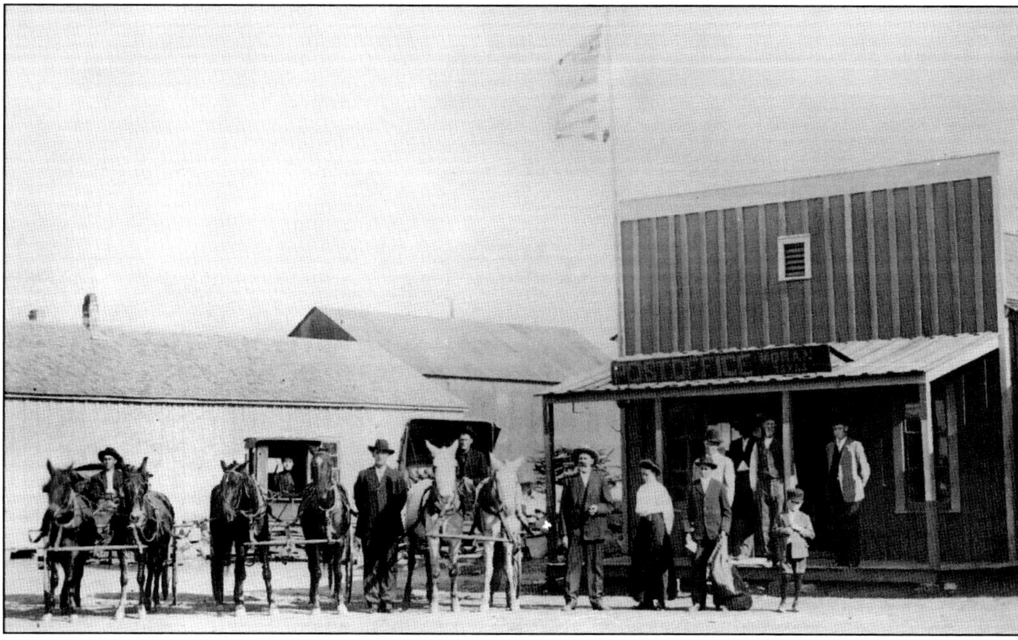

The Hulltown (later Moran) post office was established in 1883. Town founder Swope Hull served as the first postmaster. Here, a group of residents pose for the photographer in front of the building in 1910. The Moran post office has been relocated three times since then. (Courtesy of the Moran Historical Museum.)

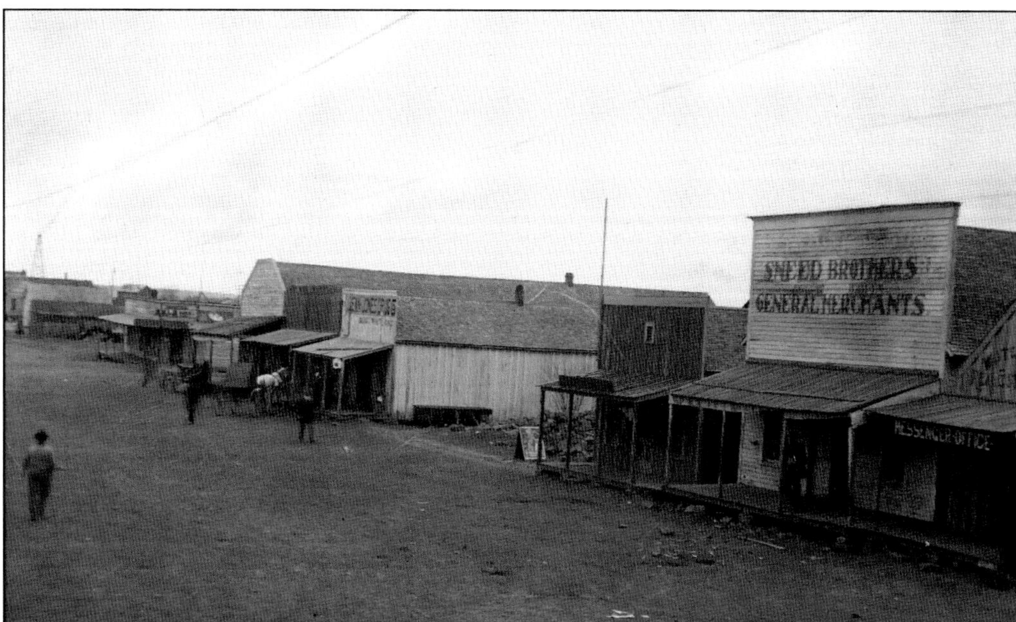

Early Moran was built around a square. Looking north, this is a view of a portion of the east side of the square. This side of the square contained many businesses housed in wooden false-front buildings. Pioneers Granville Waters and James Wild's real estate office is shown on the right, along with Sneed Brothers General Merchants next door, and the Moran post office (with the flagpole). (Courtesy of the Moran Historical Museum.)

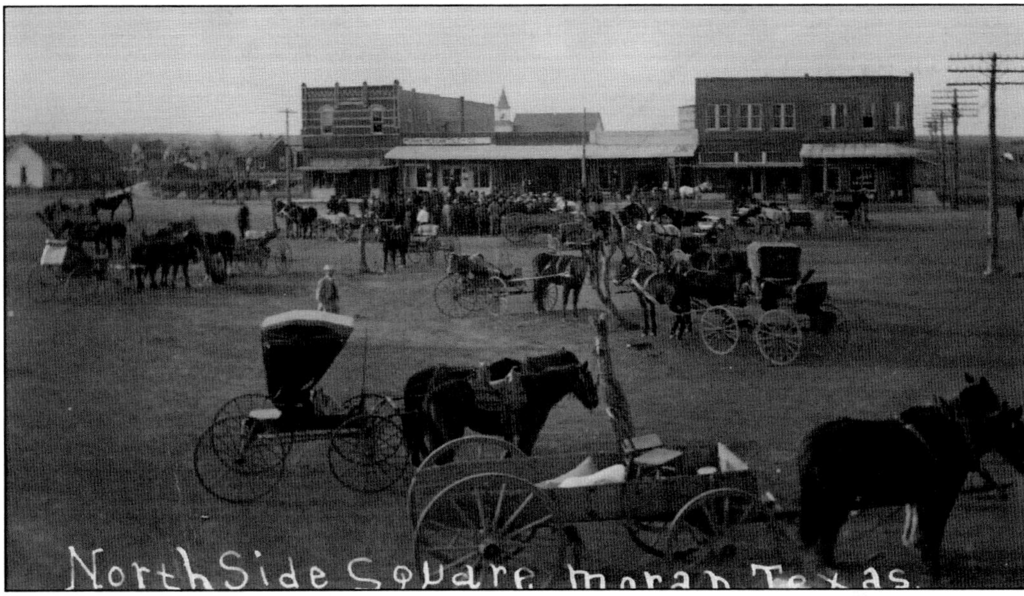

In this 1915 photograph, a gathering is taking place on the north side of the town square. Moran State Bank (later Moran National Bank) occupied the corner of the two-story brick building on the right, which is the oldest of the buildings. First Financial Bank occupies the building today. The *Moran News* was one of the businesses that occupied the two-story building on the left. In the center were the Moran Mercantile Company, M.H. Ward Hardware, and Dickson Drugs and Notions. In the background, the steeple of the Methodist church can be seen. (Courtesy of the Moran Historical Museum.)

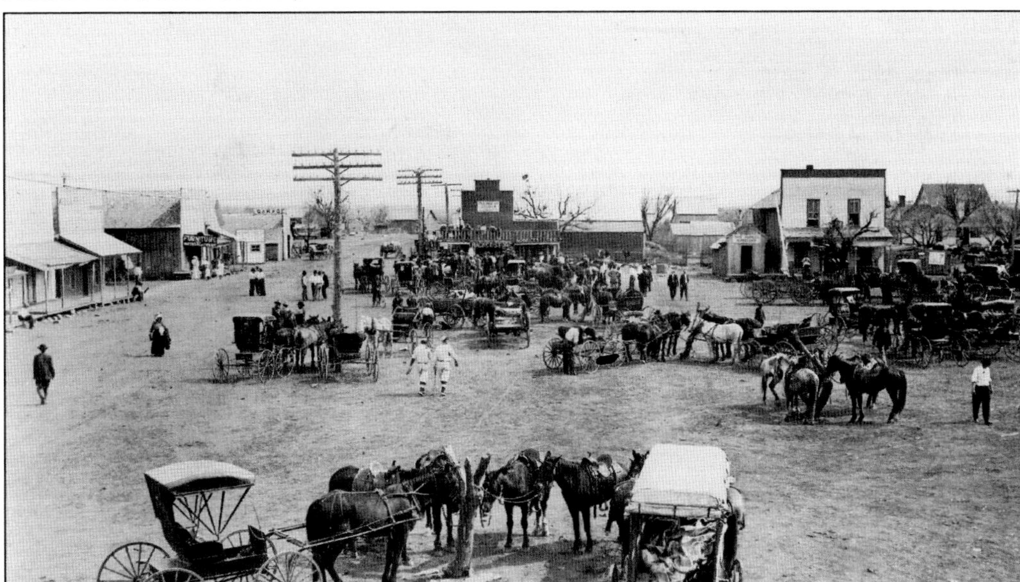

Another community gathering in 1915 is shown on the south side of the town square, in front of The Racket Store, which sold general merchandise. The second floor was occupied by The Moran Studio, owned by female photographer Mattie Cole. R.H. Townsend Furniture & Undertaking was located in the two-story building on the right. Behind it is the two-story Townsend home, which still stands today. (Courtesy of the Moran Historical Museum.)

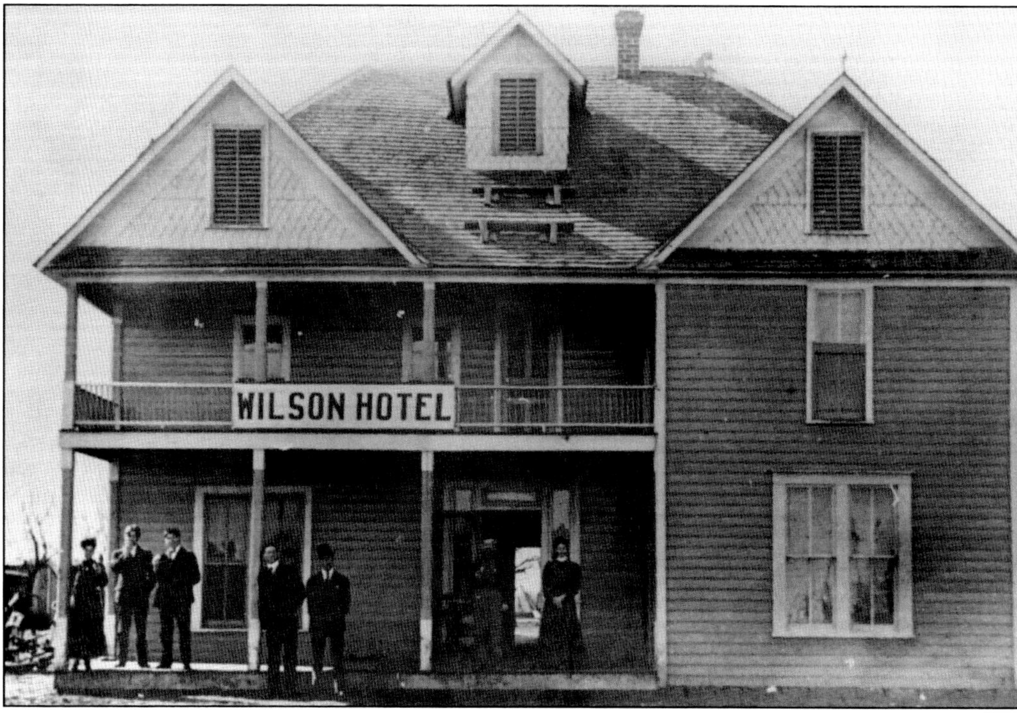

The Wilson Hotel served weary business travelers in Moran during the early oil-boom years. The hotel was located on the west side of the town square. Standing at the front door are owners John and Sarah Wilson. Their daughter Myrtle is standing on the left, among hotel guests. (Courtesy of the Moran Historical Museum.)

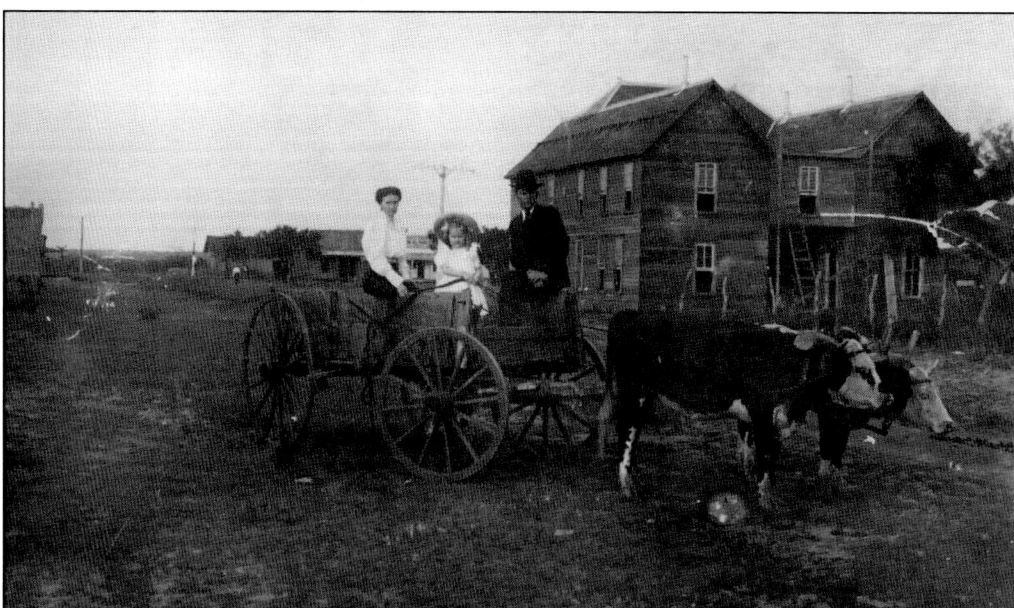

Dr. Joseph Charles Midkiff and his family pose behind the Wilson Hotel around 1907. The east side of the town square appears in the background. Moran State Bank is visible on the left edge of the photograph. (Courtesy of the Moran Historical Museum.)

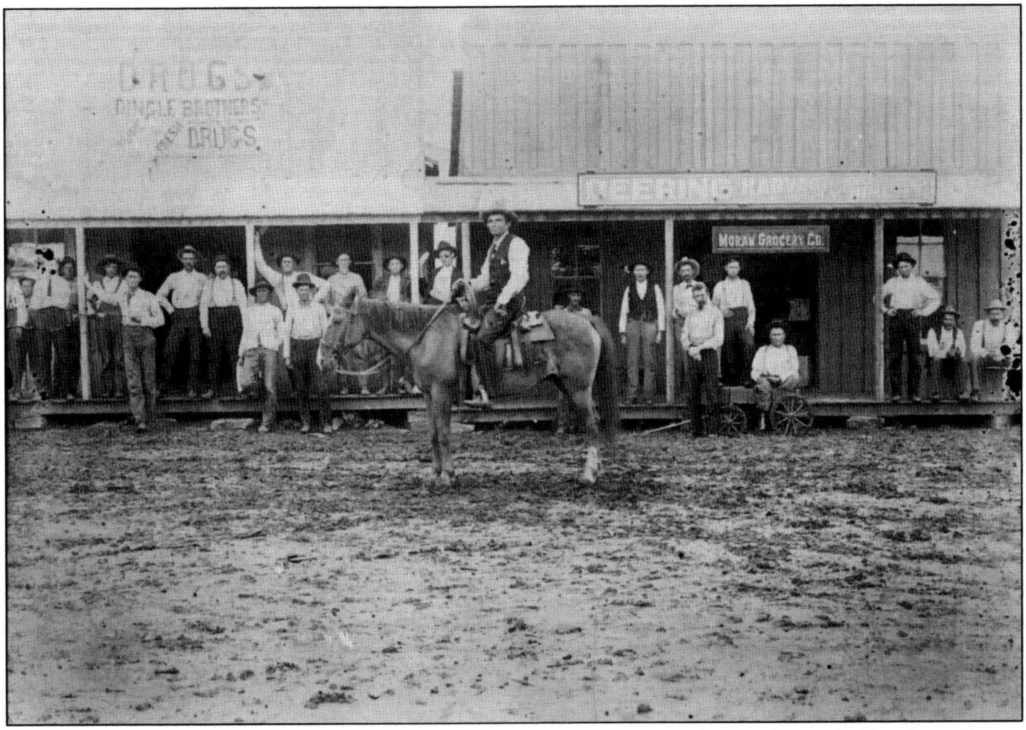

These men are gathered on the east side of the town square, in front of Dingle Brothers Drugs and the Moran Grocery Company, around 1911. (Courtesy of the Moran Historical Museum.)

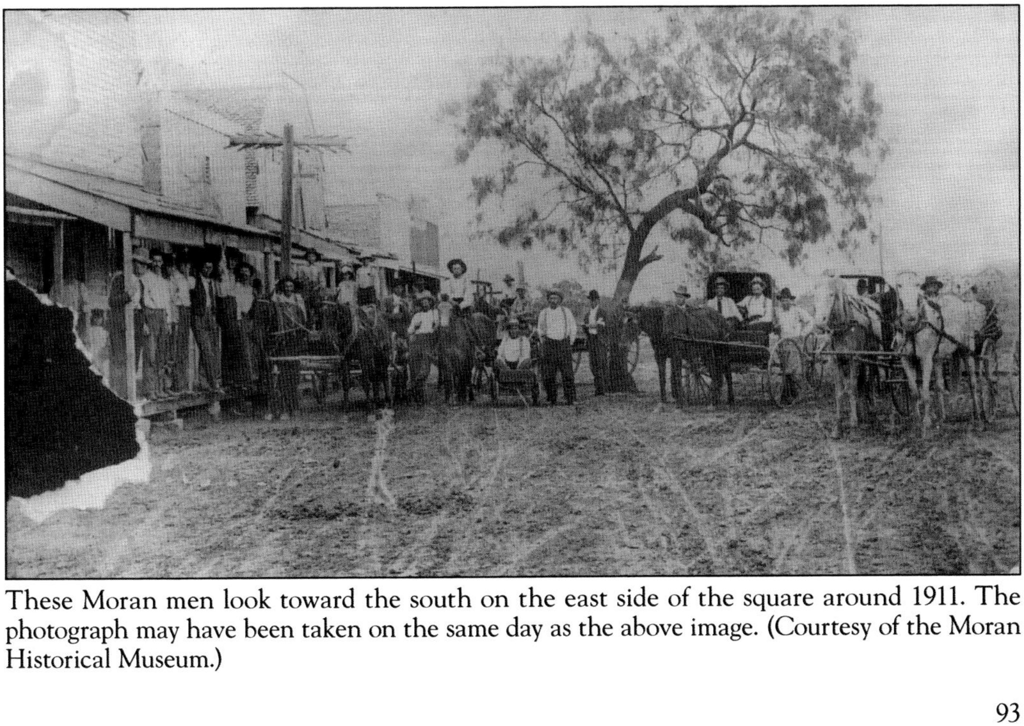

These Moran men look toward the south on the east side of the square around 1911. The photograph may have been taken on the same day as the above image. (Courtesy of the Moran Historical Museum.)

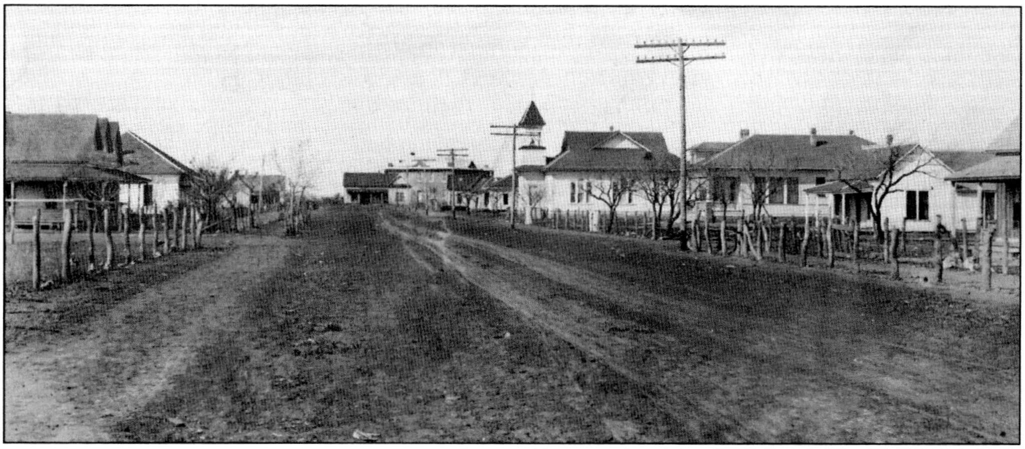

This is a west-facing view of Post Oak Street in 1913. The old wooden First Baptist Church building, which burned down in 1920 and was replaced with the current brick structure, is right of center. To the right of that is the Frank Hubbard residence, which was later extensively remodeled by oilman J.D. Meredith. It still stands today as the Thomas House. Moran's first brick school building is behind the house at the end of the street. A cattle feed lot previously occupied the school grounds. Cattle were driven down this street to the railroad to be shipped to market. The post oak fences on each side of the street kept the cattle from straying. (Courtesy of the Moran Historical Museum.)

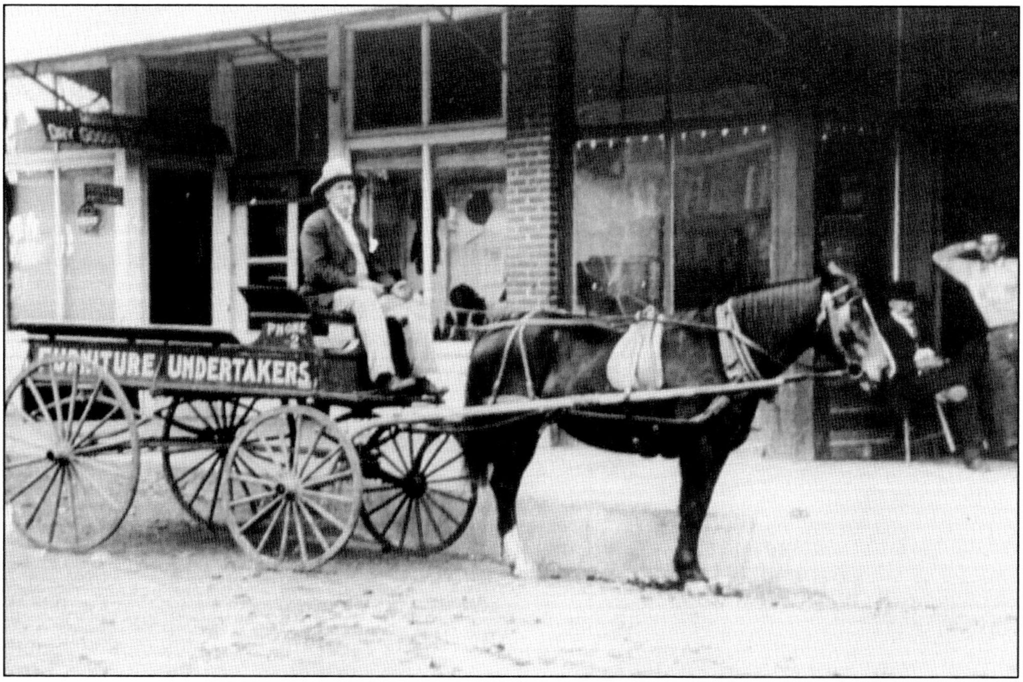

Marcus Herbert Ward Sr. poses in his wagon in front of his furniture and undertaking business on Moran's north side square in 1913. He and his son, M.H. Ward Jr., established the business two years earlier. It began as a pipe-fitting business and gradually moved into furniture, undertaking, insurance, and hardware. After the death of her husband in 1932, Ward Jr.'s widow, Derah Plummer Ward, solely operated the M.H. Ward Hardware & Variety Store until her death in 1978. (Courtesy of the Moran Historical Museum.)

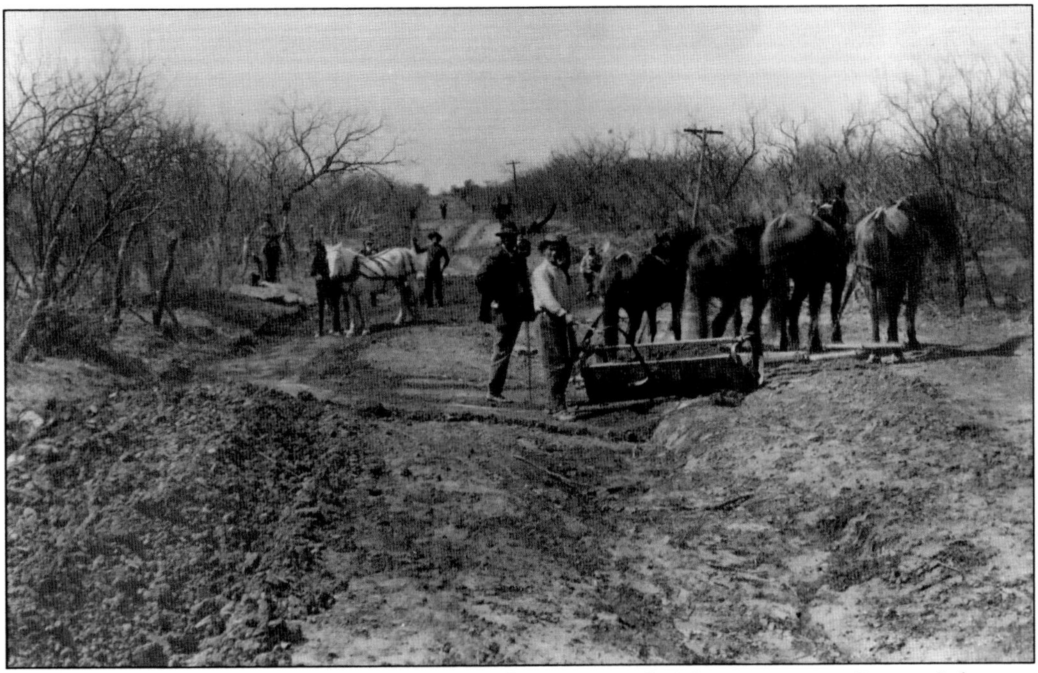

To improve the route between Moran and Albany, an early Moran pioneer, George Johnson, plowed a furrow between the two towns in the 1880s along the tracks of the railroad. Here, workers smooth out the road around 1920. The road would eventually be paved and become US Highway 283 and, later, State Highway 6.

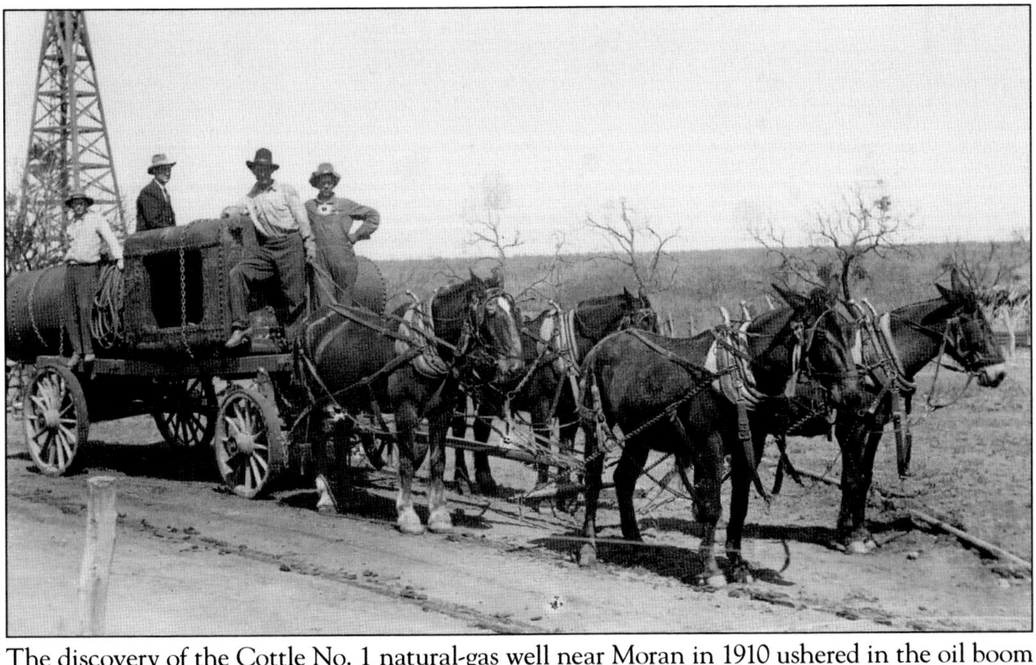

The discovery of the Cottle No. 1 natural-gas well near Moran in 1910 ushered in the oil boom in the area. Wells were drilled all around the town. The Moran Field won recognition as one of the most important sources of fossil fuels in Texas. Here, workers transport a steam engine for one of the Moran wells. (Courtesy of the Moran Historical Museum.)

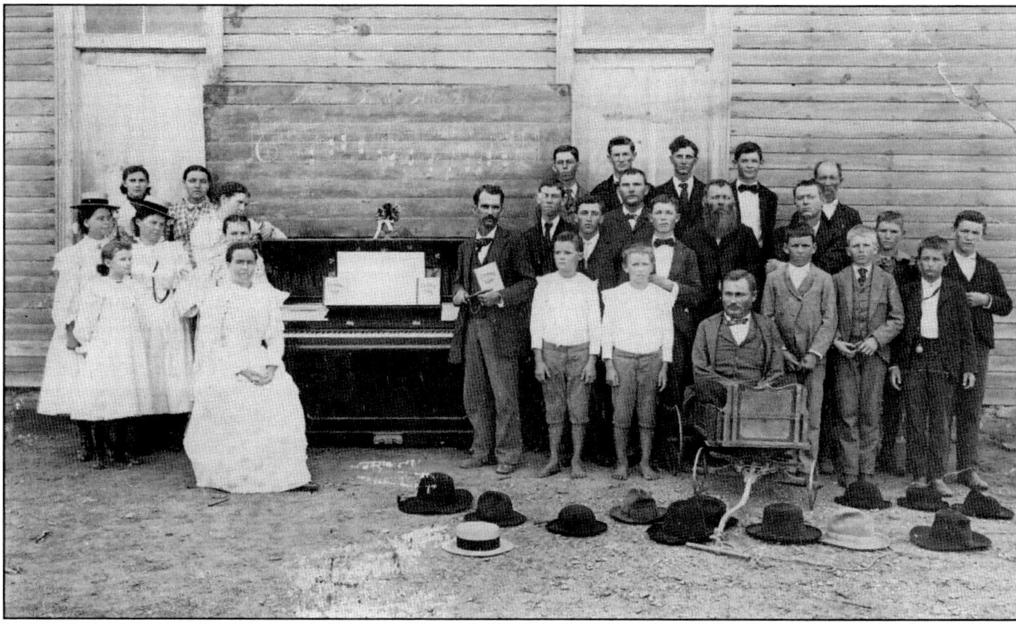

Music played an important part in early Moran life. These singers are posing with their music instructor and a piano in 1898. (Courtesy of the Moran Historical Museum.)

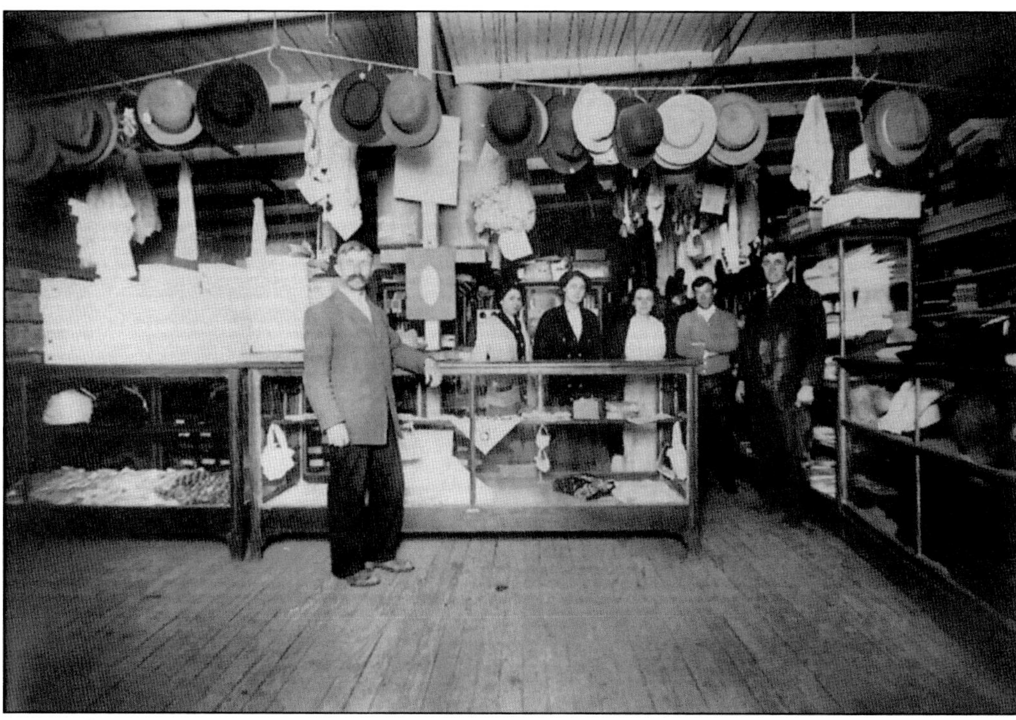

Capt. Thomas Franklin Pettus was a former Confederate military captain and later US consul to Ning-po, China, appointed during Pres. Grover Cleveland's administration. Pettus arrived in Texas in later life to establish general merchandise businesses in Albany and Moran. This photograph of the interior of his Moran store was taken in 1910. (Courtesy of Joy and Wade Roberts.)

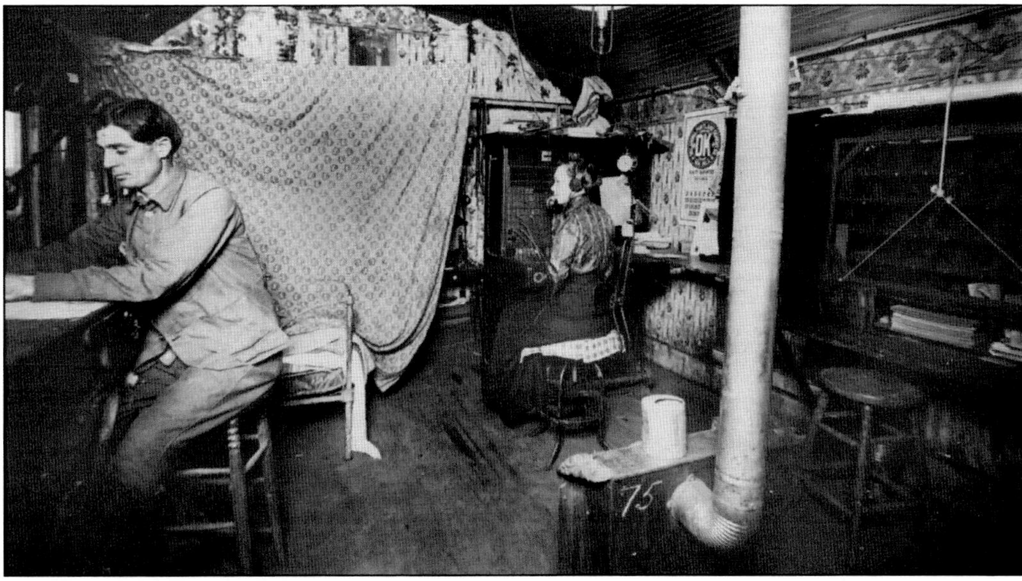

In the early 1900s, all telephone calls placed to Moran came to the switchboard office, which was located on the second floor of the bank. One of the earliest Moran switchboard operators referred to herself as "Slim" when answering calls. The operator in this c. 1915 photograph may be her. (Courtesy of the Moran Historical Museum.)

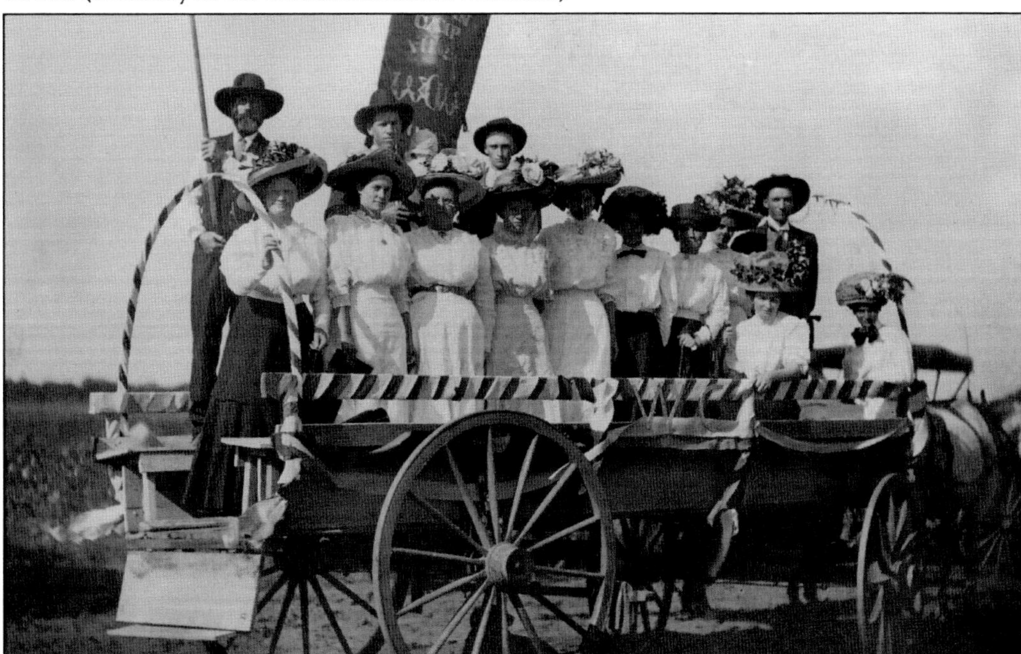

The Woodmen Circle was a women's auxiliary unit of the Woodmen of the World fraternal benefit society. Here, members of the Moran unit participate in a 1909 Memorial Day service. Shown are, from left to right, (first row) Mrs. Emri Terry, Derah Plummer, Mary Ward, Nettie Dosser, Beulah Fite, Mrs. John Coats, Mrs. Z.T. Lawhon, Belle Hayward, Almeda Anderson, and Myrtle Wilson; (second row): J.D. Fite, Emri Terry, Will Dosser, and Ben Kane. (Courtesy of the Moran Historical Museum.)

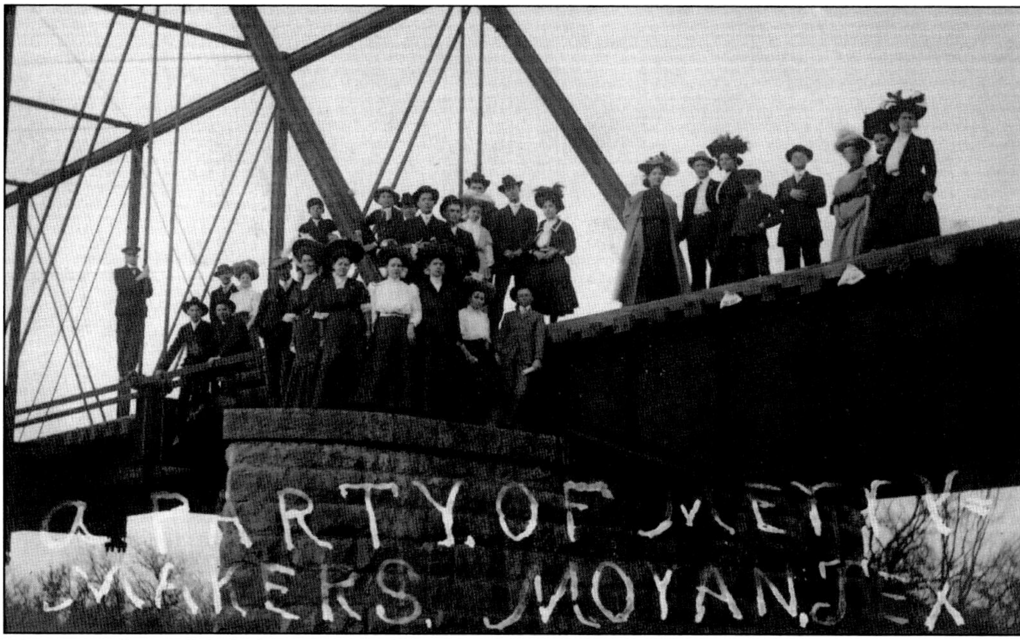

These residents, labeled "A Party of Merry Makers," are dressed in their Sunday best in 1912. They are posing on the bridge across Deep Creek, just north of Moran. (Courtesy of the Moran Historical Museum.)

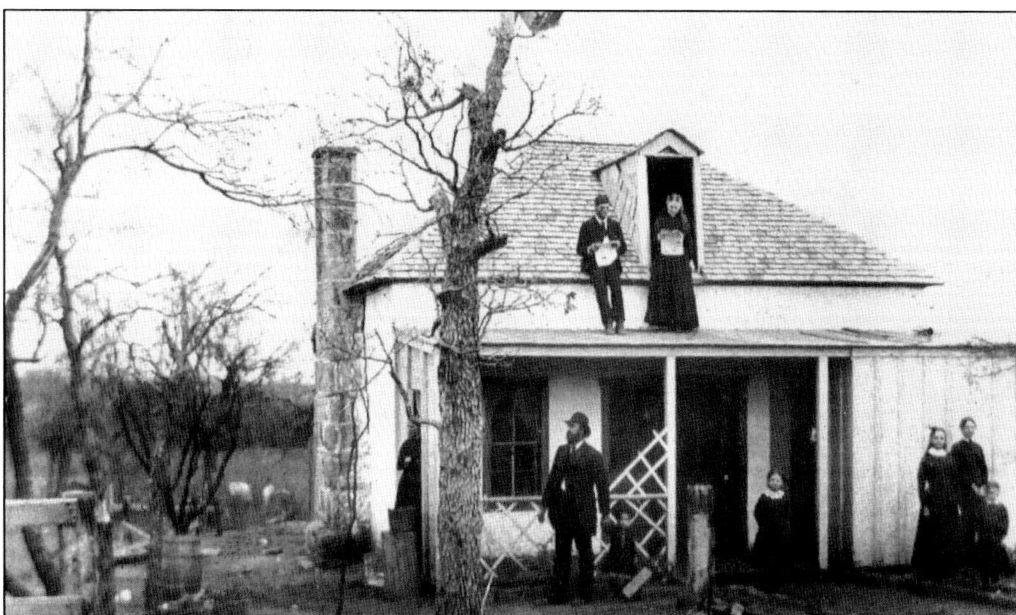

The Squire Leander and Priscilla Barker family settled along Battle Creek, southeast of Hulltown, in 1881. Barker was a farmer, stonemason, justice of the peace, and a minister for the Hulltown Christian Church (later Moran Church of Christ). Their son Elliott would become a renowned author and environmentalist, responsible for the discovery of the real Smokey Bear. The family poses in front of their home in 1888 on the wedding day of daughter Alice, who married Troupe Turner (both on the roof). (Courtesy of the Moran Historical Museum.)

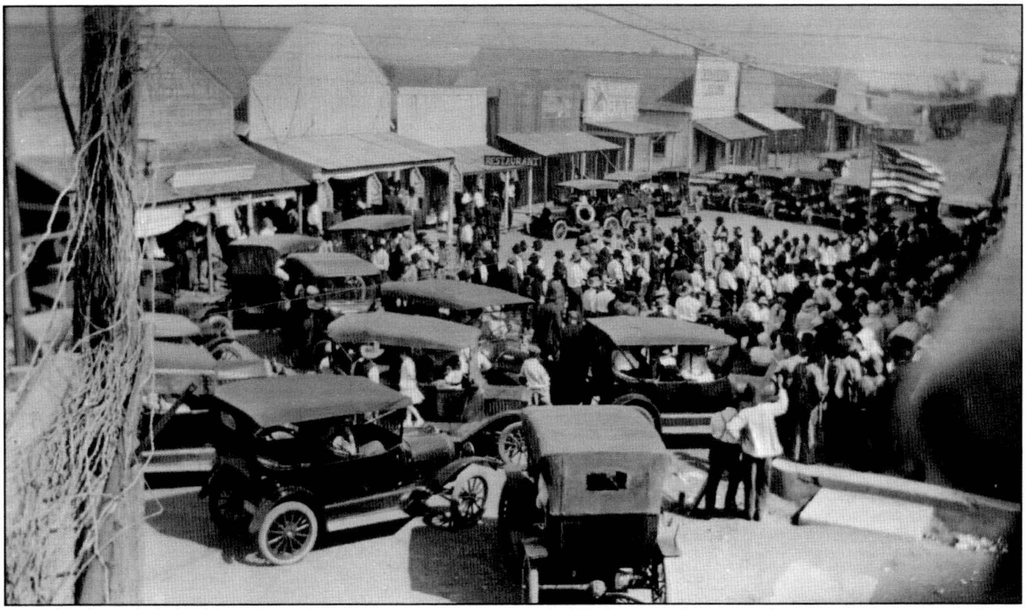

This war-bond rally in Moran in 1918, at the corner of Fisher and Ground Streets, was part of the campaign to encourage Americans to buy US treasury bonds to finance the military during World War I. The gatherings were known as war-bond drives. During the war, the federal government raised $5 billion through the sale of Liberty Bonds.

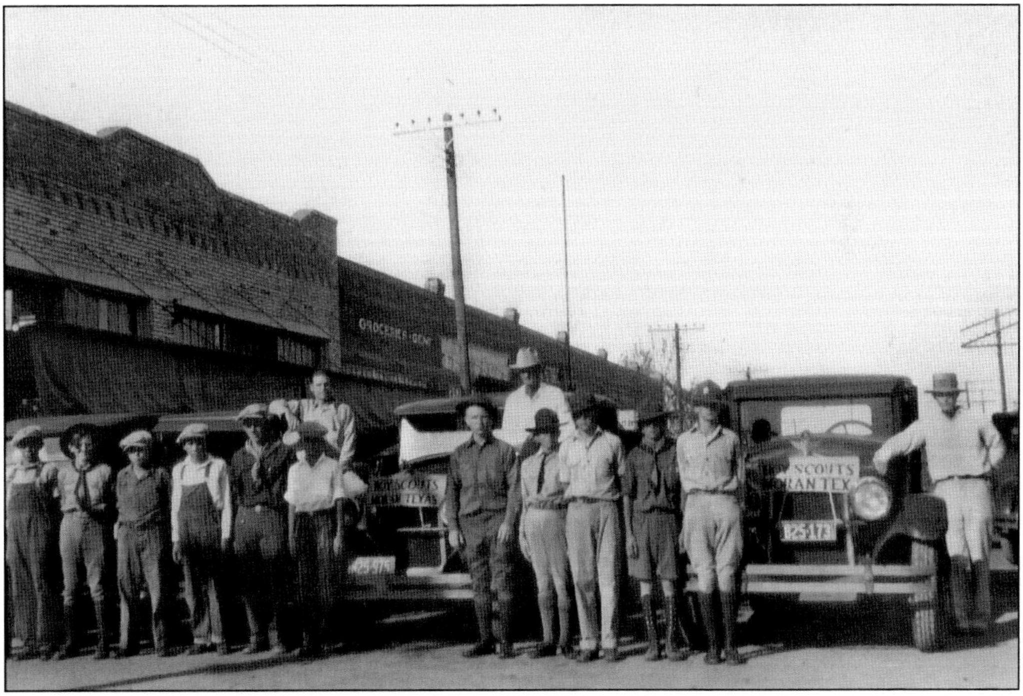

The Moran Boy Scouts pose downtown in 1928 after the group returned from a trip to New Mexico. The boys visited Carlsbad Caverns, as well as Artesia and Santa Fe. Accompanying the 15 boys were Scoutmaster C.C. Duff, Cecil Knight, A.J. Taylor, and Bert Brooks. (Courtesy of the Moran Historical Museum.)

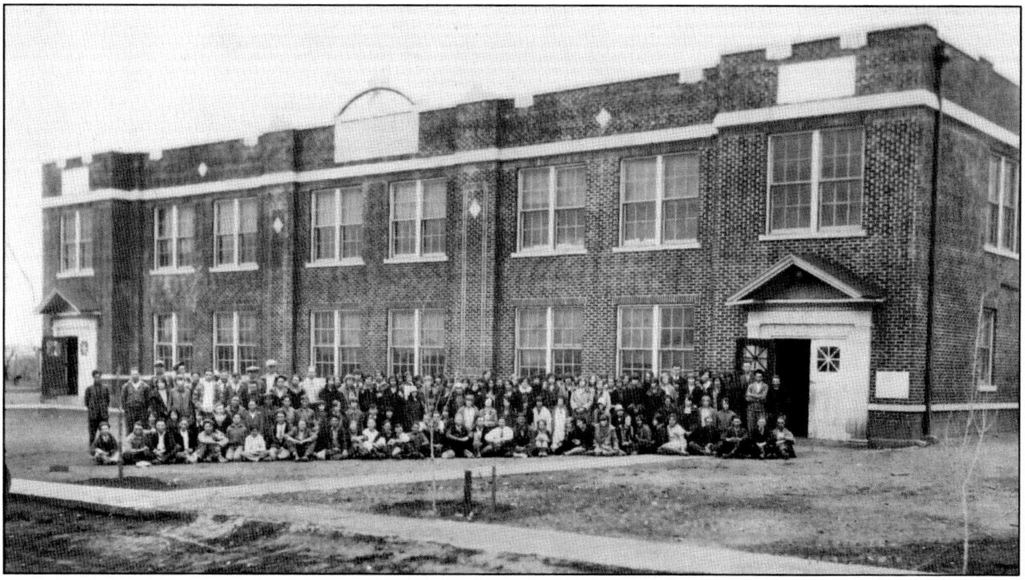

The high school body gathers together to pose for a photograph in front of the newly constructed Moran High School building in 1925. It was built in 1923 during the height of the oil boom to serve Moran's growing student population. The former high school building built in 1912 stood next to it and became the grammar school, until it was replaced by the current elementary school building in 1959. The two-story high school building was eventually replaced by the current building in 1975. (Courtesy of the Moran Historical Museum.)

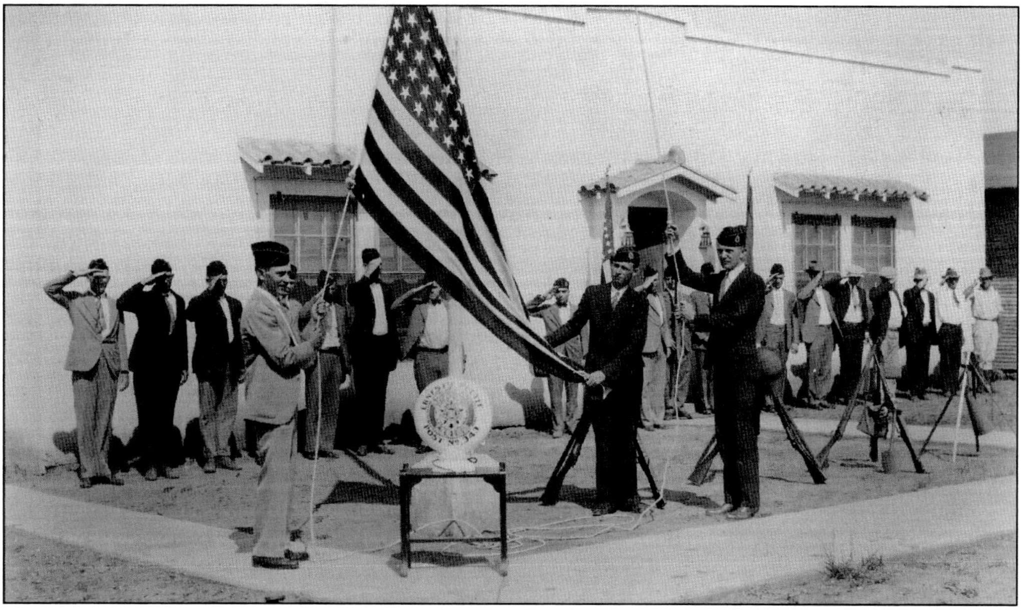

The Ernest F. Pettit Post No. 343 of the American Legion was organized in 1920 by Moran veterans following World War I. The post was named in honor of a Moran serviceman killed in 1918. This photograph depicts the day in 1922 when the newly built legion hall was dedicated by the members. In 1984, the building was enlarged with the Jimmy Strain addition (Strain was a Moran serviceman killed during the Vietnam War). The Moran post is now the last remaining active legion in Shackelford County. (Courtesy of the Moran Historical Museum.)

The Lee Weir Motor Company and Chrysler-Plymouth dealership is seen here in 1949. The business was located between the Brooks Hotel and the American Legion building on Ground Street. The company served Moran for many years as its only car dealership. (Courtesy of the Moran Historical Museum.)

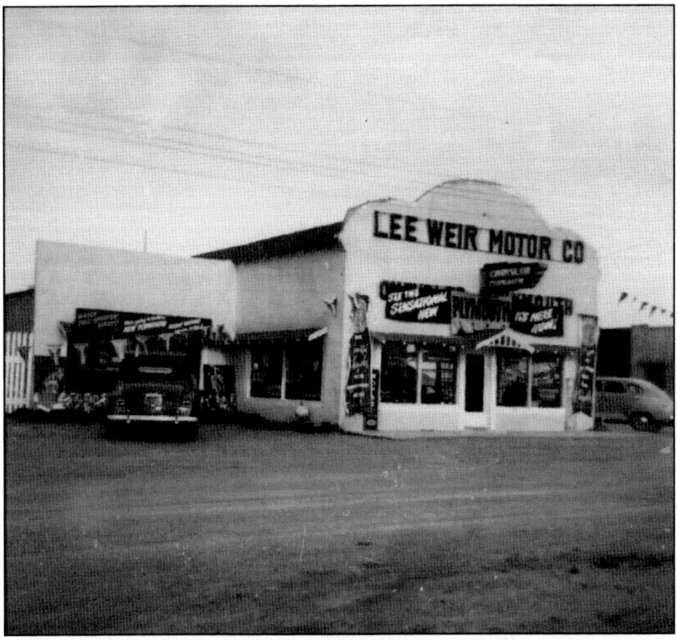

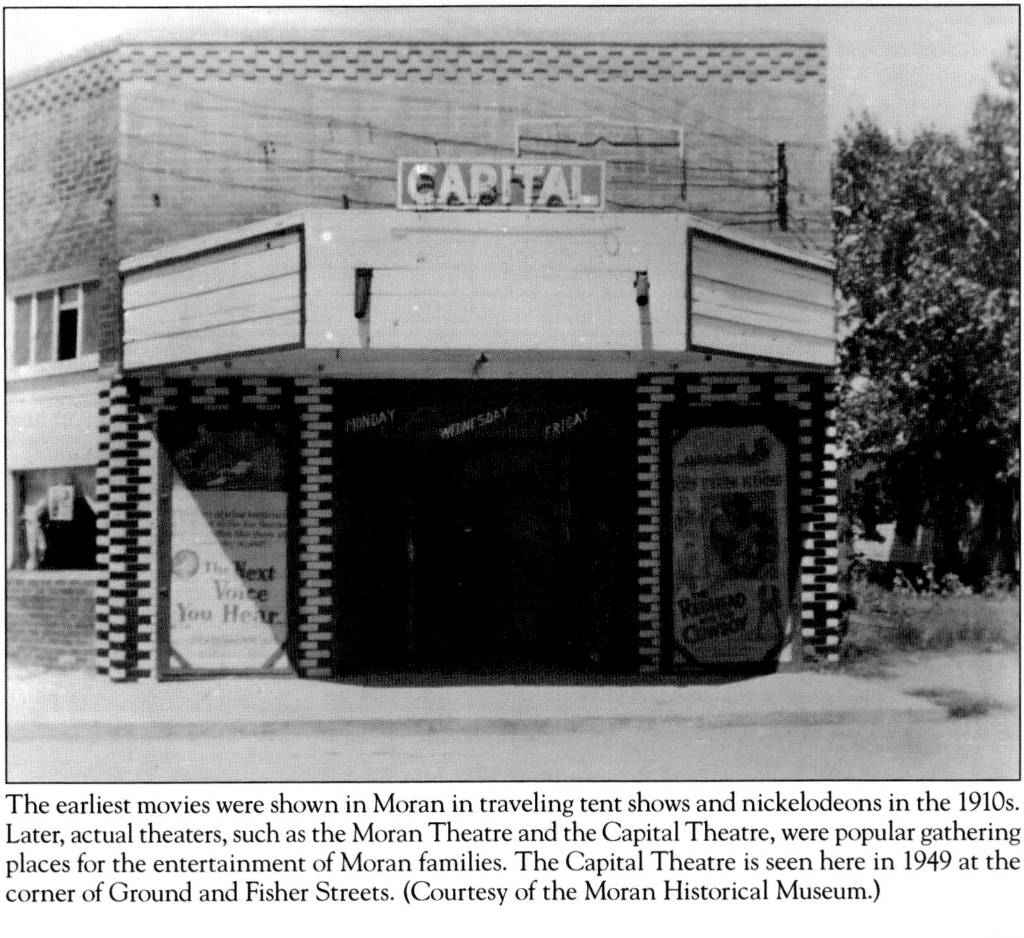

The earliest movies were shown in Moran in traveling tent shows and nickelodeons in the 1910s. Later, actual theaters, such as the Moran Theatre and the Capital Theatre, were popular gathering places for the entertainment of Moran families. The Capital Theatre is seen here in 1949 at the corner of Ground and Fisher Streets. (Courtesy of the Moran Historical Museum.)

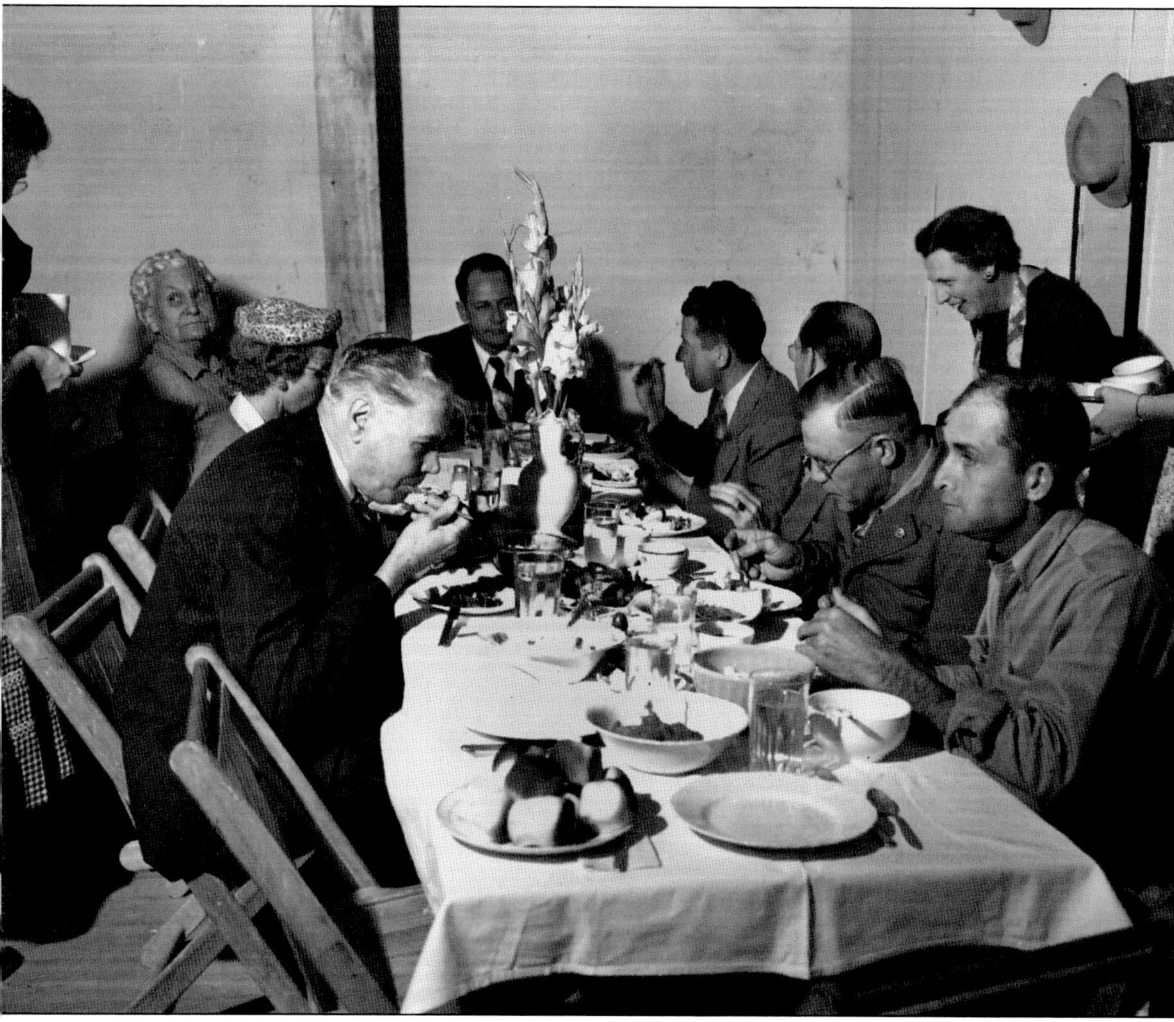

The Moran Luncheon Club served as the town's chamber of commerce from the 1920s through the 1960s. Its weekly programs and delicious luncheons, served by a rotating group of local cooks, were a popular attraction for local citizens and visitors from all over the area. (Courtesy of the Moran Historical Museum.)

Six

Making a Difference

By Lawrence Clayton, *Handbook of Texas*

The *Fort Griffin Fandangle* is an annual outdoor musical drama produced in Albany, Texas, on Thursday, Friday, and Saturday evenings of the last two weeks in June. Its focus is the historical and cultural development of the area along the Clear Fork of the Brazos River in northern Shackelford County near Fort Griffin. The military outpost stood from 1867 to 1881, providing protection for settlers in the region and giving rise to a community in the flat between the fort on the hill and the Clear Fork. The story is recalled through the memory of an old-timer of the region, a cattleman who sits on the porch of a ranch house to reveal the past as he remembers it. The production consists of a series of segments, each based on historical material introduced by the narrators and then interpreted by one or more songs and dancing.

The *Fandangle* can trace its beginning to a performance in 1937. Inspired by the Billy Rose show in Fort Worth and the Cavalcade at the State Fair of Texas in Dallas honoring the Texas centennial, Albany native Robert Edward Nail Jr. directed, with the help of local music teacher Alice Reynolds, the Lions Club Cowboy Ball. The successful show, performed in December in the high school gymnasium, raised money to benefit the needy at Christmas. The following spring, Nail produced *Dr. Shackelford's Paradise*, an outdoor musical pageant presented by the senior class that portrayed the history of Shackelford County. The play was so well received that it was expanded to include adults in the cast, and was produced that summer under the name *Fort Griffin Fandangle*. A sponsoring organization, the Fandangle Association, was incorporated in 1947. Nail established three rules: first, anybody with ties in Shackelford County could be in the show; second, the show would have to be publicized by word of mouth, not by paid promotions; and third, there would be no profanity in the show.

Alice Reynolds was active from the beginning. She wrote songs, designed sets and the numerous banners associated with the play (particularly the steer-head and fiddle emblem that represents the *Fandangle*), and sketched some of the elaborate costumes. For many years, she also played the organ in the performances. She died in May 1984. The title of the show was chosen for its alliteration and euphony. "Fandangle" is a provincial version of Spanish *fandango*, a fast dance. Originally, only traditional or folk music and dances were used, but, as the show was repeated in later years by popular demand, new material was written and included in the performances, a practice that is still followed. Although material is repeated from year to year, each season's version varies from any previous show in both content and focus. In 1979, the 66th Texas legislature designated the *Fort Griffin Fandangle* as one of four official state plays.

In addition to Nail and Reynolds, numerous other citizens have contributed significantly. Songs written by James Ball, Elsa Turner, and, later, Louann George, who replaced Reynolds as organist in 1983, have increased the content available to the production. Marge Bray, longtime choreographer for the show, assumed the directorship after James Ball, who served for four years after Nail's death in 1968. Of particular significance to the development of the *Fandangle* over the years is the work of G.P. Crutchfield, a local craftsman. He built the authentic replica of the Butterfield stagecoach, the machine representing the Texas Central Railroad train, a self-contained blacksmith shop on wheels, and the steam calliope, which is still played before performances. All of these works and many other entries, bands, and horse units appear in the annual parade, which occurs on Thursday afternoon of the second week.

The early performances were held at the local football stadium. The Prairie Theatre, west of town, was constructed in 1965 on land leased for $1 a year from the John Alexander Matthews estate. Performances have been held there since that time. Full-scale productions are held only in Albany, but short versions have been given in many locations over the years. These are usually performed in the spring and serve as the core around which the major show is built during June. These "samplers" were performed at the Lyndon B. Johnson Ranch in 1967 and 1976 and in Washington, DC, in 1984. After Marge Bray's death in 1994, Betsy Black Parsons assumed directing responsibilities. In 2008, the *Fort Griffin Fandangle* celebrated its 70th anniversary, coinciding with the sesquicentennial of Albany. A sampler show returned to perform at the LBJ Ranch that year. By that time, the *Fandangle* had grown to more than 400 cast and crew members.

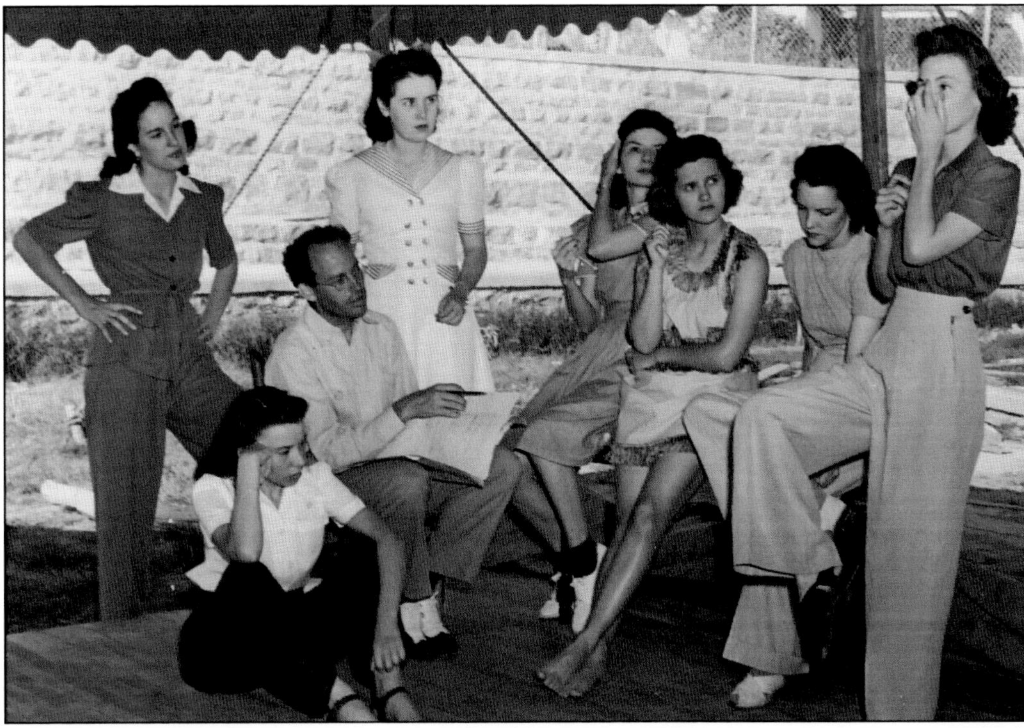

High school girls gather for rehearsal in 1938. From left to right are Jane Lieb, Betty Lieb Hill, Marilyn Howsley Myers, Janie Slay, and two unidentified women. Robert E. Nail Jr. and Alice Reynolds are seated left of center.

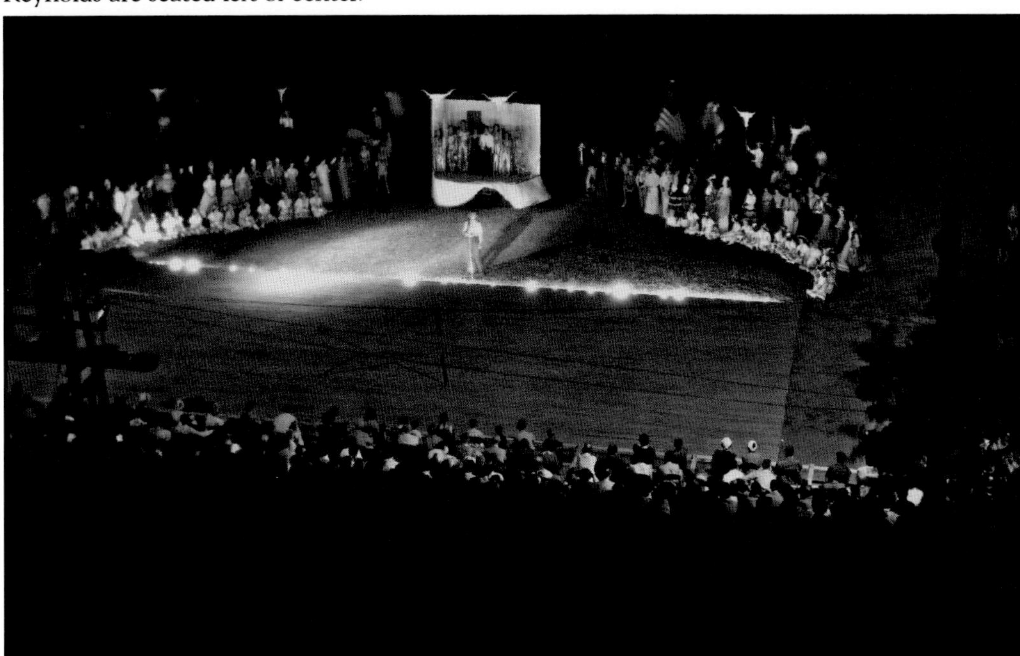

One of the earliest photographs of the *Fandangle*, this was taken during the finale of the 1939 performance. Note the large wooden stage used for performances in the football stadium.

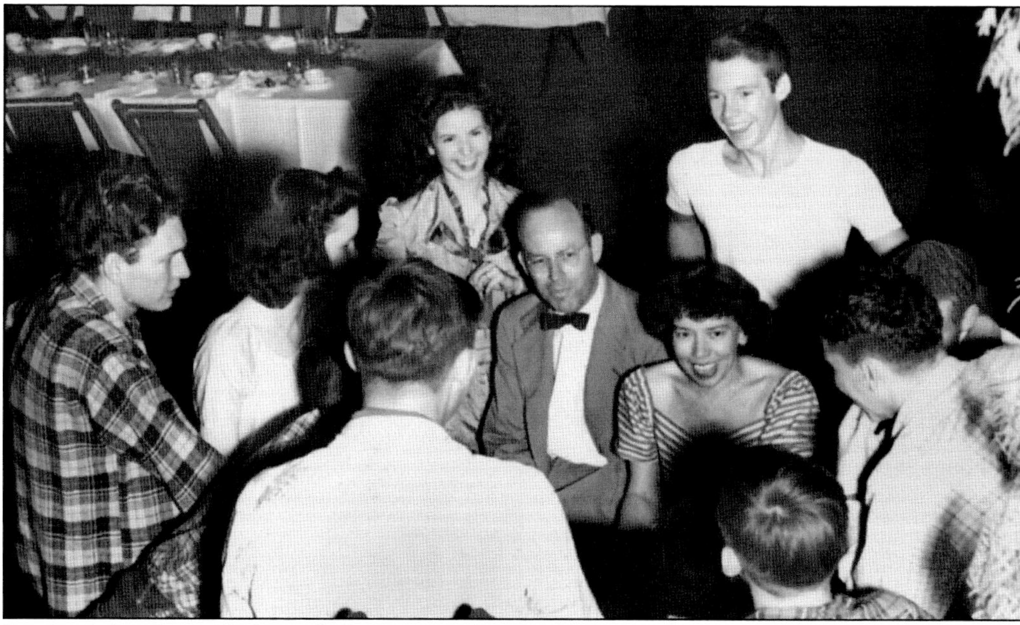

Fandangle has fostered a love of "the music and merriment in our hearts," as this group demonstrates after the Chamber of Commerce Banquet in 1947. Shown here are, from left to right, (standing, backs to camera) Bill Armstrong, Billy Webb, Jimmy Coker, and Joe Smith; (seated) Robert E. Nail Jr. (in bow tie), Alice Reynolds, and John Walker Wood; (standing, facing camera) James Ball (in profile), Jan Downing, Mary Spencer, and Jerry Ball.

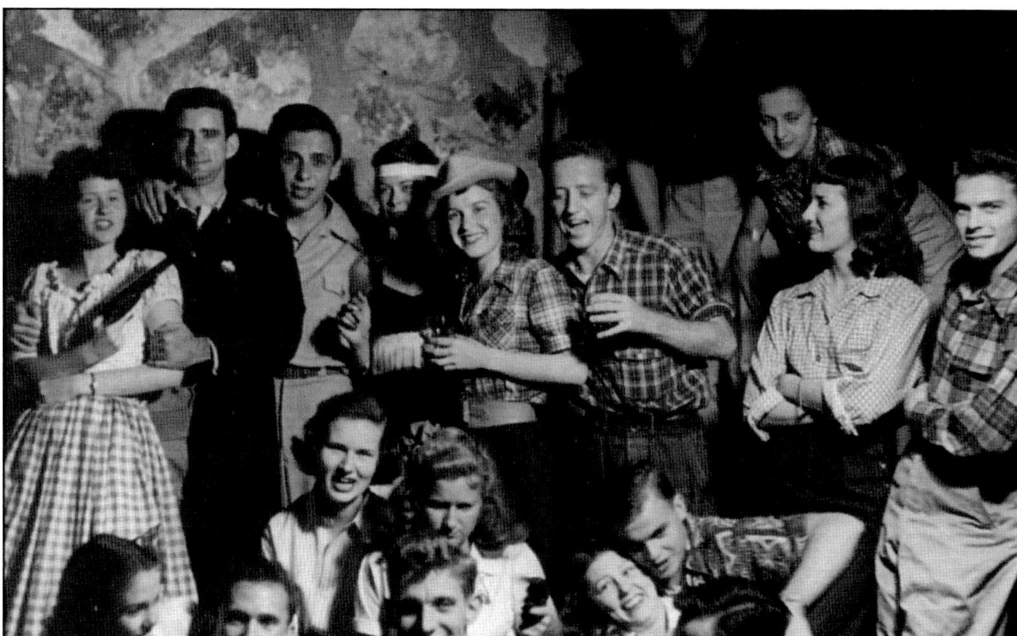

Fandangle has never been all work and no play. After-performance parties, like this one in the late 1940s, and socializing have always been a part of the fun of *Fandangle*. (Courtesy of Nancy Green.)

Bob Green, in the role of sheriff, is seen here with a young actress in the 1940s. (Courtesy of Nancy Green.)

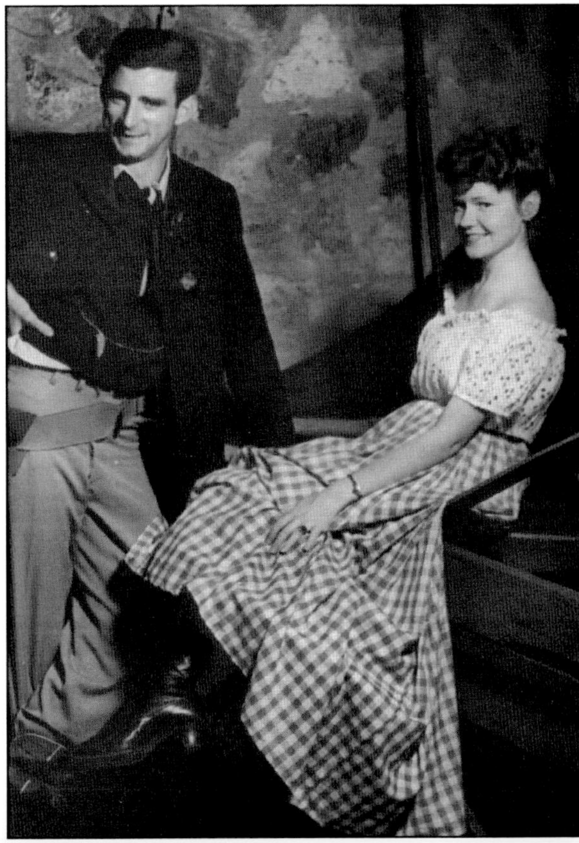

This photograph shows a finale in the 1950s. Bob Green and Marilynne Jacobs, who narrated the show for many years, are in the center of the group behind the microphone.

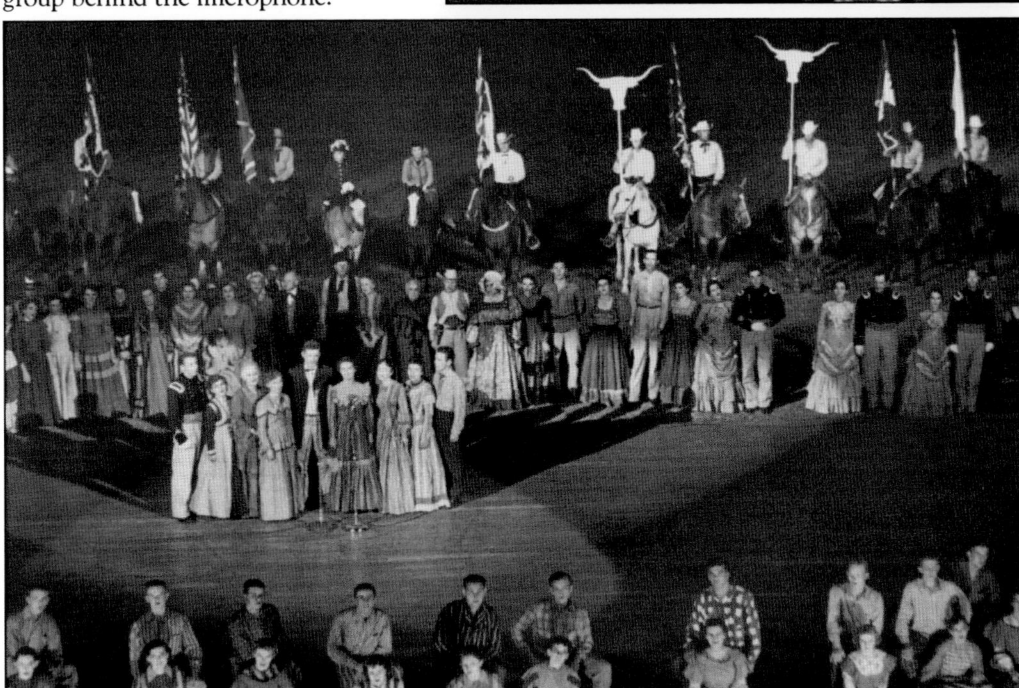

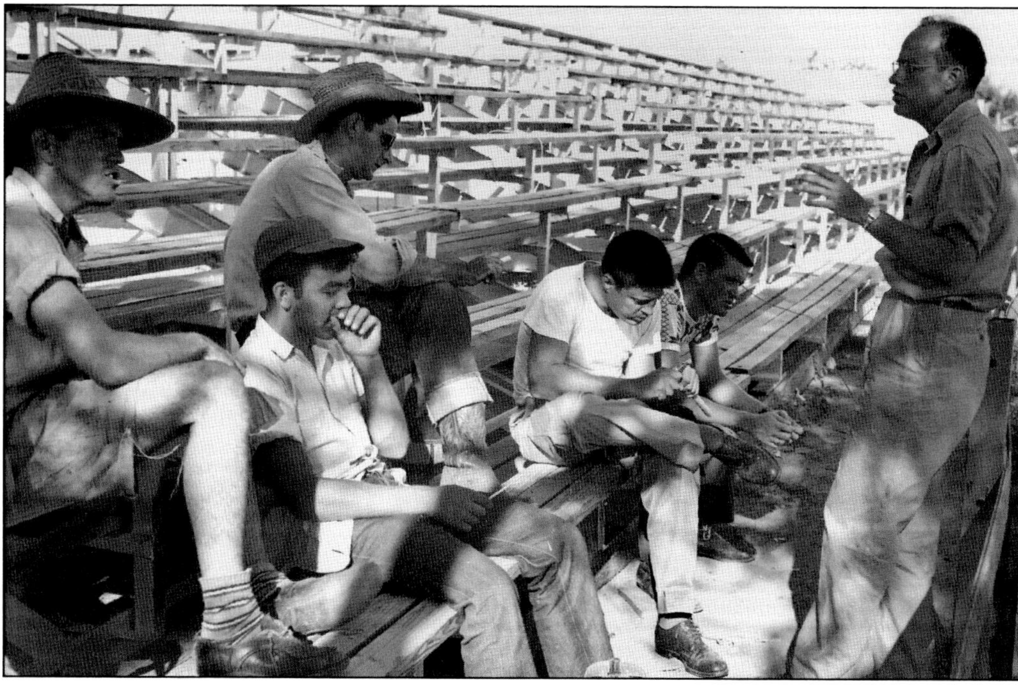

Bob Nail (right) gives instruction to young men during practice at the football field in the 1940s. The actors are, from left to right, Jackie Miller, Charles Fade, Bob Green, Winton Matthews, and ? Anderson.

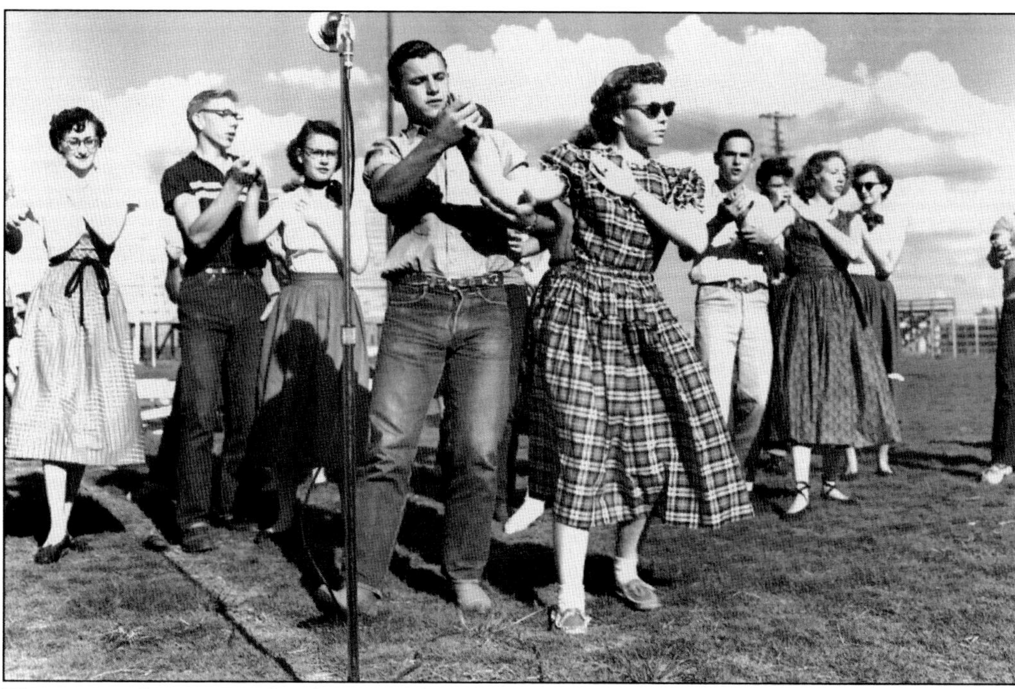

This group of young people rehearses a dance scene on the football field in 1952. The duo in front are Bonnie Millar and Barbara Daniell. The background dancers include Mary Porter, Randall Fincher, Sheila Irwin, Harry Jones, Mary Gail Pate, and Patricia Sazama.

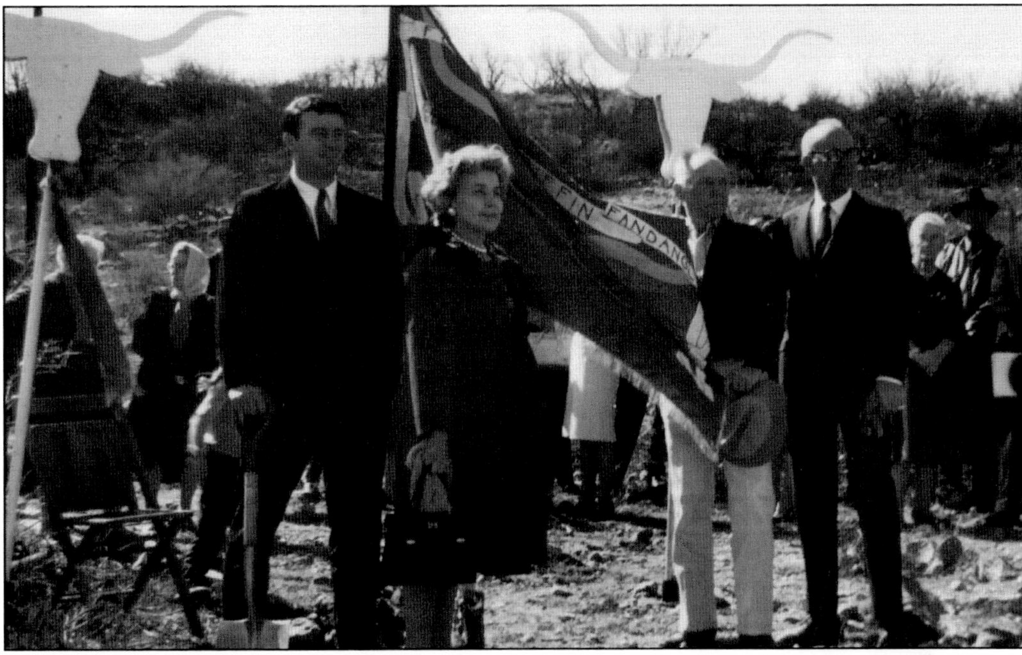

The Prairie Theatre, built on land donated by the Matthews family, provided the *Fandangle* with a permanent, custom-designed amphitheater. Attending the ground-breaking ceremonies are, from left to right, Johnny Musselman, Alice Reynolds, Watt Matthews, and Robert E. Nail Jr. (Courtesy of Nancy Green.)

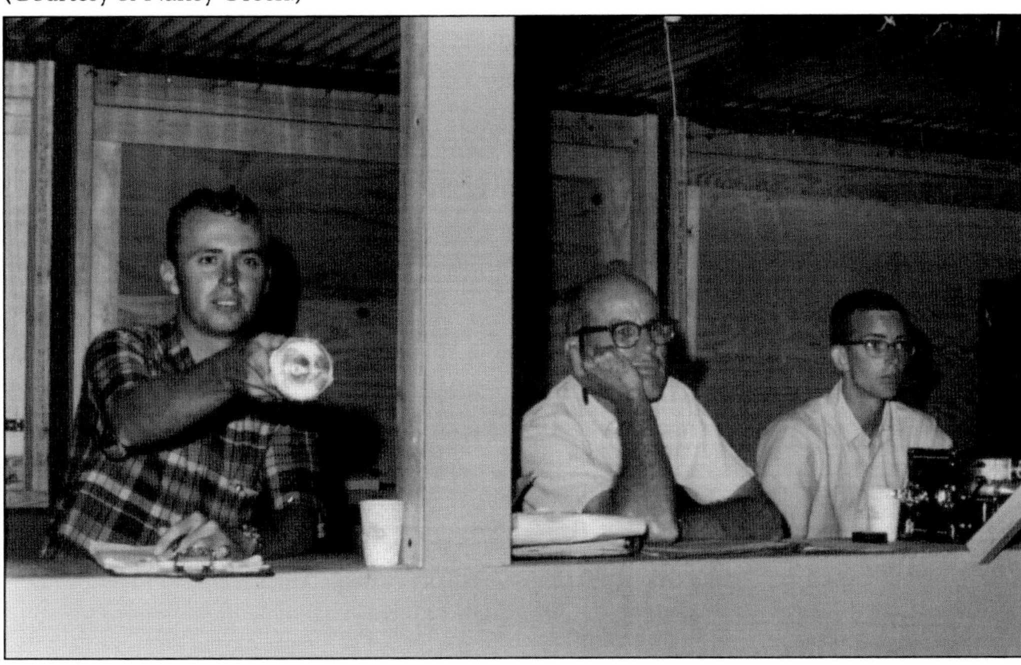

Hundreds of Albany residents come together each summer to make the production of the *Fandangle* possible. Many choose to help behind the scenes rather than share the spotlight on stage. Pictured here in the open-air crow's nest are, from left to right, Donny Hardaway, Robert E. Nail Jr., and Johnny King. (Courtesy of Nancy Green.)

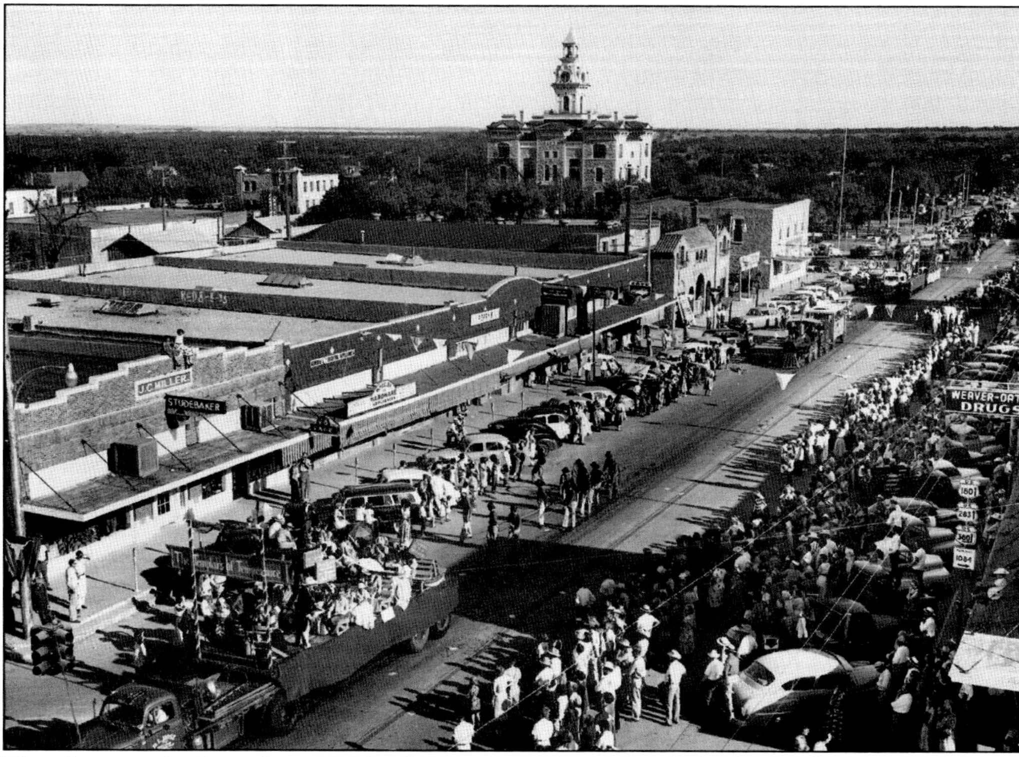

This photograph shows the east side of Main Street during a *Fandangle* parade in the early 1950s. The photograph was taken from a window at the McLemore Hotel, which is today the location of the Bank Park.

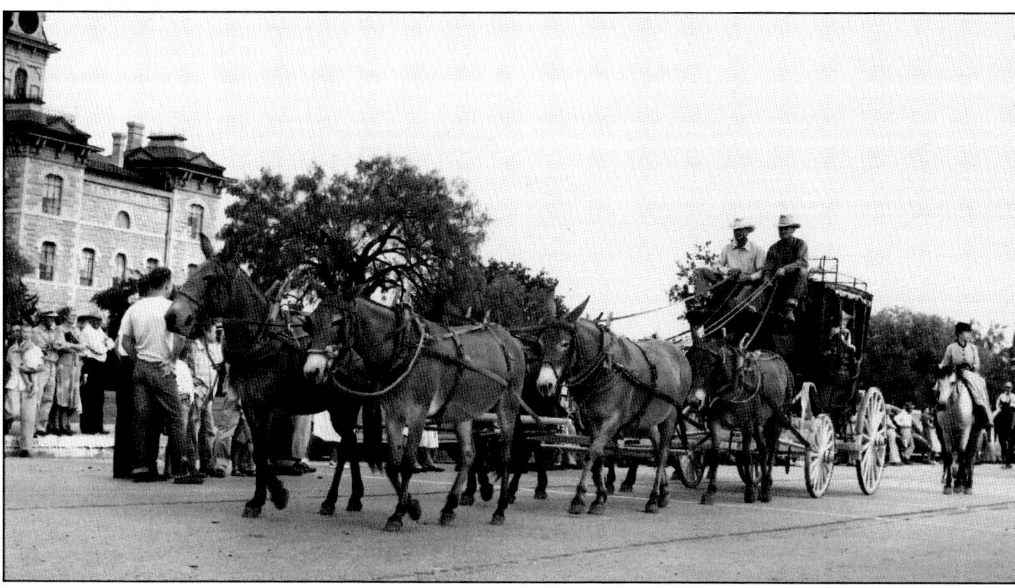

Built for the *Fandangle* by G.P. Crutchfield to fulfill a desire expressed by the director, Robert Nail, the stagecoach is a perfect replica in every detail. Crutchfield constructed the stagecoach from a set of photographs and specifications of the Concord coach, which was used on the Butterfield lines. It was completed in 1940. (Courtesy of John A. Matthews.)

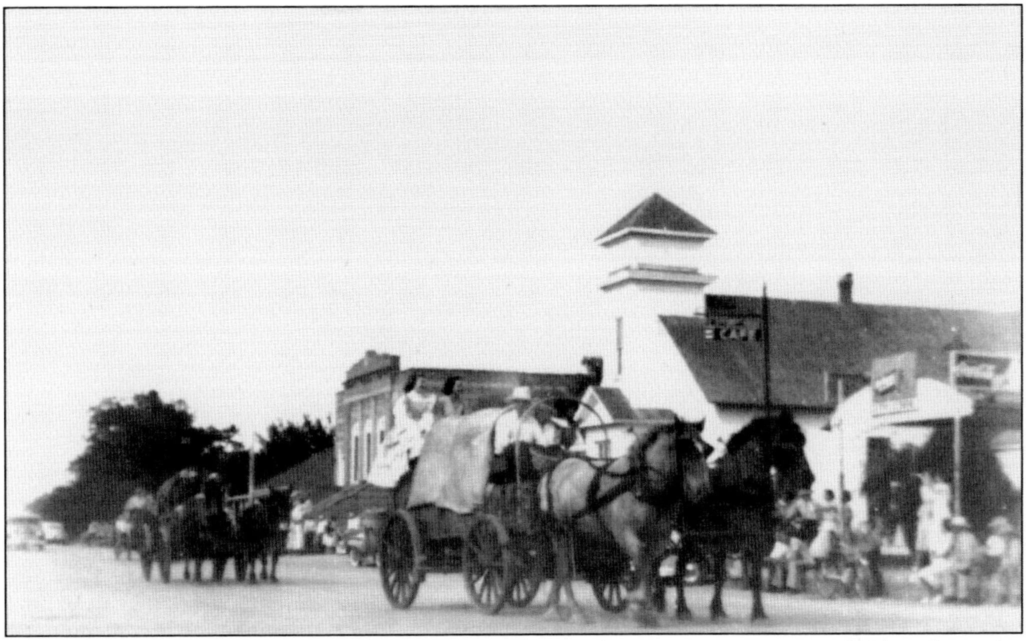

This photograph of a *Fandangle* parade in the 1940s shows Trinity Episcopal Church in the background. The church later moved to its current location at the end of North Second Street.

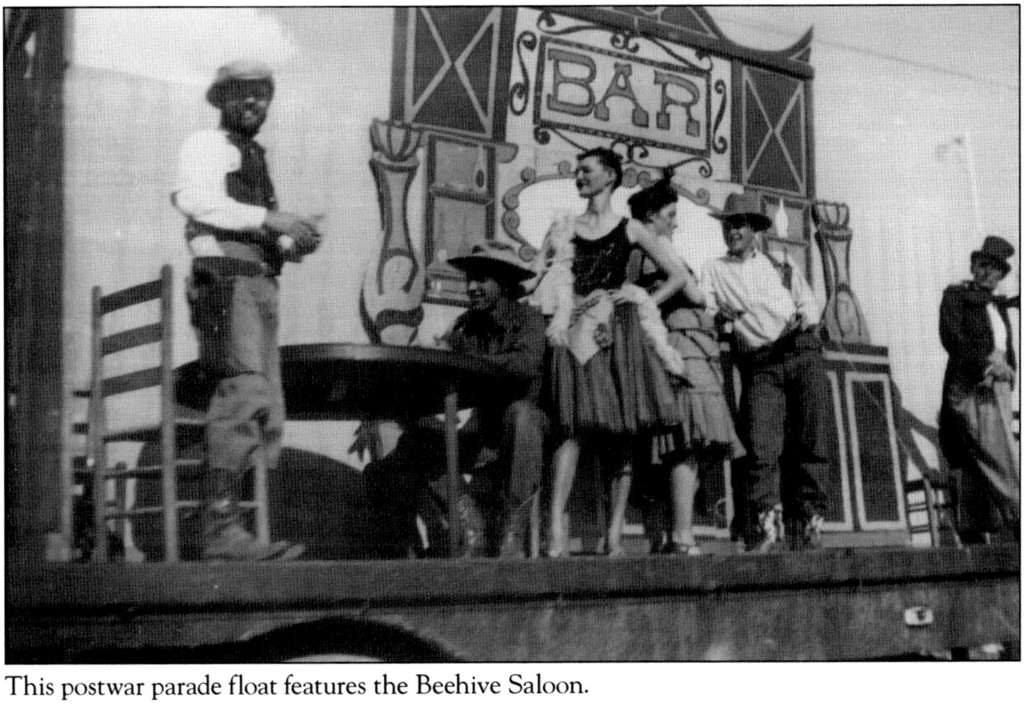

This postwar parade float features the Beehive Saloon.

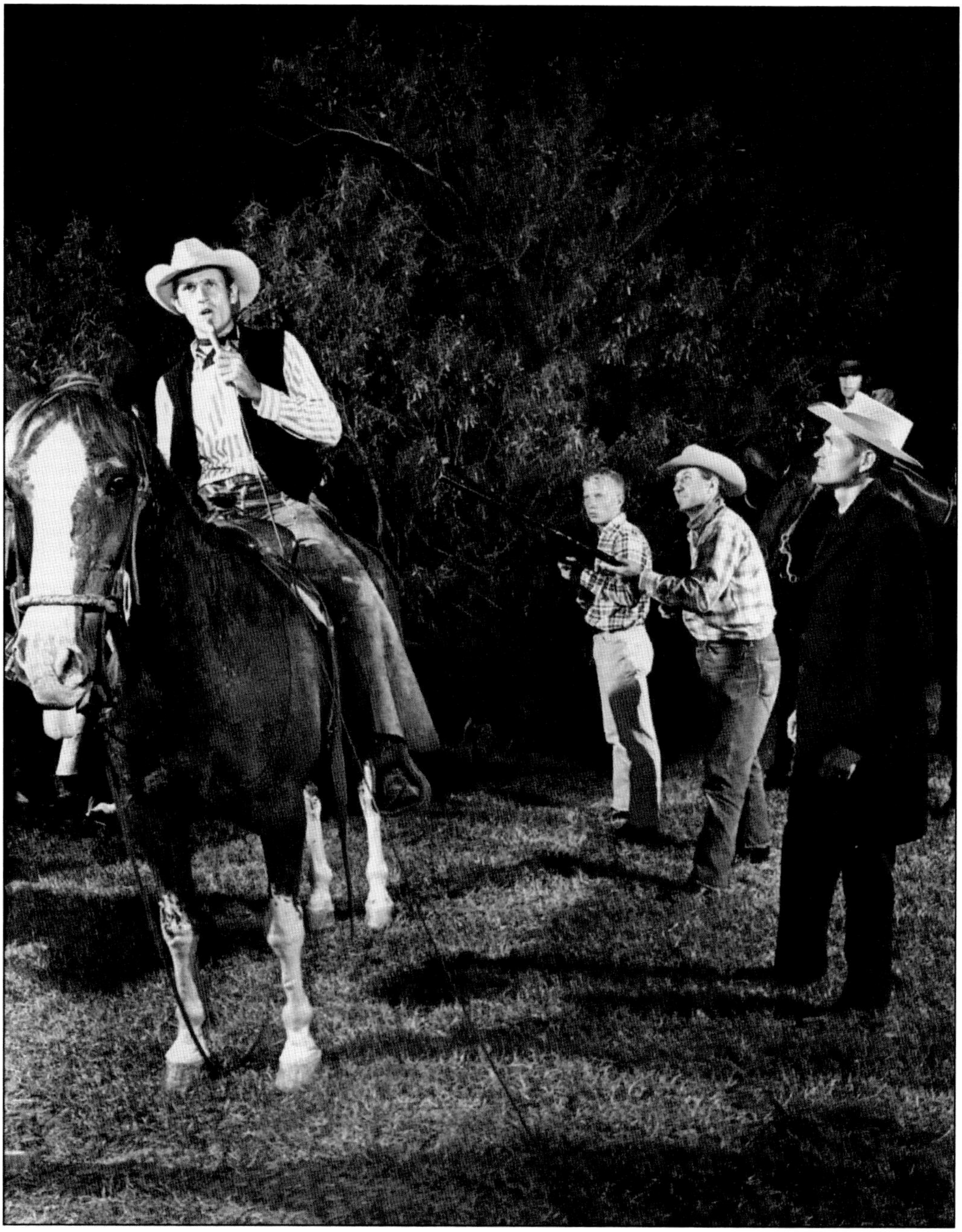

The "horse that I ride will cost me my hide." The man on horseback is Clifford Teinert. The actors on the ground are, from left to right, Mike Carnes, Harold Law, and Richard Middlebrook, portraying the judge. The horseman in the background is Bill Farmer.

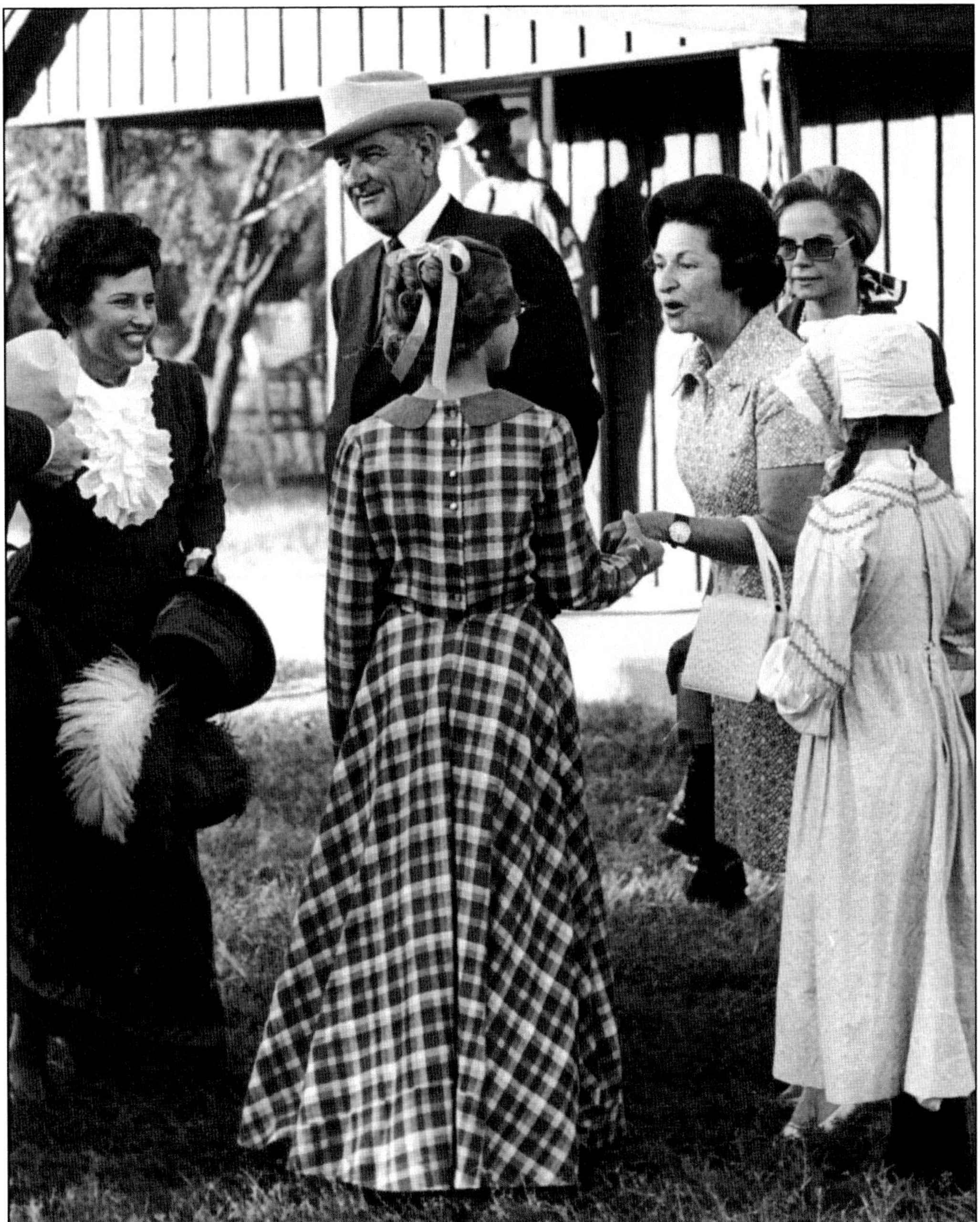

In 1970, Pres. Lyndon Johnson and his wife, Lady Bird, surprised the *Fandangle* with a visit during a sampler performance. Cast members speaking with the president and first lady are, from left to right, Elizabeth Green, Carol May Webb, and Mary Anna Green. (Courtesy of Nancy Green.)

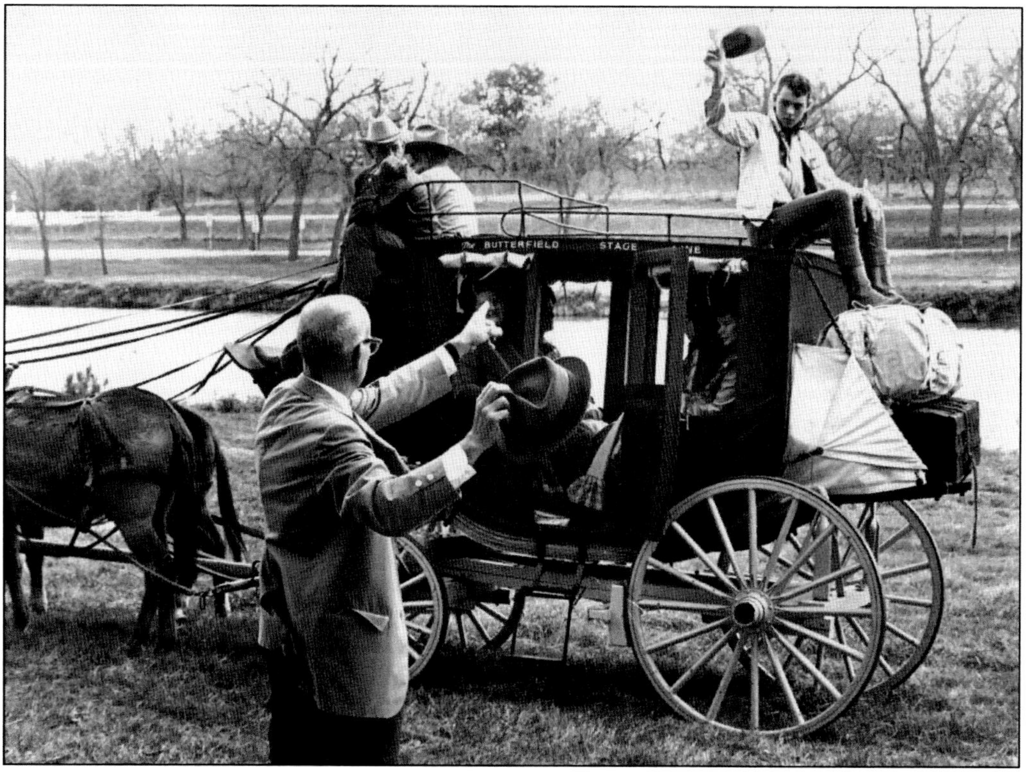

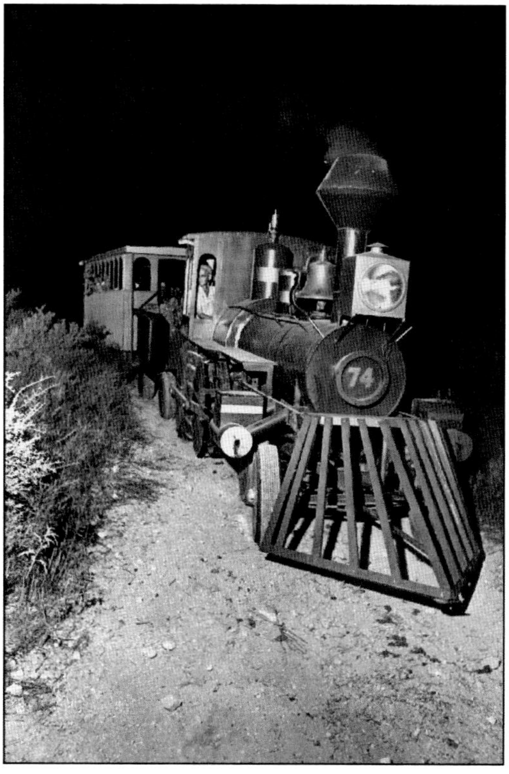

In 1967, the *Fandangle* made the first of three visits to the Lyndon B. Johnson Ranch. There, at the request of the president and first lady, a sampler was performed along the banks of the Pedernales River for Latin American dignitaries. Here, Robert Nail gives direction to Jessie White before the performance.

In 1953, at the request of Nail, Crutchfield and his crew set out to build a working train for the *Fandangle*. Using a tractor Crutchfield found in the Cook Field junk pile as the base, he and his team built the steam engine around it. To give it even more of an authentic flare, the Texas Central Railroad gave the *Fandangle* a bell and whistle. Still in use, this important prop was recently restored.

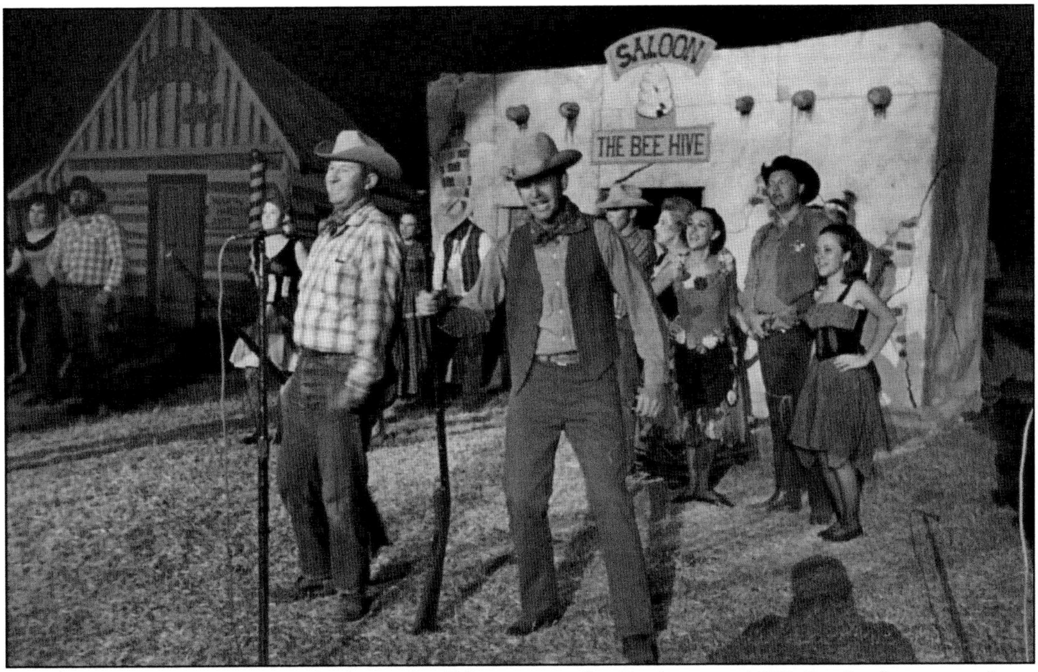

This performance photograph shows Buffalo men at the Beehive in 1970. In the foreground are veteran performers Harold Law (left) and Jon Rex Jones.

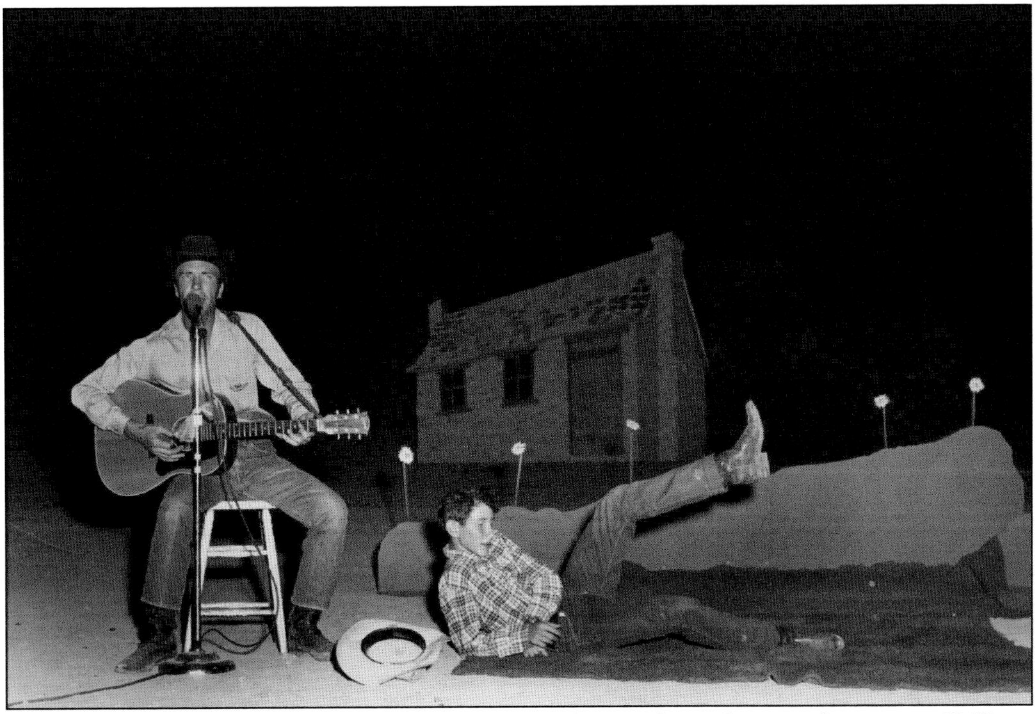

In the springtime, a young man's thoughts turn to fancy. Shown here performing in 1965 are Wayne Angel (left) and Rob Green. (Courtesy of Nancy Green.)

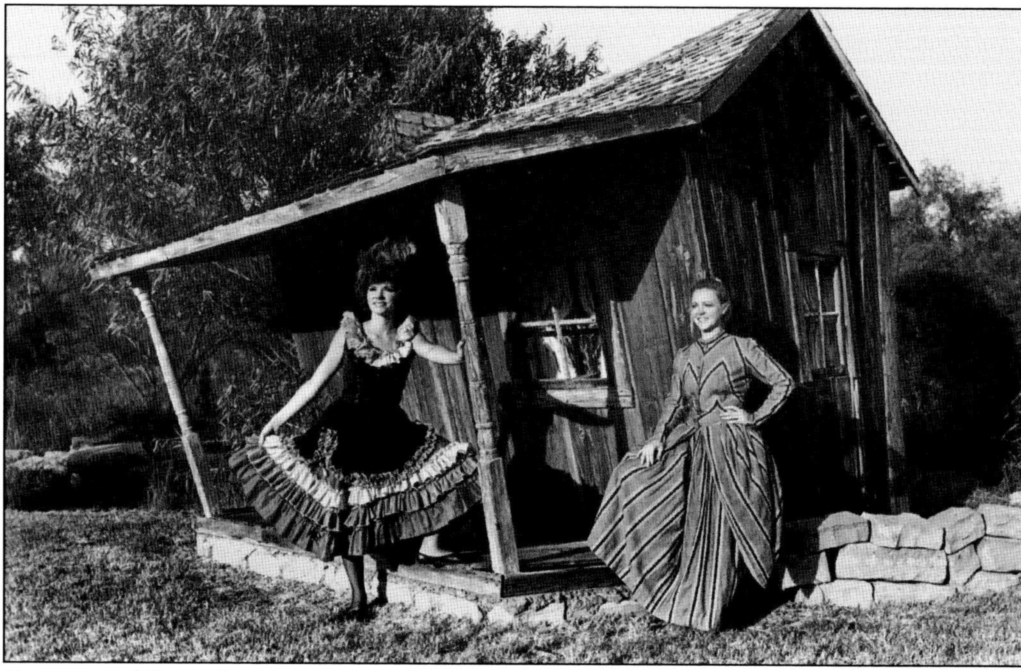

Can-can girl Betsy Parsons poses with pioneer woman Pam McComas in a 1978 promotional photograph. (Courtesy of Betsy Parsons.)

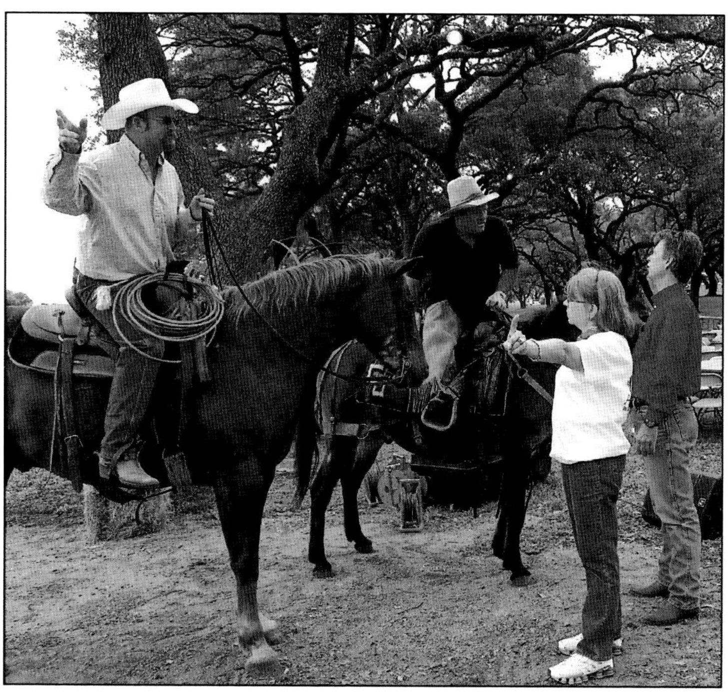

Flag Parade cowboys John Caldwell (left) and Morris D. Snyder, along with lifetime cast member Steve Waller (right), receive direction from Betsy Parsons. Parsons has served as the artistic director for 20 seasons, as of the time of publication. She was assistant director for Marge Bray for 12 years before that, and has been involved in the *Fandangle* since she was in the fifth grade. (Courtesy of *Albany News*.)

Seven

Albany Is Modern, You Can See a Change

By Melinda Lucas

Albany's population from almost the beginning has remained relatively constant, hovering around 2,000. The original industries of ranching and farming were supplemented by oil and gas in the 1920s, and since then have become more diverse, including tank manufacturing, iron foundry, wind farms, hunting, and tourism. But even natives might be surprised with a review of changes that have occurred in the last four decades.

In 1975, with the nation's bicentennial on the horizon, there was a big push to get ready for the celebration. The controversial demolition of the Western Skies hotel, Albany's tallest structure other than the Courthouse, forever changed the downtown landscape. But the addition of the Bank Park, with its Georgia Monument in honor of the state of Georgia's contributions during Texas's bid for independence, gave residents another outdoor venue. Several years after the park's dedication, the Ledbetter Pickett House was moved from the City Park to the Bank Park. Together with the monument and several markers, the historical Pickett House and the Ledbetter Salt Vats in their Bank Park setting appear as though they've been there for a hundred years, but the park is actually a relatively recent development. Down the street at the Shackelford County Courthouse, a new gazebo designed by Albany native Van Jones was also dedicated for the bicentennial celebration.

Although Albany citizens had long been conscious of their history, the downtown changes in the mid-1970s seemed to spark a renewed effort to build up the community's historical appeal. Restoration of the Lynch building, First National Bank, and Cotter Neff & Co. within that same period seemed to serve as a catalyst for other property owners.

The landscape changed again in 1978, when the remnants of Tropical Storm Amelia stalled over Shackelford County and 30-plus inches of rain fell on Albany in a 24-hour period. The ensuing flood killed nine people and destroyed dozens of houses and businesses. The flood necessitated a new sewer plant, in addition to the rebuilding of the Highway 180 bridge, which had buckled under the onslaught of floodwaters.

During the next couple of years, the town's first elementary school, a two-story structure on South First Street, was torn down to make way for a grocery store, and the First National Bank building was gutted by fire, requiring a couple of years for rebuilding. In spite of the setbacks, those years were successful ones overall, especially for the oil and gas industry; it was also during this time that interest in hunting began to grow. Hunting, along with several sell-out years of *Fandangle* performances, drew more and more visitors to town, and Albany began to gain a reputation as a weekend destination. Part of the attraction was a brand new concept housed in a very old facility, known then as the Old Jail Foundation. In 1980, the Old Jail Art Center began as a home for a couple of important collections of artwork, but the new museum grew quickly. Now the collections contain nearly 2,200 works of art and draw thousands of visitors each year.

Another big change in the 1980s was the construction of a small municipal airport, which replaced a private facility. In 2009, a $3 million project funded by a Texas Department of Transportation grant and private monies extended the runway, added a taxiway, improved lighting, and automated fuel sales. At about the same time, the Shackelford Water Supply Corporation (later Fort Griffin SUD) was formed to provide treated water to rural areas.

Also seeing some big transformations in the latter part of the 20th century and since the millennium were the local schools. A new junior high school building was constructed in the 1980s, and a cafeteria and library at the elementary campus. A bond was passed for a larger gymnasium in 1996. Two wings at Nancy Smith Elementary opened in the late 1990s. An activity center was constructed a few years later, and the 1959-era high school building was extensively renovated just after the turn of the century. Baseball and softball were added to the curriculum and a baseball field was constructed with private funds. The softball team recently moved from the city-owned park on Griffin Road to a brand-new field at Webb Park. The district has completely rebuilt the track facility and put new bleachers, a press box, and a concession stand at the football field. Technology is fully supported by the district, including individual laptops for all junior high and high school students.

Meanwhile, much of the business district was springing back to life. The handsome 1920s Aztec Theater, which was close to falling into ruin, was reborn and expanded. Several other buildings were restored or renovated, including the Hartfield and Blach buildings that house Momentum Operating, as well as the Whitney Theatre. In 2000, Shackelford County received one of the first grants given by the state for the restoration of courthouses, and in the summer of 2001, a beautiful and rejuvenated Shackelford County Courthouse was dedicated. In more recent years, the Jackson Warehouse and adjacent Sinclair station have been reenergized. Erline's and Vintage Vanilla offer more downtown charm, along with the former City Grocery and a new car museum manned by volunteers on weekends.

Over the last four decades, businesses such as EBAA Iron and Fox Tank have added specialized manufacturing plants to the economy. Oilfield service companies have also expanded. API, Concho, and Basic currently employ 500 people total, about 280 of them in Shackelford County. The most recent boom is the development of wind farms, with hundreds of turbines scattered over the county. When First Financial Bank invested in Albany in the form of a new building, it spoke clearly of expected future prospects here. And both local financial institutions offer motor banks for customer convenience.

Many new historical markers were dedicated over the last 40 years. As of February 2014, there were 37 official markers in Shackelford County, 26 of them within Albany's city limits. Several others are already approved and in the works. Local restaurants and catering firms offer a wide variety of food choices; some have earned statewide acclaim.

In recent years, private funds, often added to matching grants, have built city and rural fire department buildings, completely renovated the Shackelford County Library, established a nondenominational youth facility known as the Feed Store, and created an astounding $2 million City Park overhaul that includes a multi-feature pool, skate park, lighted walking path, athletic fields, improved playground, and more. Public funding has provided a new city water plant and county law enforcement center, a Walking Through History walkway, and a sidewalk system that extends from one end of town to the other. Events such as annual car shows, Polo on the Prairie, Christmas parades, Friends of Fort Griffin fundraisers, golf tournaments, and successful athletic activities have further strengthened the sense of community. An enduring and energetic religious infrastructure, supported by 17 local churches, also fosters a populace committed to the common good.

There have been obstacles. The hospital closed. A runaway wildfire blackened much of the county, and there was another devastating flood. Several years of drought have dried up millions of gallons of surface water. Some notable historical buildings either fell into ruin or were torn down. Businesses came and went. Families moved away. "Indispensable" community leaders were laid to rest. Through it all, Albany has maintained a stability uncommon to most small rural towns, an attractive nature that breeds pride in this community and helps anchor it for the future that lies ahead..

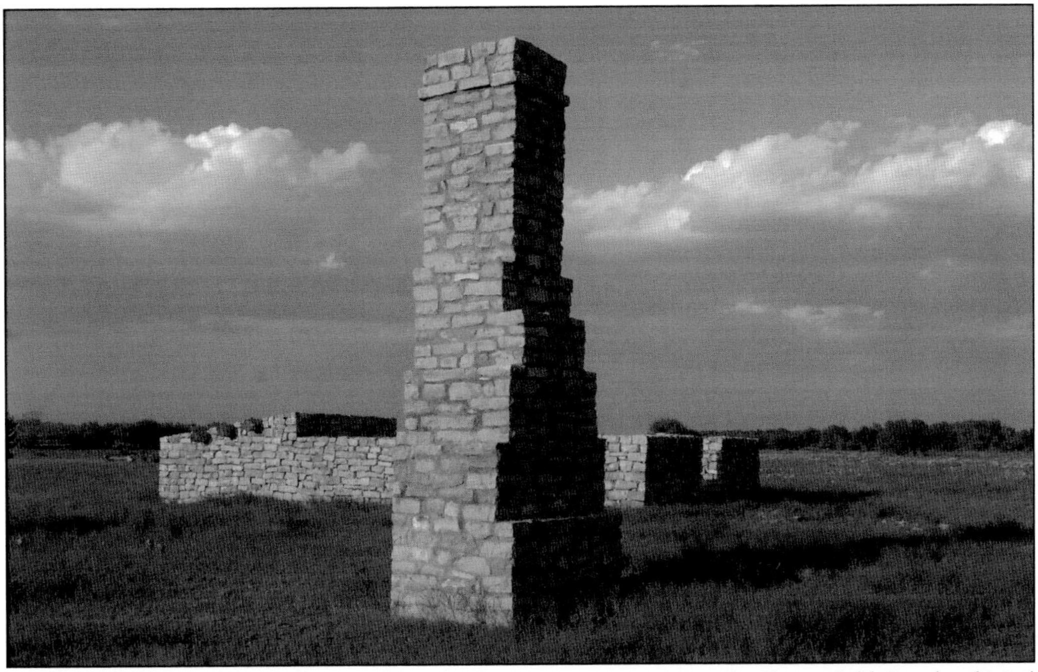

These are the reconstructed ruins of Smith's Station, a stage stop on the Butterfield Overland Mail Route that operated from 1858 to 1861. Located on the present-day Chimney Creek Ranch, it was an important stop of the early stage line that stretched from Missouri to California. Stagecoaches made the trip in less than 25 days. Smith's Station was the only Butterfield stop in present-day Shackelford County. (Courtesy of Watt Casey Jr.)

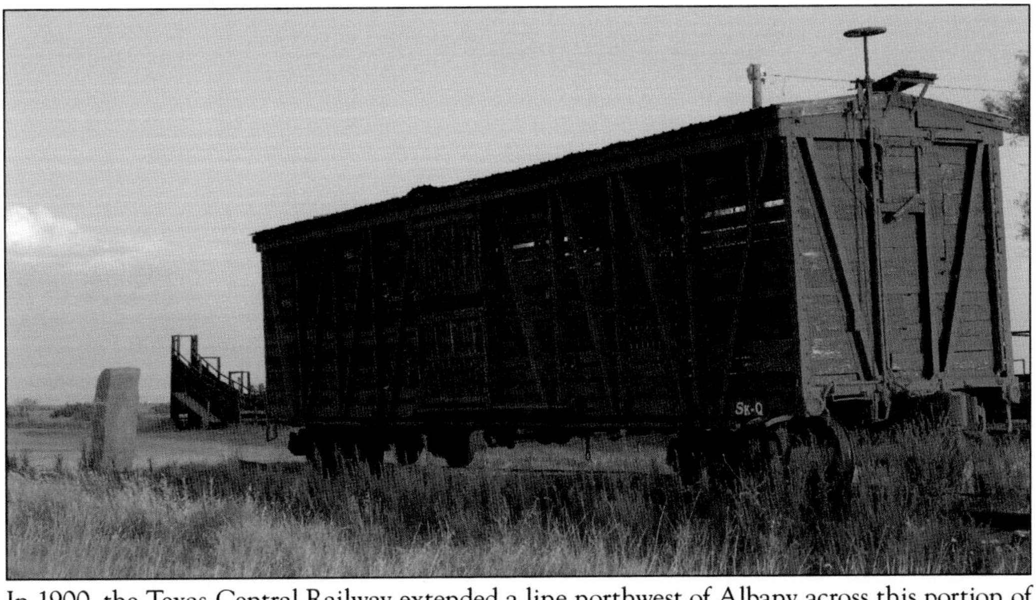

In 1900, the Texas-Central Railway extended a line northwest of Albany across this portion of Rose Ella Conrad's ranch. Ella and her brother John A. "Bud" Matthews constructed cattle pens and a loading chute at this location. Surrounding ranchers were soon shipping their cattle from this switch to markets in Fort Worth. Although the railroad ceased operations in 1967, local ranchers still load cattle onto trucks from this site. (Courtesy of Watt Casey Jr.)

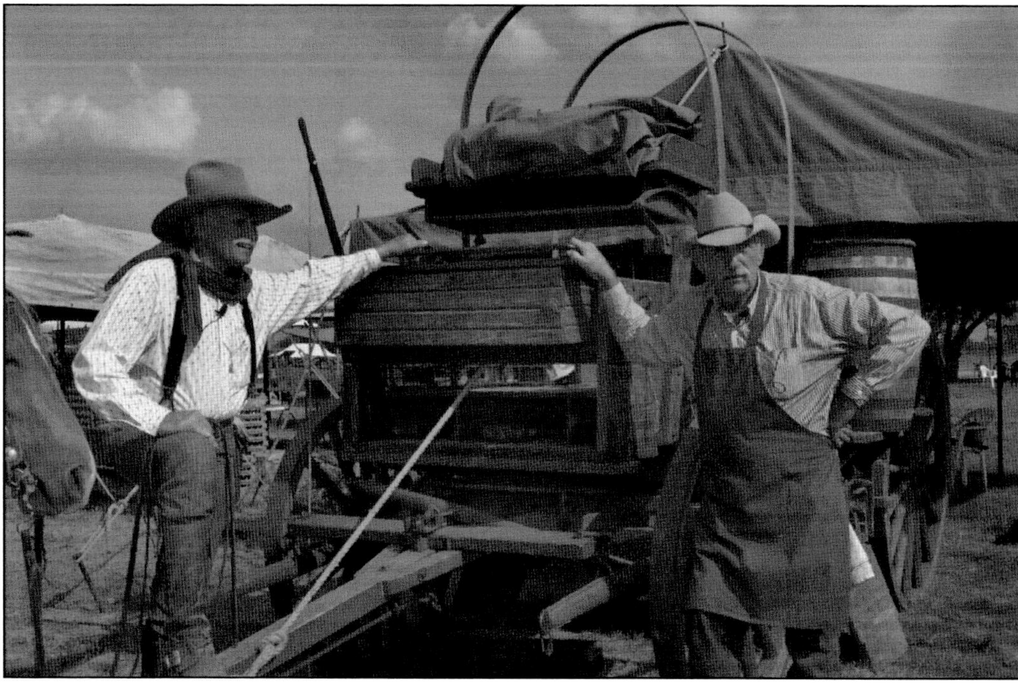

Chuck-wagon cooks Clifford Teinert (left) and Bill Cauble stand in front of an authentic chuck wagon. They are founders of the Western Chuck Wagon Association, whose contest regulations seek to uphold the authentic elements of the old chuck wagons. (Courtesy of Watt Casey Jr.)

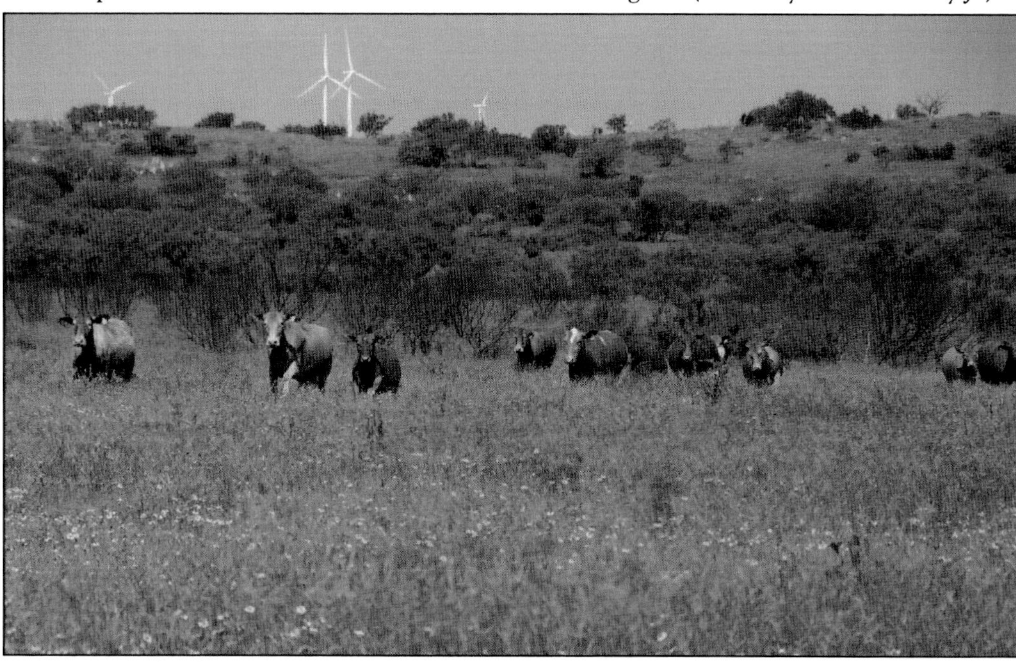

Watt Casey's beefmaster cattle graze on the Phin Reynolds Ranch, which has been in the Matthew and Reynolds families since the early 1900s. Visible in the distance are the wind turbines that generate energy and tax revenue for the surrounding communities. (Courtesy of Watt Casey Jr.)

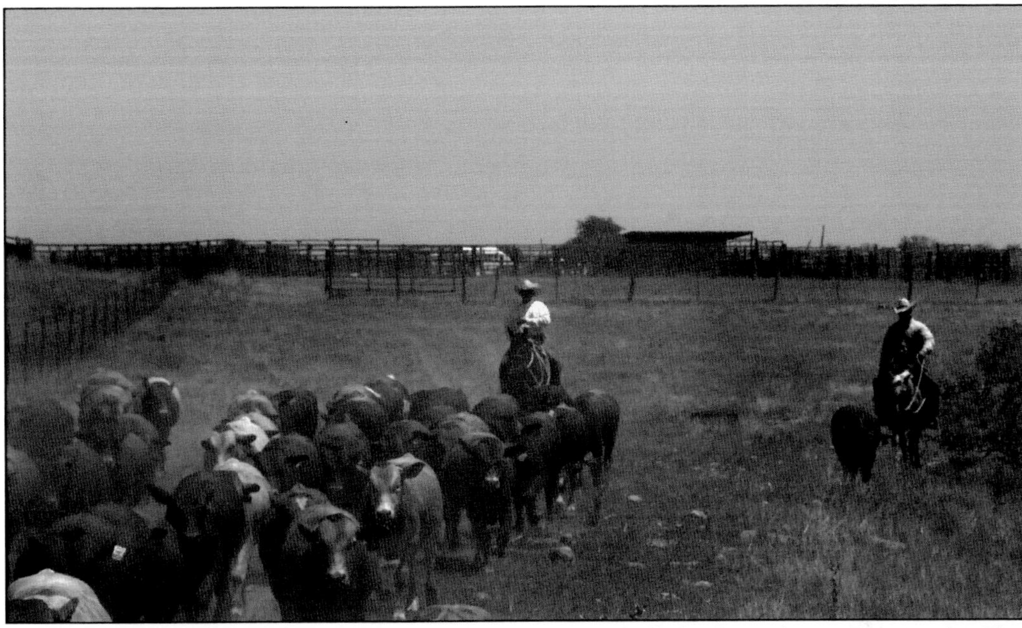

Cowboys Kyle (left) and Dunn Clement move yearling bulls back to the pasture on the Phin Reynolds ranch after they were branded. (Courtesy of Watt Casey Jr.)

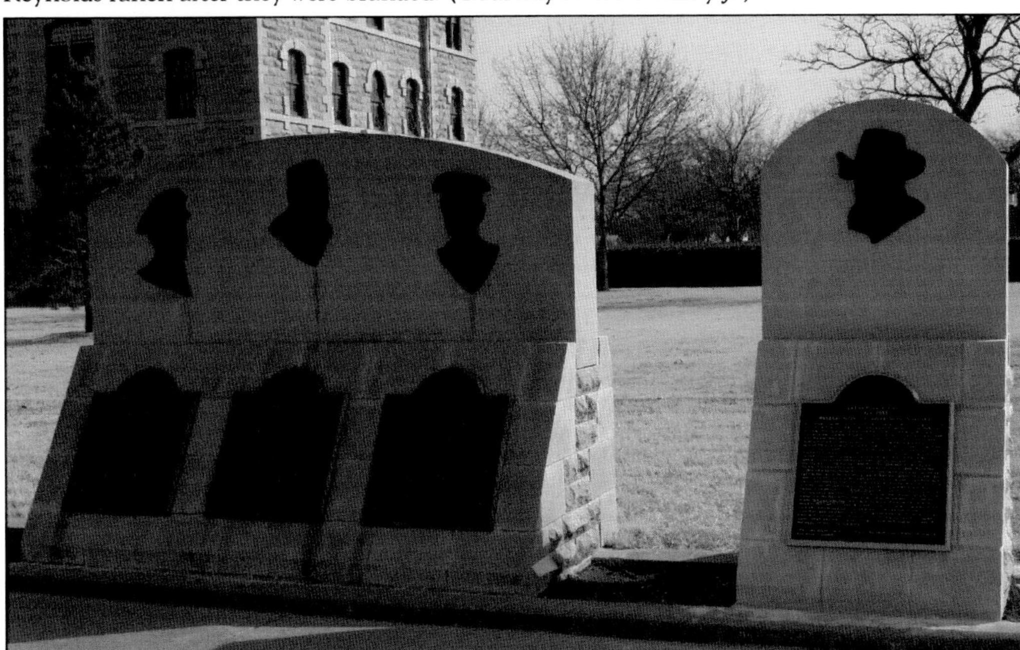

After reading Bob Green's World War II memoir *Okinawa Odyssey*, Tex Moncrief of Fort Worth was so moved that he sent Green $25,000. With that money, Green built a monument on the courthouse square for three distinguished Albany servicemen: Lt. Gen. Robert Boyd Williams (1901–1977); Col. William Edwin Dyess (1916–1943), for whom Dyess Air Force Base is named; and Rear Adm. Emory Arden Grantham (1914–1998). The monument on the right, memorializing Bob Green, was unveiled on the courthouse square on December 9, 2013. (Courtesy of Molly Sauder.)

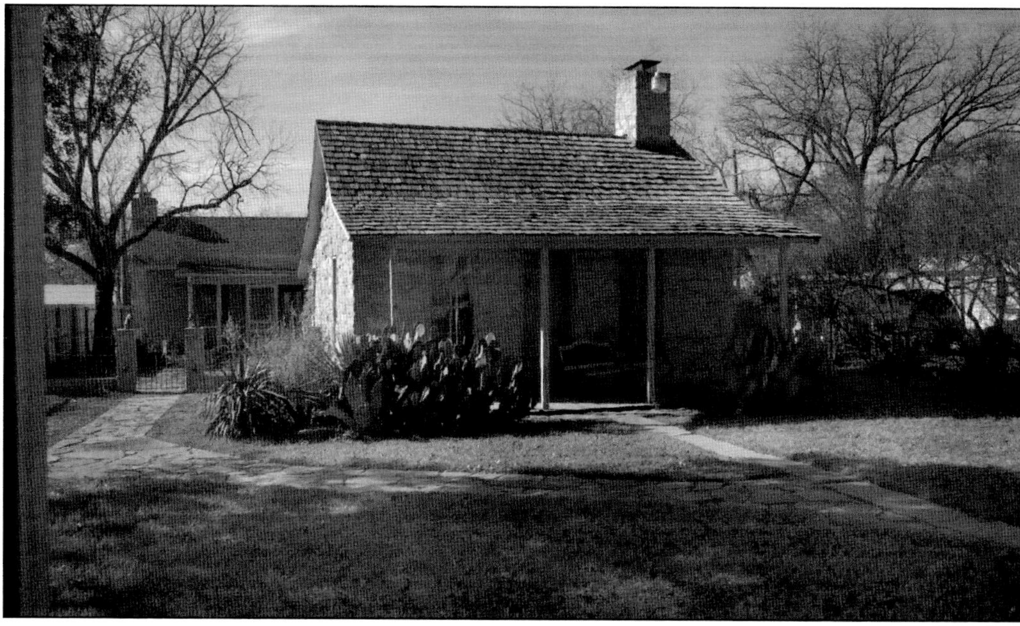

Henry Carter Jacobs (1842–1894), first sheriff of Shackelford County, built this rock house in 1875. Constructed of stone, it was the first permanent dwelling in Albany. Jacobs platted the townsite of Albany, donated the land for the courthouse and Presbyterian church, and led the initiative for a railroad to come to Albany. Today, this pioneer home has been restored and has received a marker from the Texas Historical Commission. (Courtesy of Watt Casey Jr.)

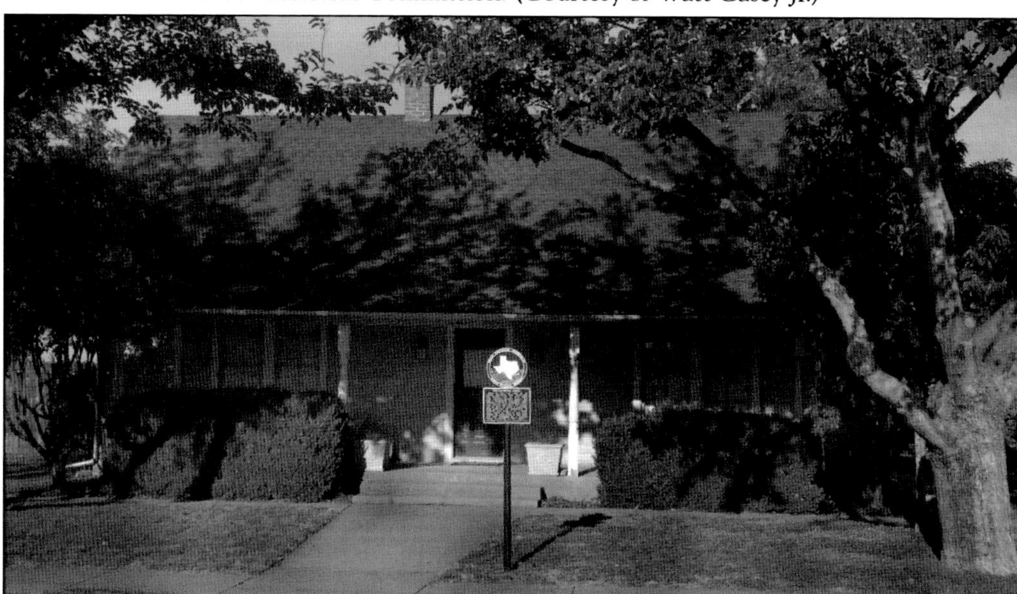

The Rye-Caperton House was built in Fort Griffin in 1874 as an office building. It was moved to Albany in 1879 by owner Edgar Rye, who soon after started the *Albany Tomahawk* newspaper. He sold the building in 1896 to Anna F. Caperton, who changed its appearance in 1902 and used it as a home. It was converted to apartments in the 1940s before finally being restored as a single-family dwelling. (Courtesy of Watt Casey Jr.)

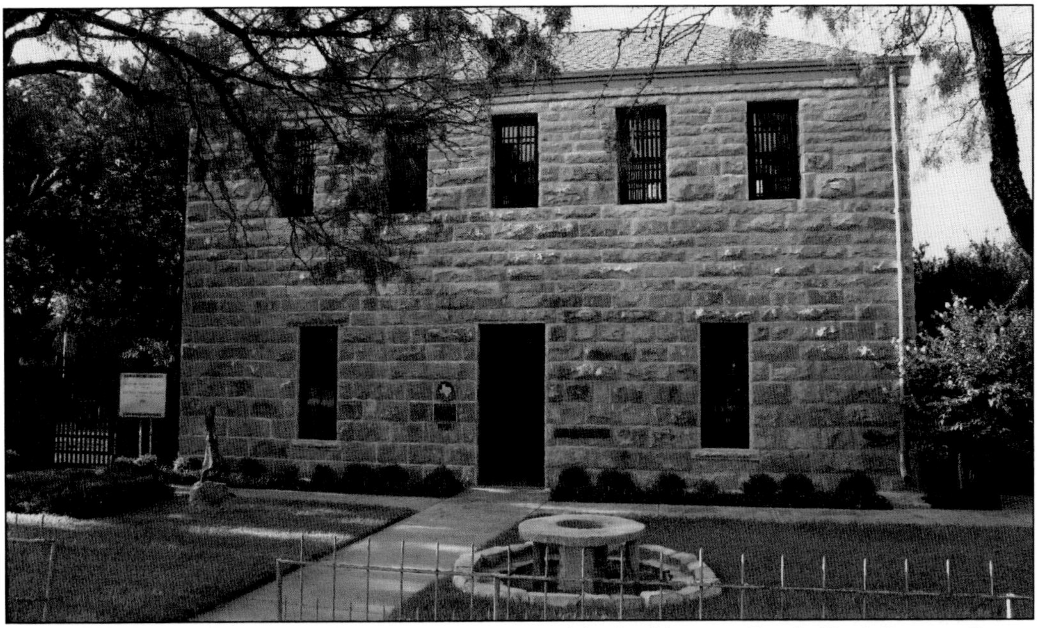

The "old jail" in Albany was the first permanent public building in Shackelford County. It was designed and built by John Thomas of Thomas & Woerner Builders, of Fort Worth. Initials on many of the native limestone blocks show masons' claims to payment for work. The old jail became abandoned in 1929, and Robert E. Nail saved it from demolition in 1940 by purchasing it from the county and using it as a writing studio. (Courtesy of Patrick Kelly.)

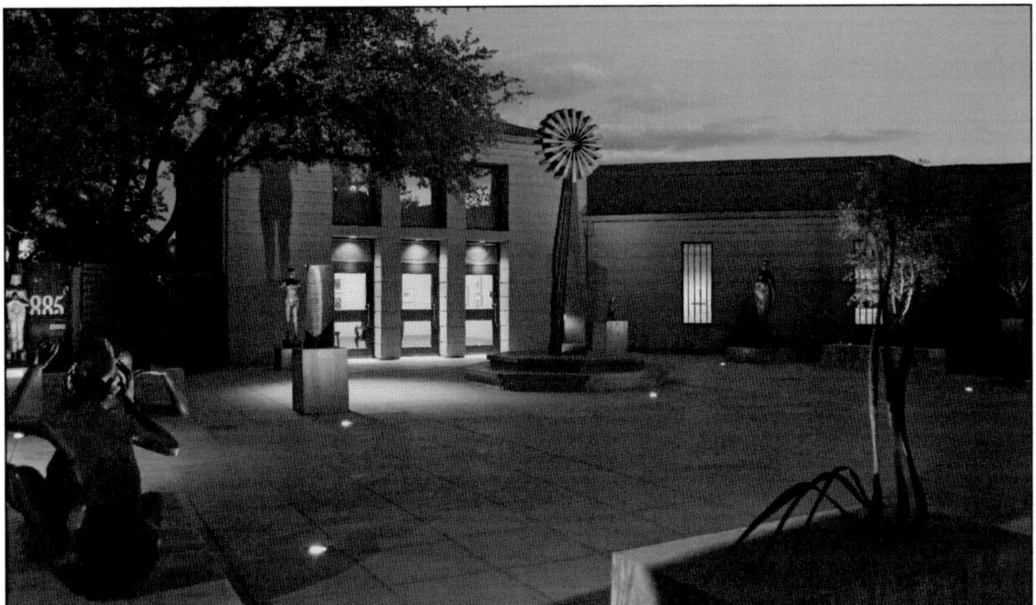

The Old Jail Art Center was opened to the public as a museum on December 19, 1980. Serving a core audience of 25 rural counties, the Old Jail Art Center is one of the only free and accredited art museums between Fort Worth and El Paso. The original rock jail portion of the museum has been designated a historical landmark and is listed in the National Register of Historic Places. (Courtesy of Patrick Kelly.)

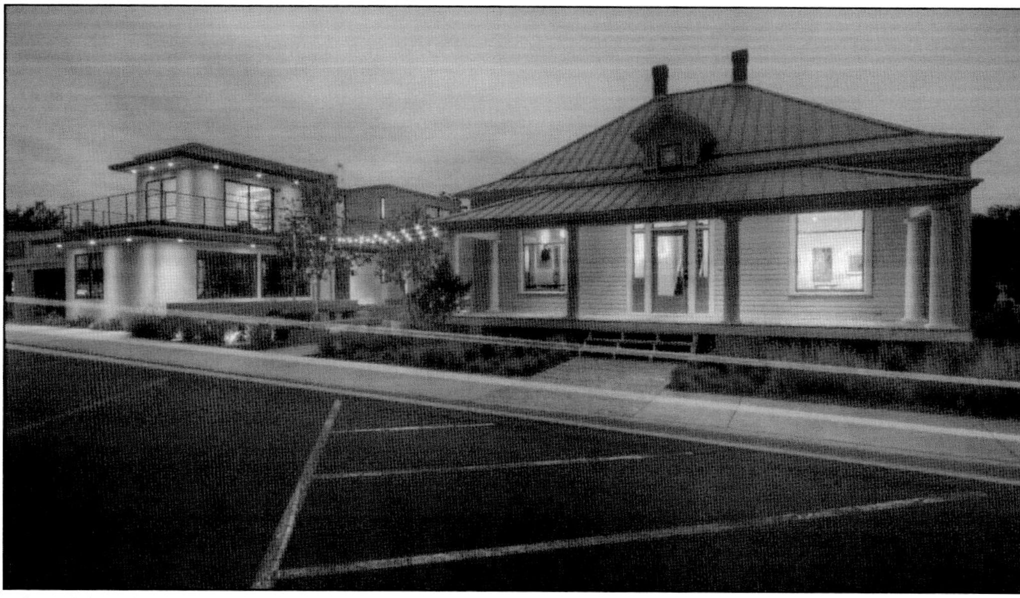

The old and new share space on the courthouse square. An AIA-award-winning compound of two contemporary houses and one historic house, one office suite, and an artist's studio was built in 2010. The site incorporates the 1907 Claude Walraven House, which was moved from next to First Christian Church and restored. Walraven (1895–1992) was a World War I veteran and an oil-field machinist. The enclave is built around a series of public and private courtyards. (Courtesy of Watt Casey Jr.)

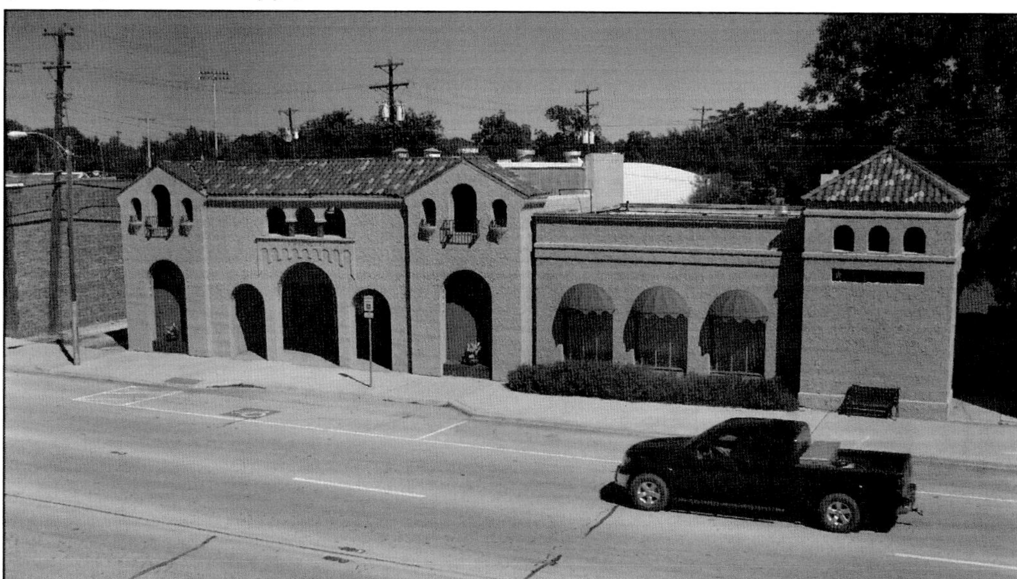

Frank Whitney built the Aztec Theatre in 1927. Showing signs of decline by the 1950s, it appeared that it would close for good in 1969. In 1971, a group of Albany citizens bought new equipment and reopened the theater. Due to concern that Albany might lose its historic stucco-and-tiled-roof structure, Dotsy Brittingham and Sally Wallace purchased the building in 1985. With locally raised funds, the theater was completely renovated. Today, it hosts plays, musicals, and community gatherings. (Courtesy of Randy Bacon.)

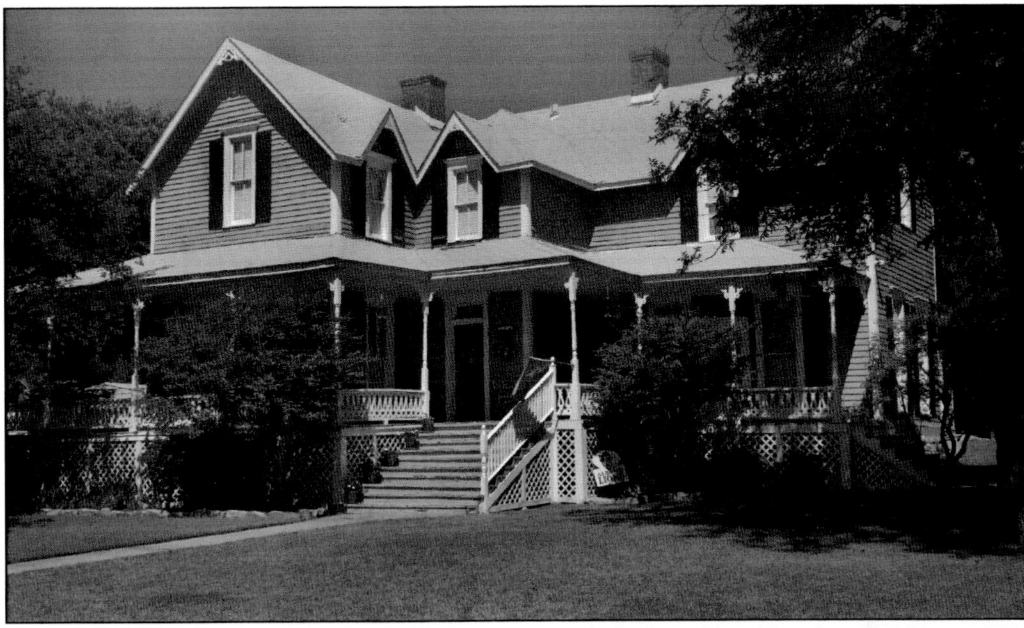

Ella Matthews Conrad (1865–1945) had this house built for herself and her four children in 1892 after her husband's death. Her parents, Mr. and Mrs. Joseph B. Matthews, moved in with her. After the death of her daughter in 1905, she sold the house to C.M. Cauble. In the ensuing years, three generations of Caubles lived in the structure. It is now known locally as the Cauble House. (Courtesy of Watt Casey Jr.)

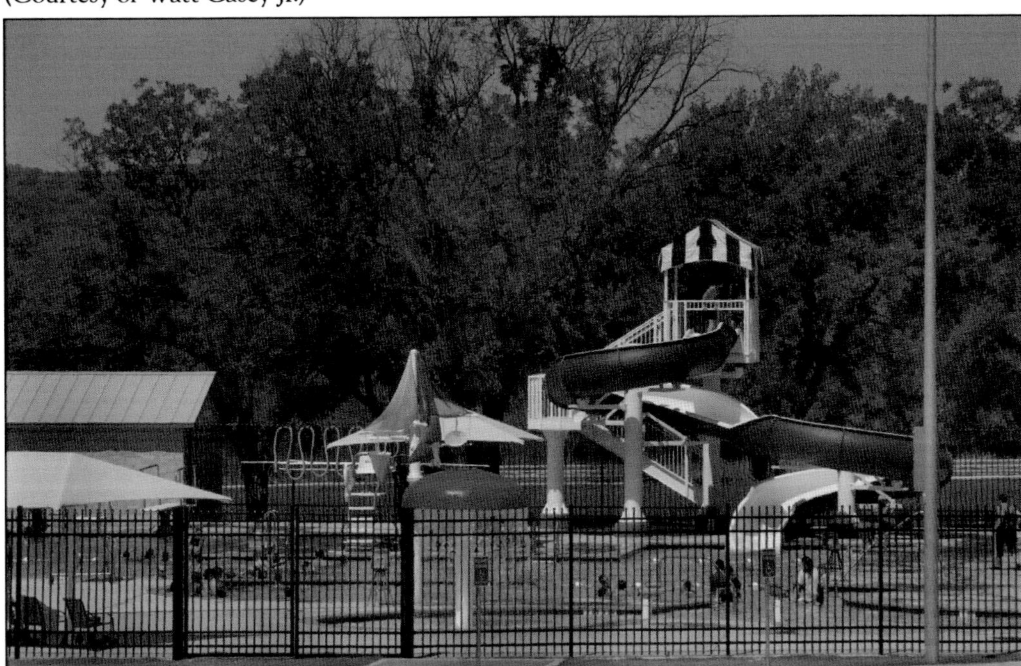

Webb Memorial Park, also called City Park, completed a full renovation in 2012. It now has a state-of-the-art swimming pool, with a water slide and bathhouse, a basketball court, a skateboard facility, a softball field, picnic tables, and a children's play area. (Courtesy of Watt Casey Jr.)

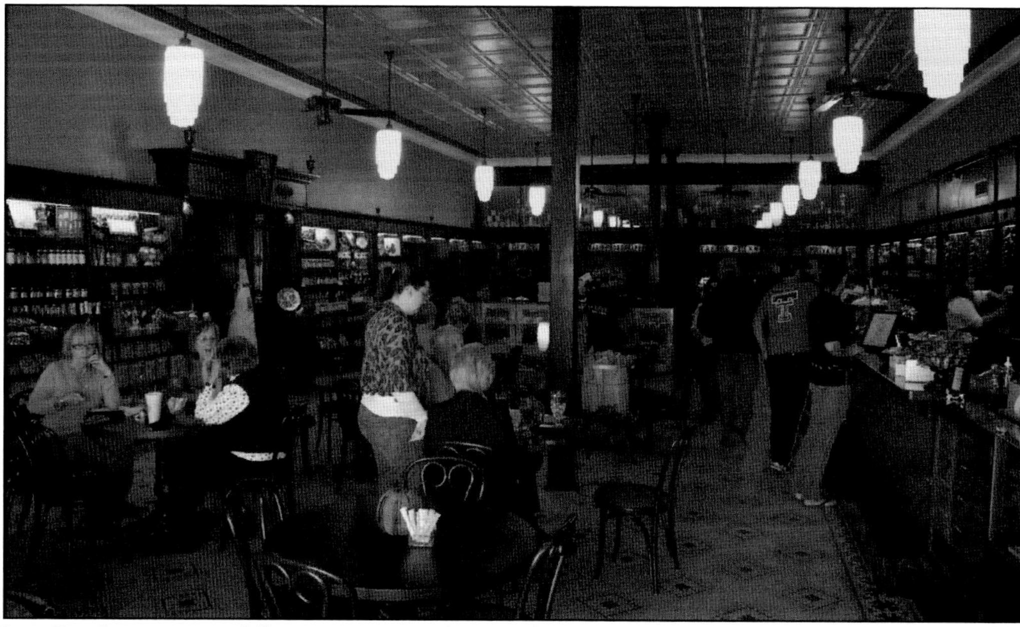

Lee Sanders came to Albany in 1916 and opened a drugstore in the current Whitney Theatre building in 1920. In 1929, he moved his business down the street to its present location. Renovated in 2009 by current owners Mike and Betsy Parsons, the drugstore looks much the same as it did when it originally opened. Soft drinks are still made from syrup and carbonated water and are served from the original marble fountain. (Courtesy of Watt Casey Jr.)

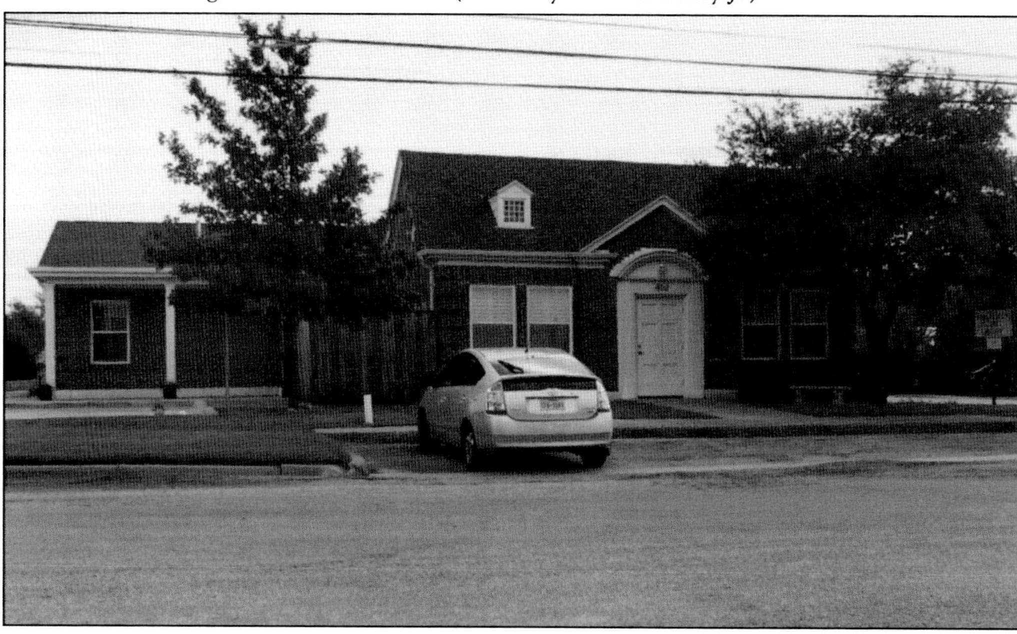

This Colonial brick building houses the Shackelford County Library, which was founded in 1956 by the Albany Study Club. Its first home was a room in the county courthouse. Elsa Turner was the first librarian. In 1961, commissioners purchased the vacant Southwestern Bell Telephone building for the library's use. A major expansion in 2009 added 1,200 square feet of space to the structure. It is still operated by the Albany Study Club. (Courtesy of Randy Bacon.)

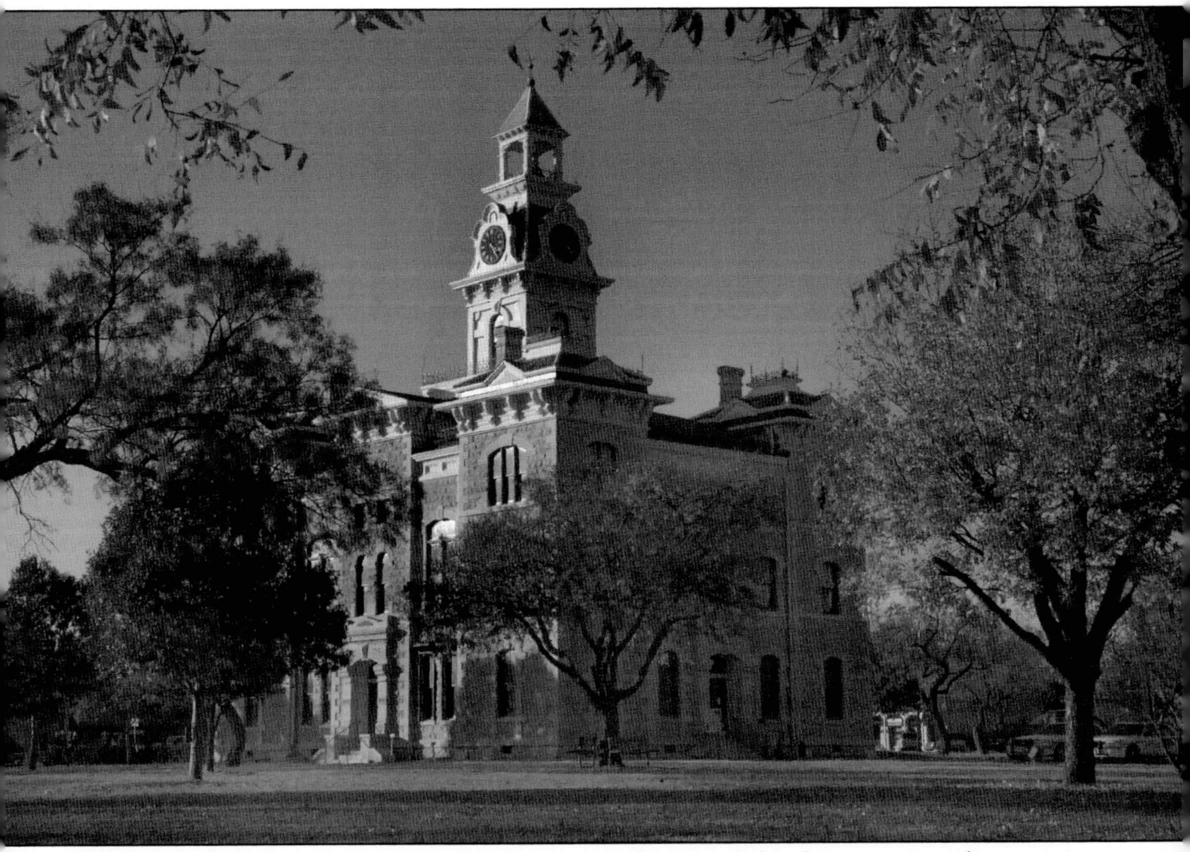

Architect J.E. Flanders is quoted as saying that the finished Shackelford County Courthouse was "generally considered the handsomest in middle Texas." A true testament to both Flanders's design and Edgar Rye's insistence on quality materials and craftsmanship, the courthouse still stands, given new life and longevity in the 21st century after an extensive renovation was completed in 2001. (Courtesy of Watt Casey Jr.)

Consistent with our mission to preserve history on a local level, this book was printed in South Carolina on American-made paper and manufactured entirely in the United States. Products carrying the accredited Forest Stewardship Council (FSC) label are printed on 100 percent FSC-certified paper.

MADE IN THE USA